Fifth Edition

Be Prepared

for the

Computer
Science
Exam in Java

Maria Litvin
Phillips Academy, Andover, Massachusetts

Gary Litvin
Skylight Publishing, Andover, Massachusetts

Skylight Publishing
Andover, Massachusetts

Library of Congress Control Number: 2012921274

ISBN 978-0-9824775-2-6

Skylight Publishing
9 Bartlet Street, Suite 70
Andover, MA 01810

web: www.skylit.com
e-mail: sales@skylit.com
          support@skylit.com

1 2 3 4 5 6 7 8 9 10   18 17 16 15 14 13

Printed in the United States of America

Brief Contents

Contents

Preface to the Fifth Edition

In this edition we have updated information about the exam format (in particular, there is no longer a penalty for wrong answers to multiple-choice questions. We have overhauled the practice exams and streamlined or replaced many of the multiple-choice and free-response questions to bring them closer to the style and difficulty level of recent AP exams. Last but not least, we have added one complete practice exam. Overall, 10 out of 20 free-response questions in this edition are new.

After solving the free-response questions with pencil and paper, students can continue working on them, individually or in groups, in a lab setting. We have included suggestions for expanding these questions into lab projects. Complete runnable files for all free-response questions are available to teachers.

Preface

The AP exam in computer science tests your understanding of basic concepts in computer science as well as your fluency in Java programming. The exam covers roughly the material of a one-semester introductory college course in computer science (CS-1). In the past, the College Board offered two computer science exams, called "A" and more advanced "AB." Starting in 2010, the College Board offers only one exam (still called "A").

Exam questions are developed by The College Board's AP Computer Science Development Committee, and exams are administered by the Educational Testing Service (ETS). The College Board currently offers exams in 34 subjects. In 2012, 2,062,205 students took 3,642,908 exams. The most up-to-date information on the AP exams offered and participation statistics can be found on The College Board's web site http://research.collegeboard.org/programs/ap/data.

In the spring of 2004, the computer science exams used Java for the first time. At the same time, the AP CS program's emphasis shifted from implementation of algorithms and coding proficiency to object-oriented software design and development. More recent exams, however, show some renewed interest in algorithms.

Answers to exam questions written in a programming language other than Java or in pseudocode will not receive credit.

A working knowledge of Java is necessary but not sufficient for a good grade on the exam. First and foremost, you must understand the basic concepts of computer science, object-oriented programming (OOP), and some common algorithms. As for Java: you don't have to know the whole language, just the subset described in

The College Board's *Computer Science A Course Description* (`www.collegeboard.com/student/testing/ap/sub_compscia.html`). You must also be familiar with The College Board's material developed specifically for the AP CS exam: the GridWorld case study.

This is a lot of material to cover, and it is certainly not the goal of this book to teach you everything you need to know from scratch. For that, you need a complete textbook with exercises and programming projects. Most students who take the exam are enrolled in an AP Computer Science course at their school. A determined student can prepare for the exam on his or her own; it may take anywhere between two and twelve months, and a good textbook will be even more important.

The goals of this book are:

- to describe the exam format and requirements
- to describe the AP Java subset
- to provide an effective review of what you should know with emphasis on the more difficult topics and on common omissions and mistakes
- to help you identify and fill the gaps in your knowledge
- to offer sample exam questions with answers, hints, and solutions for you to practice with and analyze your mistakes

The AP exam in computer science is a paper-and-pencil affair. While you need a computer with a Java compiler to learn how to program and how to implement common algorithms in Java, this book does not require the use of a computer. In fact, it is a good idea not to use one when you work on practice questions, so that you can get used to the exam's format and environment. One-hundred-percent correct Java syntax is not the emphasis here. Small mistakes (a missed semicolon or a brace) that a compiler would normally help you catch will probably not affect your exam score. You'll need a computer only to access collegeboard.com and our web site, `www.skylit.com/beprepared` for the latest updates and our solutions to the free-response questions from past exams.

Chapter 1 of this book explains the format, required materials, and the Java subset for the exam and provides information about exam grading and exam-taking hints. Chapter 2 and Chapter 3 cover the elements of Java required for the exam. Chapter 4 deals with OOP topics. Chapter 5 reviews common algorithms for searching and sorting. Chapter 6 reviews the GridWorld case study. All review chapters contain sample multiple-choice questions with detailed explanations of all the right and wrong answers. Chapter 7 is actually on the web at this book's companion web site, `www.skylit.com/beprepared/`. It offers our annotated solutions to the free-response questions from past exams. At the end of the book are five complete practice exams followed by answers and solutions.

Good luck!

Our colleague and friend Dave Wittry passed away in a tragic accident while training for a triathlon, on February 5, 2008. He was 41. Dave contributed practice exam questions for the second and third editions of this book. Dave taught at Troy High School, a magnet school for science, math, and technology in Fullerton, California, and contributed to Troy's immense success in Computer Science. In 2005 Dave moved to Taiwan and taught AP Computer Science and mathematics at the Taipei American School. He was a Reader for the AP Computer Science Exams for several years. Dave was always ready to help friends, students, and colleagues, and he developed valuable resources for computer science teachers. We miss Dave!

We are grateful to David Levine of St. Bonaventure University who recommended many important improvements, helped us catch technical and stylistic mistakes, and pointed out questions that needed clarification in the first edition of *Be Prepared*, which came out in 1999.

Roger Frank and Judy Hromcik contributed practice questions to the second and third editions; some of the questions in this book are based on their ideas. Roger also went very thoroughly over the draft of the earlier editions and recommended many corrections and improvements.

We thank teachers and students who alerted us to several mistakes in the earlier editions of this book.

Our special thanks to Margaret Litvin for making this book more readable with her thorough and thoughtful editing.

Finally, we thank the Boy Scouts of America for allowing us to allude to their motto in the book's title.

About the Authors

Maria Litvin has taught computer science and mathematics at Phillips Academy in Andover, Massachusetts, since 1987. She is an AP Computer Science exam reader and Table Leader and, as a consultant for The College Board, provides AP training for high school computer science teachers. Maria is a recipient of the 1999 Siemens Award for Advanced Placement for Mathematics, Science, and Technology for New England and of the 2003 RadioShack National Teacher Award. Prior to joining Phillips Academy, Maria taught computer science at Boston University.

Maria is the author of the earlier, C++ version of *Be Prepared* (Skylight Publishing, 1999) and co-author of *C++ for You++: An Introduction to Programming and Computer Science*, which was the leading high school textbook for AP Computer Science courses in the C++ era. In 2001, Maria and Gary Litvin co-wrote their first textbook in the *Java Methods* series. Now *Java Methods: Object-Oriented Programming and Data Structures*, Second AP Edition (Skylight Publishing, 2011) is used for AP CS courses in hundreds of schools. Maria and Gary also co-wrote *Mathematics for the Digital Age and Programming in Python* (Skylight Publishing, Second Edition, 2010).

Gary Litvin is a co-author of *C++ for You++*, the *Java Methods* series, and *Mathematics for the Digital Age and Programming in Python*. Gary has worked in many areas of software development including artificial intelligence, pattern recognition, computer graphics, and neural networks. As founder of Skylight Software, Inc., he developed SKYLIGHTS/GX, one of the first visual programming tools for C and C++ programmers. Gary led in the development of several state-of-the-art software products, including interactive touch screen development tools, OCR and handwritten character recognition systems, and credit card fraud detection software.

How to Use This Book

The companion web site

    www.skylit.com/beprepared/

is an integral part of the book. It contains annotated solutions to free-response questions from past exams, the GridWorld case study information, and relevant links. Check this web site for the current information, and be sure you have the latest edition of *Be Prepared*.

Multiple-choice questions in the review chapters are marked by their number in a box:

Their solutions are delimited by ☞ and ☜.

> **Our practice exams may be slightly more difficult than the actual exams, so don't panic if they take more time.**

⦃ Braces like these on the margins in the free-response questions in our practice exams indicate suggestions for additional lab work based on our questions.

Teachers can get access to complete runnable Java files for the free-response questions in our practice exams. To get access, e-mail support@skylit.com from your school e-mail account and include the school web page that lists your email address.

Chapter 1. Exam Format, Grading, and Tips

1.1. Exam Format and Materials

Figure 1-1 shows the format of the AP Computer Science exam. The exam takes 3 hours of test time (plus breaks and time for instructions). It is divided into two sections. Section I consists of 40 multiple-choice questions with a total allotted time of 1 hour and 15 minutes (1.5 to 2 minutes per question on average). Section II consists of four free-response questions with a total allotted time of 1 hour and 45 minutes (about 25 minutes per question). The free-response questions usually consist of two or three parts each.

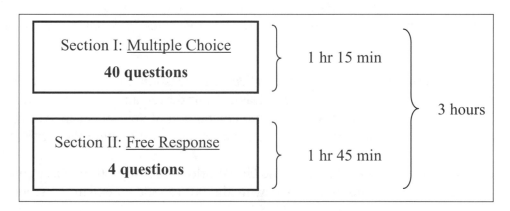

Figure 1-1. AP Computer Science exam format

> **No computers, calculators, other devices, books, or materials are allowed, only paper, pencil and an eraser.**

Pens are allowed, but we recommend that you use a pencil.

At the exam you will receive the *Quick Reference* document, both in your multiple-choice questions booklet and again in your free-response questions booklet (in other words, the same *Quick Reference* document will be given to you twice). The *Quick Reference* provides a list of the Java library classes and their methods included in the AP subset, as well as the classes and/or the documentation for the GridWorld classes that may be tested. Teachers can obtain a copy of the *Quick Reference* at *AP Central* (see "A Guide to AP Central" at www.skylit.com). This document is provided for reference — it is expected that you will already be very familiar and comfortable with the GridWorld case study and the required Java library classes before the exam.

The multiple-choice section is a mixture of questions related to general computer science terms, program design decisions, specific elements of Java syntax, logical analysis of fragments of Java code, properties of classes, OOP concepts, and five questions related to the GridWorld case study.

The free-response section aims to cover a wide range of material: Java arithmetic, algorithms, one- and two-dimensional arrays, strings, classes and interfaces, Java library classes (within the AP subset), and so on. In past exams, students were asked to write a constructor or a method that performs a specified task under a given header for the method. The second part of the question often refers to the class or method implemented in the first part, but each part is graded separately, and your implementation of Part (a) does not have to be correct in order for you to get full credit for Part (b). Part (c) may ask questions about your implementation or ask you to write an additional method that uses Parts (a) and/or (b). In that case you are to assume that the methods in the previous parts work as intended, regardless of what you wrote for them.

Free-response questions may also include a "design" question, in which you are asked to design and write a complete small Java class. Your design and implementation will be graded based on the correctness of the implementation of your class, including the encapsulation principle (declaring all instance variables private), and other criteria.

One free-response question is based on the GridWorld case study. It may ask you to extend a case study class and to write a new method or rewrite an existing method.

1.2. The Java Subset

The Development Committee has defined a restricted subset of Java to be tested on the exam. The purpose of the subset is to focus the AP CS program more on general concepts than on the specifics of Java and to limit the scope, especially of material related to the peculiarities of Java. The subset is described in The College Board's *Computer Science A Course Description*; we have a link to it from this book's web site www.skylit.com/beprepared/.

What is in the subset? Actually, quite a bit:

- `boolean`, `int`, and `double` primitive data types. `(int)` and `(double)` casts. **Other primitive data types, including `char`, are not in the subset and should be avoided on the exam.**

- Assignment (=), arithmetic (+, -, *, /, %), increment/decrement (++, --), compound assignment (+=, -=, *=, /=, %=), relational (<, >, <=, >=, ==, !=), and logical (&&, ||, !) operators. **Use only the postfix form of ++ and -- (k++ or k--), and do not use them in expressions**.

- + and += operators for concatenating strings. `String`'s `compareTo`, `equals`, `length`, `substring`, and `indexOf(String s)` methods. `\n`, `\\`, and `\"` escape sequences in literal strings.

- `System.out.print` and `System.out.println`.

- One- and two-dimensional arrays, `array.length`, arrays of objects, initialized arrays such as `int[] x = {1, 2, 3};`

- `if-else`, `for`, including the "for each" form, `for(type x : values)...`, `while`, `return`. **But do-while and switch are not included.**

- Classes. Constructors, the `new` operator, `public` and `private` methods, `static` methods, `static` variables and `static final` variables (constants), overloaded methods, `null`. **All instance variables are private.** Default initialization rules are <u>not</u> in the subset and won't come up on the exam.

- Inheritance, interfaces and abstract classes, `extends`, `implements`. Calling a superclass's constructor from a subclass (as in `super(...)`). Calling a superclass's method from a subclass (as in `super.someMethod(...)`). Passing `this` object to a method (as in `otherObject.someMethod(this)`).

- `NullPointerException`, `ArrayIndexOutOfBoundsException`, `ArithmeticException`, `IllegalArgumentException`, `ClassCastException`.

- Library classes, methods, and constants:
  - **String**: `length()`, `substring(...)`, `indexOf(String s)`
  - **Integer**: `Integer(int x)`, `intValue()`; `Integer.MIN_VALUE` and `Integer.MAX_VALUE`.
  - **Double**: `Double(double x)`, `doubleValue()`
  - **Math**: `abs(int x)`, `abs(double x)`, `pow(double base, double exp)`, `sqrt(double x)`, `random()`

  Also understand `toString` methods for all objects, the `equals` and `compareTo` methods for `String`, `Integer`, and `Double`. **Comparable<*T*> interface is <u>not</u> in the subset**, but is worth knowing.

- The `List<E>` interface and the `ArrayList<E>` class (see Section 2.6).

> **If you feel you must stray from the subset in your free-response solution, you might have misunderstood the problem and be making it harder than it is.**

At the same time, it is OK to use such features outside the subset as `Math.min(...)` and `Math.max(...)` methods, `ArrayList`'s `contains` and `remove(object)` methods, and other simple tools that all exam readers are familiar with.

Things that are <u>not</u> in the AP subset and should be avoided include the following:

- Java syntax abominations, such as the `?_:_` operator and the "comma" operator

- `++` and `--` in expressions (as in `a[i++]`)

- Primitive data types other than `boolean`, `int`, and `double` (`char` is <u>not</u> in the subset)

- Bitwise logical operators and shift operators: `~`, `&`, `|`, `^`, `<<`, `>>`.

Also not in the subset and will not be tested:

- The `switch` statement, the `do-while` loop, `continue` in loops

- The prefix form of `++` and `--` operators (`++k`, `--k`)

- Library classes (such as `StringBuffer`, `Arrays`, `DecimalFormat`, etc.), unless specifically listed in the subset

- checked exceptions and `try-catch-finally` statements

- `System.in` and `Scanner`; any input and output other than `System.out.print` and `System.out.println`

- `enum` data types

1.3. Grading

The exam is graded on a scale from 1 to 5. Grades of 5 and 4 are called "extremely well qualified" and "well qualified," respectively, and usually will be honored by colleges that give credit or placement for the AP exam in computer science. A grade of 3, "qualified," may be denied credit or placement at some colleges. Grades of 2, "possibly qualified," and 1, "no recommendation," will not get you college credit or placement.

Table 1-1 presents published statistics and grade distributions for the 2011 and 2012 exams. In 2012, 26,103 candidates took the exam; 48 percent scored 4 or 5.

AP Computer Science A	2012		2011	
	Number	%	Number	%
Students	26,103	100.0	22,176	100.0
Grade:				
5	6,171	23.6	5,521	24.9
4	6,351	24.3	5,510	24.8
3	4,075	15.6	3,143	14.2
2	2,013	7.7	1,748	7.9
1	7,493	28.7	6,254	28.2
4 or 5	12,522	48.0	11,031	49.7

Table 1-1. 2012 and 2011 grade distributions

▌**The multiple-choice and free-response sections weigh equally in the final grade.**

The College Board uses a weighted combination of the multiple-choice (MC) and free-response (FR) scores to determine the final total score:

```
totalScore =
     MC_coeff * countCorrect + FR_coeff * FR_score;
```

One point is given for each correct answer to a multiple-choice question.

▌**There is no penalty for giving a wrong answer to a multiple-choice question, so it is a good strategy not to leave any answers blank.**

Solutions to free-response questions are graded by a group of high school teachers and college professors. Scores are based on a *rubric* established by the Chief Reader, Exam Leader, and Question Leaders. Each free-response question is graded out of 9 points, with partial credit given according to the rubric.

The final score is obtained by adding the MC and FR weighted scores. The MC and FR coefficients are chosen in such a way that they give equal weights to the multiple-choice and free-response sections of the exam. For example, if the exam has 40 multiple-choice questions and 4 free-response questions, weights of 1.0 for multiple-choice and 1.1111 for free-response will give each section a maximum total of 40, for a maximum possible total score of 80.

Every year over the summer the College Board releases sample solutions to free-response questions and grading rubrics. Every few years the College Board releases a complete exam, including a diagnostic guide for multiple-choice questions, grading rubrics for free-response questions, and the cut-off points for grades.[*] Table 1-2 shows the cut-off points used for the 2004 and 2009 exams. The maximum possible composite score was 80 (1.00 * MC + 1.1111 * FR). In those years there was a 1/4 point penalty for incorrect answers to multiple-choice questions; there is no penalty now. The table shows both the actual cut-offs and the cut-offs adjusted for no-penalty grading. The cut-off points are determined by the Chief Reader in consultation with the College Board and may vary slightly from year to year based on the score distributions and close examination of a sample of individual exams. In 2009, 77.5 percent or more would get you a 5.

	2004			2009	
AP Grade	Actual	Adjusted for no penalty	AP Grade	Actual	Adjusted for no penalty
5	63 - 80	65 - 80	5	60 -80	62 - 80
4	49 - 62	52 - 64	4	44 - 59	47 - 61
3	39 - 48	43 - 51	3	33 - 43	37 - 46
2	32 - 38	36 - 42	2	25 - 32	29 - 36
1	0 - 31	0 - 35	1	0 - 24	0 - 28

Table 1-2. Score-to-grade conversion.

Statistical analysis of the 2009 exam shows that over 98.5 percent of students who answered correctly at least 27 out of 40 questions on the multiple-choice section received a 4 or a 5 for the whole exam.

1.4. College Credit

Most colleges will take your AP courses and exam grades into account in admission decisions if you take your exams before your senior year. But acceptance of AP exam results for credit and/or placement varies widely among colleges. In general, the AP Computer Science course corresponds to a CS-1 course (Introductory Computer Science or Computer Programming I), a one-semester course for computer science majors. Some colleges may base their decision on your grade, and some may not give any credit at all.

---

[*] When this book went to print, 2009 was the last released exam. See `www.skylit.com/beprepared` for the latest updates.

The AP program in computer science is a rigorous and demanding program that is comparable to or exceeds the level of the respective first-semester computer science courses at most colleges.

> **If you plan to major in computer science and your college of choice does not recognize a good grade on the AP exam for credit and/or placement, you should examine the reasons carefully. Decide for yourself whether these reasons are valid or just stem from the bias of that college or its computer science department.**

1.5. Exam Taking Tips

Some things are obvious:

- If you took the time to read a multiple-choice question and all the answer choices, take an extra ten seconds and guess. Most likely you have eliminated one or two wrong answers even without noticing. **Do not leave any multiple-choice answers blank: there is no penalty for wrong answers**.

- If a common paragraph refers to a group of questions and you took the time to read it, try each question in the group.

- Do read the question before jumping to the code included in the question. Notes to multiple-choice questions in our practice exams might show you some shortcuts.

- In questions with I, II, III options, work from the answers; for example, you might be able to eliminate two or three answer choices if you are sure that Option I doesn't work.

There are a few important things to know about answering free-response questions.

> **Remember that all free-response questions have equal weight. Don't assume that the first question is the easiest and the last is the hardest.**

> **In a nutshell: be neat, straightforward, and professional; keep your exam reader in mind; don't show off.**

More specifically:

1. Stay within the AP Java subset, except for a few obvious shortcuts, such as `Math.max(...)` and `Math.min(...)`.

2. Remember that the elegance of your code <u>does not</u> count. More often than not, a brute-force approach is the best. You may waste a lot of time writing tricky, non-standard code and trick yourself in the process or mislead your exam reader who, after all, is only human. Your exam reader will read your solution, but will not test it on a computer.

3. Superior efficiency of your code does not count, unless the desired performance of the solution is specifically stated in the question.

4. Remember that Parts (b) and (c) of a question are graded independently from the previous parts, and may actually be easier: Part (a) may ask you to write a method, while Part (b) or Part (c) may simply ask you to use it. It is common for method(s) specified in Part (a) to be called in subsequent parts. Do so, even if your Part (a) is incorrect or left blank. <u>Do not</u> re-implement code from earlier parts in later parts — you will waste valuable time and may lose points for doing so.

5. If a question presents a partial definition of a class with certain methods described but not implemented ("implementation not shown"), call these methods whenever appropriate in your code — do not write equivalent code yourself.

6. Bits of "good thinking" count. You may not know the whole solution, but if you have read and understood the question, go ahead and write fragments of code that may earn you partial credit points. But don't spend too much time improvising incorrect code.

7. Don't waste your time erasing large portions of work. Instead, cross out your work neatly, <u>but only after you have something better to replace it with</u>. Do not cross out a solution if you have no time to redo it, even if you think it is wrong. You <u>won't</u> be penalized for incorrect code and may get partial credit for it. Exam readers are instructed not to read any code that you have crossed out. But if you wrote two solutions, be sure to cross one out: otherwise only the first one on the page will be graded.

8. Read the comment above the method header quickly — it usually restates the task in a more formal way and sometimes gives hints. <u>Assume that all preconditions are satisfied — don't add unnecessary checks to your code</u>.

9. One common mistake is to forget a `return` statement in a non-`void` method. Make sure the returned value matches the specified type.

10. Do not ignore any hints in the question description. If an algorithm is suggested for a method (as in "you may use the following algorithm"), don't fight it, just use it!

11. Remember that the exam readers grade a vast number of exams in quick succession during a marathon grading session every June. Write as neatly as possible. Space out your code (don't save paper).

12. Always indent your code properly. This helps you and your exam reader. If you miss a brace but your code is properly indented, the reader (as opposed to a Java compiler) may accept it as correct. Similarly, if you put each statement on a separate line, a forgotten semicolon may not be held against you.

13. Follow the Java naming convention: the names of all methods, variables, and parameters start with a lowercase letter. Use meaningful, but not too verbose, names for variables. `count` may be better than `a`; `sum` may be better than `temp`; `row`, `col` may be better than `i`, `j`. But `k` is better than `loopControlVariable`. If the question contains examples of code with names, use the same names when appropriate.

14. Don't bother with comments; they do not count and you will lose valuable time. Occasionally you can put a very brief comment that indicates your intentions for the fragment of code that follows. For example:

```
// Find the first empty seat:
   ...
   ...
```

15. Don't worry about `imports` — assume that all the necessary Java library and GridWorld classes are imported.

16. Code strictly according to the specifications and preconditions and postconditions. Avoid extraneous "bells and whistles" — you will lose points. Never add `System.out.print/println` in solutions unless specifically asked to do so. Do not read any data in your method — it is passed in as a parameter.

17. Do not use in your code specific numbers, strings, or dimensions of arrays given as examples in explanations of questions. If the question says: "For example, a two-dimensional array `pixelValues` may contain the following image" and shows an array of 4 rows by 5 columns, do <u>not</u> use 4 and 5 in your code — make your code work with an array of any size.

18. Don't try to catch the exam authors on ambiguities: there will be no one to hear your case, and you'll waste your time. Instead, try to grasp quickly what was <u>meant</u> and write your answer.

19. Don't quit until the time is up. Use all the time you have and keep trying. The test will be over before you know it.

Chapter 2. Java Features, Part 1

2.1. Variables; Arithmetic, Relational, and Logical Operators

Primitive data types included in the subset are `boolean`, `int`, and `double`. In Java, an `int` always takes four bytes, regardless of a particular computer or Java compiler, and its range is from -2^{31} to $2^{31} - 1$. The smallest and the largest integer values are defined in Java as symbolic constants `Integer.MIN_VALUE` and `Integer.MAX_VALUE`; use these symbolic constants if you need to refer to the limits of the `int` range. A `double` takes 8 bytes and has a huge range, but its precision is about 15 significant digits.

Remember to declare local variables.

If you declare a variable inside a nested block, make sure it is used only in that block. If you declare a variable in a `for` loop, it will be undefined outside that loop.

For example:

```java
public int countMins(int[] a)
{
  if (a.length > 0)
  {
    int iMin = 0;

    for (int i = 1; i < a.length; i++)
    {
      if (a[i] < a[iMin])
        iMin = i;
    }

    int count = 0;

    for (i = 0; i < a.length; i++)
    {
      if (a[i] == a[iMin])
        count++;
    }
  }
  return count;
}
```

Error: `i` *is undefined*

Error: `count` *is undefined here*

A safer version:

```
public int countMins(int[] a)
{
  int iMin = 0;
  int count = 0;

  if (a.length > 0)
  {
    iMin = 0;
    for (int i = 1; i < a.length; i++)
    {
      if (a[i] < a[iMin])
        iMin = i;
    }

    count = 0;

    for (int i = 0; i < a.length; i++)
    {
      if (a[i] == a[iMin])
        count++;
    }
  }
  return count;
}
```

> *Do not declare* count *here:*
> **int** count = 0;
> *would be a mistake*

You won't be penalized for declarations inside blocks of code, but if you declare important variables near the top of the method's code, it makes it easier to read and may help you avoid mistakes.

Which of the following statements is true?

(A)   In Java, data types in declarations of symbolic constants are needed only for documentation purposes.
(B)   When a Java interpreter is running, variables of the `double` data type are represented in memory as strings of decimal digits with a decimal point and an optional sign.
(C)   A variable's data type determines where it is stored in computer memory when the program is running.
(D)   A variable's data type determines whether that variable may be passed as a parameter to a particular method.
(E)   A variable of the `int` type cannot serve as an operand for the / operator.

☞ This question gives us a chance to review what we know about data types.

Choice A is false: the data type of a symbolic constant is used by the compiler. In this sense, symbolic constants are not so different from variables. The difference is that a constant declaration includes the keyword `final`. Class constants are often declared as `static final` variables. For example:

```
public static final double LBS_IN_KG = 2.20462262;
public static final int maxNumSeats = 120;
```

Choice B is false, too. While real numbers may be written in programs in decimal notation, a Java compiler converts them into a special floating-point format that takes eight bytes and is convenient for computations.

Choice C is false. The data type by itself does not determine where the variable is stored. Its location in memory is determined by where and how the variable is declared: whether it is a local variable in a method or an instance variable of a class or a static variable.

Choice E is false, too. In Java, you can write `a/b`, where both `a` and `b` are of type `int`. The result is truncated to an integer.

Choice D is true. For example a value of the type `String` cannot be passed to a method that expects an `int` as a parameter. Sometimes, though, a parameter of a different type may be promoted to the type expected by the method (for example, an `int` can be promoted to a `double` when you call, say, `Math.sqrt(x)` for an `int x`). The answer is D. ☜

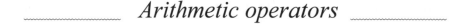

Arithmetic operators

> **The most important thing to remember about Java's arithmetic operators is that the data type of the result, even each intermediate result, is the same as the data type of the operands. In particular, the result of division of one integer by another integer is truncated to an integer.**

For example:

```
int n = 3;
double result;

result = (n + 1) * n / 2;        // result is 6.0
result = (n / 2) * (n + 1);      // result is 4.0
result = (1 / 2) * n * (n + 1);  // result is 0.0
```

To avoid truncation you have to watch the data types and sometimes use the *cast operator*. For example:

```
int a, b;
double ratio;
...
ratio = (double)a / b;          // Or: a / (double)b;
// But not ratio = (double)(a/b) -- this is a cast applied too late!
```

If at least one of the operands is a `double`, there is no need to cast the other one — it is promoted to a `double` automatically. For example:

```
int factor = 3;
double x = 2.0 / factor;  // Result: x = 0.6666...
```

2

Which of the following expressions does not evaluate to 0.4?

(A)   `(int)4.5 / (double)10;`
(B)   `(double)(4 / 10);`
(C)   `4.0 / 10;`
(D)   `4 / 10.0;`
(E)   `(double)4 / (double)10;`

 In B the cast to `double` is applied too late — after the ratio is truncated to 0 — so it evaluates to 0. The answer is B.

In the real world we have to worry about the range of values for different data types. For example, a method that calculates the factorial of *n* as an `int` may overflow the result, even for a relatively small *n*. In Java, arithmetic overflow is not reported in any way: there is no warning or exception. If an `int` result is greater than or equal to 2^{31}, the leftmost bit, which is the sign bit, may be set to 1, and the result becomes negative.

> **For the AP exam, you have to be aware of what overflow is, and you need to be aware of the `Integer.MIN_VALUE` and `Integer.MAX_VALUE` constants, but you don't have to know their specific values.**

Modulo division

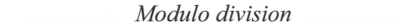

> **The `%` (modulo division) operator usually applies to two integers: it calculates the remainder when the first operand is divided by the second.**

For example:

```
int r;
r = 17 % 3;   // r is set to 2
r = 8 % 2;    // r is set to 0
r = 4 % 5;    // r is set to 4
```

Compound assignments, ++ *and* --

Compound assignment operators are +=, -=, *= , /=, and %=. x += y is the same as x = x + y. Other operations follow the same pattern.

There are two forms of the ++ and -- operators in Java. The prefix form ("++k") increments (or decrements) the variable before its value is used in the rest of the expression; the postfix form increments (or decrements) it afterwards.

> **The AP CS Development Committee discourages the use of ++ and -- in expressions. Use ++ and -- only in separate statements and only in the postfix form, such as in k++ or k--.**

For example:

```
while (i <= n)          while (i <= n)
{                       {
                            sum += i;
    sum += i++;             i++;
}                       }
```

Too much!   O.K.

You won't lose points over ++ or -- in expressions if you use them correctly, but they won't earn you any extra credit, either.

> **It is bad style _not_ to use increment or compound assignment operators where appropriate.**

For example:

```
for (int i = 0; i < n; i = i + 1)     for (int i = 0; i < n; i++)
{                                     {
   count = count + 1;                     count++;
   sum = sum + a[i];                      sum += a[i];
}                                     }
```

Works, but looks bad   Better

Again, this incurs no penalty but doesn't look good.

Arithmetic expressions are too easy to be tested alone. You may encounter them in questions that combine them with logic, iterations, recursion, and so on.

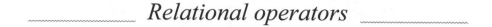

Relational operators

In the AP subset, the relational operators ==, !=, <, >, <=, >= apply to `ints` and `doubles`. Remember that "is equal to" is represented by == (not to be confused with =, the assignment operator). `a != b` is equivalent to `!(a == b)`, but `!=` is stylistically better.

> **The == and != operators can be also applied to two objects, but their meanings are different from what you might expect: they compare the <u>addresses</u> of the objects. The result of == is true if and only if the two variables refer to exactly the same object. You rarely care about that: most likely you want to compare the <u>contents</u> of two objects, for instance two strings. Then you need to use the `equals` or `compareTo` method.**

For example:

```
if (str.equals("Stop")) ...
```

> **On the other hand, == or != must be used when you compare an object to `null`.**

`null` is a Java reserved word that stands for a reference with a zero value. It is used to indicate that a variable currently does not refer to any valid object. For example:

```
if (str != null && str.equals("Stop")) ...
// str != null avoids NullPointerException --
// can't call a null's method
```

You can write instead:

```
if ("Stop".equals(str)) ...
```

This works because `"Stop"` is not `null`; it works even if `str` is `null`.

Logical operators

The logical operators `&&`, `||`, and `!` normally apply to Boolean values and expressions. For example:

```
boolean found = false;          boolean found = false;
...                             ...
while (i >= 0 && !found)        while (i >= 0 && found == false)
{                               {
  ...                             ...
}                               }
```

Works, but is more verbose

Do not write

```
while (... && !found == true)
```

— this works, but "`== true`" is redundant.

3

Assuming that `x`, `y`, and `z` are integer variables, which of the following three logical expressions are equivalent to each other, that is, have equal values for all possible values of `x`, `y`, and `z`?

  I.   `(x == y && x != z) || (x != y && x == z)`

 II.   `(x == y || x == z) && (x != y || x != z)`

III.   `(x == y) != (x == z)`

(A)   None of the three
(B)   I and II only
(C)   II and III only
(D)   I and III only
(E)   I, II, and III

☞ Expression III is the key to the answer: all three expressions state the fact that exactly one out of the two equalities, `x == y` or `x == z`, is true. Expression I states that either the first and not the second or the second and not the first is true. Expression II states that one of the two is true and one of the two is false. Expression III simply states that they have different values. All three boil down to the same thing. The answer is E. ☜

De Morgan's Laws

The exam is likely to include questions on De Morgan's Laws:

> `!(a && b)` is the same as `!a || !b`
> `!(a || b)` is the same as `!a && !b`

4

The expression `!((x <= y) && (y > 5))` is equivalent to which of the following?

(A) `(x <= y) && (y > 5)`
(B) `(x <= y) || (y > 5)`
(C) `(x >= y) || (y < 5)`
(D) `(x > y) || (y <= 5)`
(E) `(x > y) && (y <= 5)`

☞ The given expression is pretty long, so if you try to plug in specific numbers you may lose a lot of time. Use De Morgan's Laws instead:

$$!((x <= y) \quad \&\& \quad (y > 5))$$

$$!(x <= y) \quad || \quad !(y > 5)$$

$$(x > y) \quad || \quad (y <= 5)$$

> *When* `!` *is distributed,* `&&` *changes into* `||` *and vice-versa*

The answer is D.

Short-circuit evaluation

> An important thing to remember about the logical operators `&&` and `||` is *short-circuit evaluation*. If the value of the first operand is sufficient to determine the result, then the second operand is **not** evaluated.

Consider the following code segment:

```
int x = 0, y = 3;
String op = "/";

if (op.equals("/") && (x != 0) && (y/x > 2))
{
  System.out.println("OK");
}
else
{
  System.out.println("Failed");
}
```

Which of the following statements about this code is true?

(A)   There will be a compile error because `String` and `int` variables are intermixed in the same condition.
(B)   There will be a run-time divide-by-zero error.
(C)   The code will compile and execute without error; the output will be `OK`.
(D)   The code will compile and execute without error; the output will be `Failed`.
(E)   The code will compile and execute without error; there will be no output.

☞   Choices A and E are just filler answers. Since `x` is equal to 0, the condition cannot be true, so C should be rejected, too. The question remains whether it crashes or executes. In Java, once `x != 0` fails, the rest of the condition, `y/x > 2`, won't be evaluated, and `y/x` won't be computed. The answer is D. ☜

The relational expressions in the above question are parenthesized. This is not necessary because relational operators always take precedence over logical operators. If you are used to lots of parentheses, use them, but you can skip them as well. For example, the Boolean expression from Question 5 can be written with fewer parentheses:

```
if (op.equals("/") && x != 0 && y/x > 2) ...
```

`&&` also takes precedence over `||`, but it's clearer to use parentheses when `&&` and `||` appear in the same expression. For example:

```
if ((0 < a && a < top) || (0 < b && b < top)) ...
```

Bitwise logical operators

> The bitwise logical operators, &, |, ^, and ~, are **not** in the AP Java subset and are **not** tested on the AP exam. You don't have to worry about them.

Programmers use these operators to perform logical operations on individual bits, usually in `int` values. Unfortunately, Java also allows you to apply these operators to `boolean` values, and, when used that way, these operators do not comply with short-circuit evaluation. This may lead to a nasty bug if you inadvertently write & instead of && or | instead of ||. For example,

```
if (x != 0 & y/x > 2)
```

Error: & instead of &&

results in a division by 0 exception when x = 0.

2.2. Conditional Statements and Loops

> You can use simplified indentation for **if-else-if** statements.

For example:

```
if (score >= 70)
  grade = 5;
else if (score >= 60)
  grade = 4;
...
else
  grade = 1;
```

But don't forget braces and proper indentation for nested `if`s. For example:

```
if (exam.equals("Calculus AB"))
{
  if (score >= 60)
    grade = 5;
  else if ...
    ...
}
else if (exam.equals("Calculus BC"))
{
  if (score >= 70)
    grade = 5;
  else if ...
    ...
}
```

6

Consider the following code segment, where m is a variable of the type int:

```
if (m > 0)
{
  if ((1000 / m) % 2 == 0)
    System.out.println("even");
  else
    System.out.println("odd");
}
else
  System.out.println("not positive");
```

Which of the following code segments are equivalent to the one above (that is, produce the same output as the one above regardless of the value of m)?

I.
```
if (m <= 0)
    System.out.println("not positive");
else if ((1000 / m) % 2 == 0)
    System.out.println("even");
else
    System.out.println("odd");
```

II.
```
if (m > 0 && (1000 / m) % 2 == 0)
    System.out.println("even");
else if (m <= 0)
    System.out.println("not positive");
else
    System.out.println("odd");
```

III.
```
if ((1000 / m) % 2 == 0)
{
  if (m <= 0)
    System.out.println("not positive");
  else
    System.out.println("even");
}
else
{
  if (m <= 0)
    System.out.println("not positive");
  else
    System.out.println("odd");
}
```

(A) I only
(B) II only
(C) I and II only
(D) II and III only
(E) I, II, and III

☞ Segment I can actually be reformatted as:

```
if (m <= 0)
  System.out.println("not positive");
else
{
  if ((1000 / m) % 2 == 0)
    System.out.println("even");
  else
    System.out.println("odd");
}
```

So it's the same as the given segment with the condition negated and `if` and `else` swapped. Segment II restructures the sequence, but gives the same result. To see that, we can try different combinations of true/false for `m <= 0` and `(1000 / m) % 2 == 0`. Segment III would work, too, but it has a catch: it doesn't work when `m` is equal to 0. The answer is C. ⏎

⁓⁓⁓ for *and* while *loops* ⁓⁓⁓

The `for` loop,

```
for (initialize; condition; change)
{
    ...    // Do something
}
```

is equivalent to the `while` loop:

```
initialize;
while (condition)
{
    ...    // Do something
    change;
}
```

change can mean any change in the values of the variables that control the loop, such as incrementing or decrementing an index or a counter.

`for` loops are shorter and more idiomatic than `while` loops in many situations. For example:

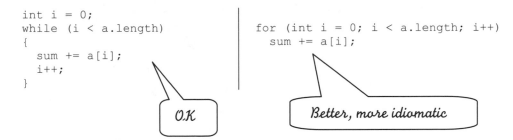

```
int i = 0;
while (i < a.length)
{
    sum += a[i];
    i++;
}
```
O.K

```
for (int i = 0; i < a.length; i++)
    sum += a[i];
```
Better, more idiomatic

> **In a `for` or `while` loop, the condition is evaluated at the beginning of the loop and the program does not go inside the loop if the condition is false. Thus, the body of the loop may be skipped entirely if the condition is false at the very beginning.**

7

Consider the following methods:

```
public int fun1(int n)
{
    int product = 1;
    for (int k = 2; k <= n; k++)
    {
        product *= k;
    }
    return product;
}
```

```
public int fun2(int n)
{
    int product = 1;
    int k = 2;
    while (k <= n)
    {
        product *= k;
        k++;
    }
    return product;
}
```

For which integer values of n do `fun1(n)` and `fun2(n)` return the same result?

(A)   Only n > 1
(B)   Only n < 1
(C)   Only n == 1
(D)   Only n >= 1
(E)   Any integer n

☞   The best approach here is purely formal: since the initialization, condition, and increment in the `for` loop in `fun1` are the same as the ones used with the `while` loop in `fun2`, the two methods are equivalent. The answer is E.

8

Consider the following code segment:

```
while (x > y)
{
  x--;
  y++;
}
System.out.println(x - y);
```

Assume that x and y are int variables and their values satisfy the conditions $0 \le x \le 2$ and $0 \le y \le 2$. Which of the following describes the set of all possible outputs?

(A)   0
(B)   –1, 1
(C)   –1, –2
(D)   0, –1, –2
(E)   0, –1, 1, –2, 2

☞ If $x \le y$ to begin with, then the while loop is never entered and the possible outputs are 0, –1, and –2 (for the pairs (0, 0), (0, 1), (0, 2), (1, 1), (1, 2), (2, 2)). If $x > y$, then the loop is entered and after the loop we must have $x \le y$, so $x - y$ cannot be positive. The answer is D. ☜

OBOBs

When coding loops, beware of the so-called "off-by-one bugs" ("OBOBs"). These are mistakes of running through the loop one time too many or one time too few.

Suppose the `isPrime` method is defined:

```
// Returns true if p is a prime, false otherwise.
// Precondition: p >= 2
public static boolean isPrime(int p) { < implementation not shown > }
```

Given

```
int n = 101;
int sum = 0;
```

Which of the following code segments correctly computes the sum of all prime numbers from 2 to 101, inclusive?

(A)
```
while (n != 2)
{
  n--;
  if (isPrime(n)) sum += n;
}
```

(B)
```
while (n >= 2)
{
  n--;
  if (isPrime(n)) sum += n;
}
```

(C)
```
while (n != 2)
{
  if (isPrime(n)) sum += n;
  n--;
}
```

(D)
```
while (n >= 2)
{
  if (isPrime(n)) sum += n;
  n--;
}
```

(E)
```
while (n >= 2 && isPrime(n))
{
  sum += n;
  n--;
}
```

☞ It is bad style to start the body of a loop with a decrement, so Choices A and B are most likely wrong. Indeed, both A and B miss 101 (which happens to be a prime) because `n` is decremented too early. In addition, Choice B eventually calls `isPrime(1)`, violating `isPrime`'s precondition. Choice C misses 2 — an OBOB on the other end. Choice E might look plausible for a moment, but it actually quits as soon at it encounters the first non-prime number. The answer is D. ↵

The "for each" loop

The "for each" loop was first introduced in Java 5.0. This loop has the form

```
for (SomeType x : a)  // read: "for each x in a"
{
   ...   // do something
}
```

where `a` is an array or an `ArrayList` (or another `List` or "collection") that holds values of *SomeType*.

For example:

```
int[] scores = {87, 95, 76};
for (int score : scores)
   System.out.print(score + " ");
```

works the same way as

```
int[] scores = {87, 95, 76};
for (int i = 0; i < scores.length; i++)
{
   int score = scores[i];
   System.out.print(score + " ");
}
```

Both will display

```
87 95 76
```

Another example:

```
List<String> plants = new ArrayList<String>();
plants.add("Bougainvillea");
plants.add("Hibiscus");
plants.add("Poinciana");

for (String name : plants)
  System.out.print(name + " ");
```

will display

```
Bougainvillea Hibiscus Poinciana
```

Note that the "for each" loop traverses the array or list only in the forward direction and does not give you access to the indices of the values stored in the array or list. For example, a "for each" loop won't be very useful if you need to find the <u>position</u> of the first occurrence of a target value in a list.

If you need access to indices, use a `for` or `while` loop.

A "for each" loop does not allow you to set an element of an array to a new value, because it works with a <u>copy</u> of the element's value, and so the original values of an array will remain unchanged.

For example, given an `int` array `arr`,

```
for (int x : arr)
  x = 1;
```

will leave `arr` unchanged.

If you need to replace or delete elements in an array or list, use a `for` or `while` loop.

If an array or list holds objects, then you can call an object's method inside a "for each" loop, so you can potentially change object's state if the method changes it.

_____ break *and* return *in loops* _____

In Java it is okay to use break and return inside loops. return immediately quits the method from any place inside or outside a loop. This may be a convenient shortcut, especially when you have to quit a method from within a nested loop. For example:

```java
// Returns true if all values in list are different, false otherwise
public boolean allDifferent(int[] list)
{
  for (int i = 0; i < list.length; i++)
    for (int j = i + 1; j < list.length; j++)
      if (list[i] == list[j])
        return false;
  return true;
}
```

You can also use break, but it may be dangerous and is not in the AP subset. Remember that in a nested loop, break takes you out of the inner loop but not out of the outer loop. Avoid redundant, verbose, and incorrect code like this:

```java
// Returns true if all values in list are different, false otherwise
public boolean allDifferent(int[] list)
{
  boolean foundDuplicates;

  for (int i = 0; i < list.length; i++)
  {
    for (int j = i + 1; j < list.length; j++)
    {
      if (list[i] == list[j])
      {
        foundDuplicates = true;
        break;
      }
      else
      {
        foundDuplicates = false;
      }
    }
  }
  if (foundDuplicates == true)
    return false;
  else
    return true;
}
```

Out of the inner for *but still in the outer* for.

If you insist on using Boolean flags, you need to be extra careful:

```
// Returns true if all values in list are different, false otherwise
public boolean allDifferent(int[] list)
{
  boolean foundDuplicates = false;

  for (int i = 0; i < list.length; i++)
  {
    for (int j = i + 1; j < list.length; j++)
    {
      if (list[i] == list[j])
      {
        foundDuplicates = true;
        break;
      }
    }
  }
  return !foundDuplicates;
}
```

The `continue` statement is not in the AP subset and should be avoided.

2.3. Strings

In Java, a string is an object of the type `String`, and, as with other types of objects, a `String` variable holds a reference to (the address of) the string.

Strings are immutable: no string methods can change the string.

An assignment statement

```
str1 = str2;
```

copies the reference from `str2` into `str1`, so they both refer to the same memory location.

A *literal string* is a string of characters within double quotes. A literal string may include "escape sequences" \n (newline), \" (a double quote), \\ (one backslash), and other escapes. For example,

```
System.out.print("Hello\n");
```

has the same effect as

```
System.out.println("Hello");
```

The String class supports the + and += operators for concatenating strings.

> **String is the only class in Java that supports special syntax for using operators on its objects (only + and +=).**

The operator

```
s1 += s2;
```

appends s2 to s1. In reality it creates a new string by concatenating s1 and s2 and then sets s1 to refer to the new string. It is equivalent to

```
s1 = s1 + s2;
```

10

What is the output of the following code segment?

```
String str1 = "Happy ";
String str2 = str1;
str2 += "New Year! ";
str2.substring(6);
System.out.println(str1 + str2);
```

(A) Happy New Year!
(B) Happy Happy New Year!
(C) Happy New Year! New Year!
(D) Happy New Year! Happy New Year!
(E) Happy New Year! Happy

  After str2 = str1, str1 and str2 point to the same memory location that contains "Happy ". But after str2 += "New Year! ", these variables point to different things: str1 remains "Happy " (strings are immutable) while str2 becomes "Happy New Year! ". str2.substring(6) does not change str2 — it calls its substring method but does not use the returned value (a common beginner's mistake: again, strings are immutable). The answer is B.

String *methods*

The `String` methods included in the AP subset are:

```
int length()
boolean equals(Object other)
int compareTo(String other)
String substring(int from)
String substring(int from, int to)
int indexOf(String s)
```

> **Always use the `equals` method to compare a string to another string. The == and != operators, applied to two strings, compare their <u>addresses</u>, not their values.**

`str1.equals(str2)` returns `true` if and only if `str1` and `str2` have the same values (that is, consist of the same characters in the same order).

`str1.compareTo(str2)` returns a positive number if `str1` is greater than `str2` (lexicographically), zero if they are equal, and a negative number if `str1` is less than `str2`.

`str.substring(from)` returns a substring of `str` starting at the `from` position to the end, and `str.substring(from, to)` returns `str`'s substring starting at the `from` position and up to but <u>not including</u> the `to` position (so the length of the returned substring is `to - from`). Positions are counted from 0. For example, `"Happy".substring(1, 4)` would return `"app"`.

`str.indexOf(s)` returns the starting position of the first occurrence of the substring `s` in `str`, or `-1` if not found.

11

Consider the following method:

```
public String process(String msg, String delim)
{
  int pos = msg.indexOf(delim);
  while (pos >= 0)
  {
    msg = msg.substring(0, pos) + " "
                      + msg.substring(pos + delim.length());
    pos = msg.indexOf(delim);
  }
  return msg;
}
```

What is the output of the following code segment?

```
String rhyme = "Twinkle\ntwinkle\nlittle star";
String rhyme2 = process(rhyme, "\n");
System.out.println(rhyme + "\n" + rhyme2);
```

(A) little star
     Twinkle twinkle little star

(B) little star
     Twinkle
     twinkle
     little star

(C) Twinkle
     twinkle
     little star
     Twinkle winkle ittle tar

(D) Twinkle
     twinkle
     little star
     Twinkle twinkle
     little star

(E) Twinkle
     twinkle
     little star
     Twinkle twinkle little star

process receives and works with a <u>copy</u> of a reference to the original string (see Section 3.3). The method can reassign the copy, as it does here, but the original reference still refers to the same string. This consideration, combined with immutability of strings, assures us that rhyme remains unchanged after the call process(rhyme).

The rhyme string includes two newline characters, and, when printed, it produces

```
Twinkle
twinkle
little star
```

So the only possible answers are C, D or E. Note that we can come to this conclusion before we even look at the process method! This method repeatedly finds the first occurrence of delim in msg, cuts it out, and replaces it with a space. No other characters are replaced or lost. The resulting message prints on one line. The answer is E.

2.4. Integer and Double Classes

In Java, variables of primitive data types (int, double, etc.) are not objects. In some situations it is convenient to represent numbers as objects. For example, you might want to store numeric values in an ArrayList (see Section 2.6), but the elements of an ArrayList must be objects. The java.lang package provides several "wrapper" classes that represent primitive data types as objects. Two of these classes, Integer and Double, are in the AP subset.

The Integer class has a constructor that takes an int value and creates an Integer object representing that value. The intValue method of an Integer object returns the value represented by that object as an int. For example:

```
Integer obj = new Integer(123);
...
int num = obj.intValue();   // num gets the value of 123
```

Likewise, Double's constructor creates a Double object that represents a given double value. The method doubleValue returns the double represented by a Double object:

```
Double obj = new Double(123.45);
...
double x = obj.doubleValue();   // x gets the value of 123.45
```

The `Integer` class also provides two symbolic constants that describe the range for `int` values:

```
public static final int MIN_VALUE = -2147483648;
public static final int MAX_VALUE = 2147483647;
```

> **Use the `equals` method of the `Integer` or of the `Double` class if you want to compare two `Integer` or two `Double` variables, respectively.**

For example:

```
Integer a = new Integer(...);
Integer b = new Integer(...);
...
if (a.equals(b))
   ...
```

If you apply a relational operator `==` or `!=` to two `Integer` or two `Double` variables, you will compare their <u>addresses</u>, not values. This is rarely, if ever, what you want to do.

The `Integer` and `Double` classes implement the `Comparable<Integer>` and `Comparable<Double>` interfaces, respectively (see Section 4.6), so each of these classes has a `compareTo` method. As usual, `obj1.compareTo(obj2)` returns a positive integer if `obj1` is greater than `obj2` (that is, `obj1`'s numeric value is greater than `obj2`'s numeric value), a negative integer if `obj1` is less than `obj2`, and zero if their numeric values are equal.

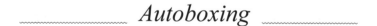

Autoboxing

Starting with Java 5.0, the compiler in certain situations automatically converts values of primitive data types, (`int`, `double`, etc.) into the corresponding wrapper types (`Integer`, `Double`, etc.). This feature is called *autoboxing* (or *autowrapping*). For example, in

```
ArrayList<Integer> numbers = new ArrayList<Integer>();
numbers.add(5);
```

the second line is compiled as

```
numbers.add(new Integer(5));
```

Likewise, where appropriate, the compiler performs *autounboxing*. For example,

```
int num = numbers.get(0);
```

in effect compiles as

```
int num = numbers.get(0).intValue();
```

> **Autoboxing and autounboxing are <u>not</u> in the AP subset, but you won't be penalized for relying on them.**

2.5. Arrays

There are two ways to declare and create a one-dimensional array:

```
SomeType[] a = new SomeType[size];
SomeType[] b = {value_0, value_1, ..., value_{n-1}};
```

For example:

```
double[] samples = new double[100];
int[] numbers = {1, 2, 3};
String[] cities = {"Atlanta", "Boston", "Cincinnati", "Dallas"};
```

The first declaration declares an array of `double`s of size 100. Its elements get default values (zeroes), but this fact is not in the AP subset. The second declaration creates an array of `int`s of size 3 with its elements initialized to the values 1, 2, and 3. The third declaration declares and initializes an array of four given strings.

We can refer to `a`'s elements as `a[i]`, where `a` is the name of the array and `i` is an index (subscript), which can be an integer constant, variable, or expression.

> **Indices start from 0.**

`a.length` refers to the size of the array. (In an array, `length` is not a method, but rather works like a public instance variable, hence <u>no parentheses</u>.)

> **`a[a.length-1]` refers to the last element.**

Once an array is created, its size cannot be changed. The only way to expand an array is to create a bigger array and copy the contents of the original array into the new one. The old array is discarded (or, more precisely, recycled by a process called "garbage collection"). For example:

```
int[] a = new int[100];
...
int[] temp = new int[a.length * 2];
for (int i = 0; i < a.length; i++)
  temp[i] = a[i];
a = temp;    // reassign a to the new array; the old array is discarded
```

> **If a and b are arrays, a = b does not copy elements from b into a: it just reassigns the reference a to b, so that both a and b refer to the same array.**

The following method reverses the order of elements in an array of strings:

```
public void reverse(String[] words)
{
  int i = 0, j = words.length - 1;

  while (i < j)
  {
    String temp = words[i]; words[i] = words[j]; words[j] = temp;
    i++;
    j--;
  }
}
```

The Java Virtual Machine (the run-time interpreter) checks that an array index is within the valid range, from 0 to `array.length-1`. If an index value is invalid, the interpreter "throws" an `ArrayIndexOutOfBoundsException` — reports a run-time error, the line number for the offending program statement, and a trace of the method calls that led to it.

> **An *exception* is a run-time error, not a compile-time error.**

The compiler cannot catch errors that will be caused by certain circumstances that occur during program execution, such as a variable used as an array index whose value has gone out of the allowed range.

12

Suppose the method int sign(int x) returns 1 if x is positive, −1 if x is negative, and 0 if x is 0. Given

```
int[] nums = {-2, -1, 0, 1, 2};
```

what are the values of the elements of nums after the following code is executed?

```
for (int k = 0; k < nums.length; k++)
{
  nums[k] -= sign(nums[k]);
  nums[k] += sign(nums[k]);
}
```

(A) -2, -1, 0, 1, 2
(B) -1, 0, 0, 0, 1
(C)   0, 0, 0, 0, 0
(D) -2, 0, 0, 2, 3
(E) -2, 0, 0, 0, 2

☞ Remember that the first statement within the loop changes nums[k], which may change the sign of nums[k], too. Jot down a little table:

Before		After -=		After +=
a[k]	sign of a[k]	a[k]	sign of a[k]	a[k]
-2	-1	-1	-1	-2
-1	-1	0	0	0
0	0	0	0	0
1	1	0	0	0
2	1	1	1	2

The answer is E. ↵

| 13 |

Consider the following method:

```
// Returns true if there are no two elements among
// counts[0], ... counts[n-1], whose values are the same
// or are consecutive integers; otherwise, returns false.
// Precondition: counts contains n values, n > 1
public boolean isSparse(int[] counts, int n)
{
  < missing code >
}
```

Which of the following code segments can be used to replace *< missing code >* so that the method `isSparse` works as specified?

I.
```
for (int j = 0; j < n; j++)
{
  for (int k = j + 1; k < n; k++)
  {
    int diff = counts[j] - counts[k];
    if (diff >= -1 && diff <= 1)
      return false;
  }
}
return true;
```

II.
```
for (int j = 1; j < n; j++)
{
  for (int k = 0; k < j; k++)
  {
    int diff = counts[j] - counts[k];
    if (diff >= -1 && diff <= 1)
      return false;
  }
}
return true;
```

III.
```
for (int j = 0; j < n; j++)
{
  for (int k = 1; k < n; k++)
  {
    int diff = counts[j] - counts[k];
    if (Math.abs(diff) <= 1)
      return false;
  }
}
return true;
```

(A)   I only
(B)   II only
(C)   I and II only
(D)   I and III only
(E)   I, II, and III

   Note that in this question not all `counts.length` elements of `counts` are used, just the first n. Their subscripts range from 0 to n-1. The precondition states that n > 1, so there is no need to worry about an empty array or an array of just one element. Looking at the inner loop in each segment you can quickly see that they work the same way. So the difference is how the loops are set up; more precisely, the limits in which the indices vary. In Option I the outer loop starts with the first item in the list; the inner loop compares it with each of the subsequent items. In Option II the outer loop starts with the second item in the list; the inner loop compares it with each of the preceding items. Both of these are correct and quite standard in similar algorithms. This eliminates A, B, and D. Option III at first seems harmless, too, but it has a catch: the inner loop doesn't set a limit for k that depends on j, so when j is greater than 0, k may eventually take the same value as j (such as j = 1, k = 1). The method will erroneously detect the same value in `counts` when it is actually comparing an item to itself. The answer is C.

Array return type

Occasionally you may need to return an array from a method. Suppose you want to restructure the `reverse` method above so that it <u>returns</u> a new array containing the values from a given array in reverse order. The original array remains unchanged. The method can be coded as follows:

```
public String[] reverse(String[] words)
{
  String[] result = new String[words.length];

  for (int i = 0; i < words.length; i++)
    result[i] = words[words.length - 1 - i];

  return result;
}
```

Two-dimensional arrays

The AP subset includes rectangular two-dimensional arrays. These are similar to one-dimensional arrays but use two indices, one for the row and one for the column. For example:

```
double[][] matrix = new double[3][5]; // 3 rows by 5 cols
int r, c;
...
matrix[r][c] = 1.23;
```

> If m is a two-dimensional array, m.length represents the number of rows and m[0].length (that is, the length of the first row) represents the number of columns.

Only rectangular 2-D arrays are considered in the AP subset; therefore, the lengths of all the rows are the same, and m[0].length represents the length of any row.

The following method calculates the sums of the values in each column of a 2-D array, places these sums into a new 1-D array of sums, and returns that array:

```
// Returns a 1-D array containing sums of all the values
// in each column of table
public double[] totalsByColumn(double[][] table)
{
  int nRows = table.length;
  int nCols = table[0].length;
  double[] totals = new double[nCols];

  for (int c = 0; c < nCols; c++)
  {
    totals[c] = 0.0;    // optional: default
    for (int r = 0; r < nRows; r++)
      totals[c] += table[r][c];
  }
  return totals;
}
```

14

Consider the following code segment:

```
String[][] m = new String[6][3];

for (int k = 0; k < m.length; k++)
{
  m[k][m[0].length - 1] = "*";
}
```

Which of the following best describes the result when this code segment is executed?

(A) All elements in the first row of m are set to "*"
(B) All elements in the last row of m are set to "*"
(C) All elements in the last column of m are set to "*"
(D) The code has no effect
(E) `ArrayIndexOutOfBoundsException` is reported

☞ The first index is the row, and the `for` loop is set up for all rows. The answer is C. ☜

> **Note that in Java, a two-dimensional array is treated as an array of one-dimensional arrays, its rows. So a naive "for each" loop won't work for traversing a 2-D array.**

To make a "for each" loop work on a 2-D array, you need nested loops. For example:

```
int[][] a = {{1, 2, 3}, {4, 5, 6}};

for (int[] row : a)
{
  for (int x : row)
    System.out.print(x + " ");
  System.out.println();
}
```

However, traversing a 2-D array with nested "for each" loops is not in the AP subset.

2.6.   The `List` Interface and the `ArrayList` Class

`java.util.List<E>` is a Java library interface that defines a list of objects of some type *E*.

> **Starting with Java 5.0, a `List<E>` holds objects of the specified type `E` (for example, `Strings` or `Integers`).**

Java developers say that in Java 5.0, `List` and other *collections* have become *generic*. The term implies that the same code works with collections of elements of different data types. As we see it, collections have become type-specific: a collection holds elements of a specified type. (Before the 5.0 release, Java collection classes and interfaces only worked with elements of the `Object` type.)

The Java library provides two classes that implement `List<E>`: `java.util.ArrayList<E>` and `java.util.LinkedList<E>`. An `ArrayList` stores the items in an array; a `LinkedList` uses a linked list structure.

> **The `java.util.LinkedList<E>` class is <u>not</u> included in the AP subset.**

Note the syntax for declaring an `ArrayList` introduced in Java 5.0. The class name is `ArrayList` followed by angle brackets that hold the data type of the objects stored in the list. For example:

```
ArrayList<Student> list = new ArrayList<Student>();
```

Since `ArrayList<E>` implements the `List<E>` interface, you can also write:

```
List<Student> list = new ArrayList<Student>();
```

> **You cannot instantiate an interface, so it is a mistake to write something like this:**
>
> ```
> List<String> list = new List<String>();  // Error!
> ```

> **An `ArrayList` cannot hold values of a primitive data type. For instance, `ArrayList<int>` or `ArrayList<double>` will result in a syntax error.**

However, an `int` or `double` value can be added to an `ArrayList<Integer>` or `ArrayList<Double>` respectively, due to autoboxing. For example:

```
List<Double> prices = new ArrayList<Double>();
prices.add(29.95);
```

`ArrayList` provides methods for getting and setting the value of a particular element, adding a value at the end of the list, removing a value, and inserting a value at a given position. As in standard arrays, indices start from 0.

An `ArrayList` is automatically resized when it runs out of space for added elements. `ArrayList`'s "no-args" constructor (that is, the constructor that takes no parameters) allocates an array of some default initial capacity and sets the size to 0 (no values stored in the `ArrayList` yet). As values are added, their number may exceed the current capacity. Then a new array is allocated with twice the capacity, the old values are copied into the new array, and the old array is discarded. All this happens behind the scenes — you don't have to worry about any of it.

The AP subset includes the following methods of `List<E>` and `ArrayList<E>`:

`int size()`	Returns the number of values currently stored in the list
`boolean add(E x)`	Adds x at the end of the list; returns `true`
`E get(int index)`	Returns the value stored at `index`
`E set(int index, E x)`	Sets the value of the element at `index` to x; returns the old value stored at `index`
`E remove(int index)`	Removes the value at `index` and shifts the subsequent values toward the beginning of the list; returns the old value stored at `index`
`void add(int index, E x)`	Inserts x at `index`, shifting the current value stored at `index` and all the subsequent values toward the end of the list

The `add` and `remove` methods adjust the size of the `ArrayList` appropriately. The methods that take an `index` parameter check that the index is in the valid range, from 0 to `size()-1` (0 to `size()` for `add(x)`) and "throw" `IndexOutOfBoundsException` if the index is not in that range.

It might be helpful for you to know and use on the AP exam three additional methods of `List` and `ArrayList`, which are not in the AP subset:

`boolean contains(Object obj)`	Returns `true` if one of the elements in the list is equal to `obj`
`int indexOf(Object obj)`	Returns the index of the first occurrence of `obj` in the list, or –1, if the list does not contain `obj`
`boolean remove(Object obj)`	If the list contains `obj`, removes the first occurrence of `obj` and returns `true`; otherwise returns `false`

Since the compiler knows what type of objects are stored in an `ArrayList`, it automatically casts values retrieved from the list into their type. For example:

```
List<Fish> list = new ArrayList<Fish>();
...
Fish f = list.get(i);
```

15

What is the output of the following code segment?

```
ArrayList<String> list = new ArrayList<String>();
list.add("A");
list.add("B");
list.add("C");
list.add("D");
list.add("E");

for (int k = 1; k <= 3; k++)
{
  list.remove(1);
}

for (int k = 1; k <= 3; k++)
{
  list.add(1, "*");
}

for (String word : list)
{
  System.out.print(word + " ");
}
```

(A)   A C D E * * *
(B)   * * * B C D E
(C)   A * * * E
(D)   A E * * *
(E)   IndexOutOfBoundsException

☞   This question is not as tricky as it might seem. First we create an empty list and add five values to it: "A", "B", "C", "D", "E". Then we remove the value at index 1 three times. This is the second element and each time we remove it, the subsequent values are shifted toward the beginning by one position. "A" and "E" remain. Then we insert three asterisks. Note that we always insert at index 1. After the first insertion we get "A", "*", "E". After the second we get "A", "*", "*", "E". The third insertion produces "A", "*", "*", "*", "E". The third loop (a "for each" loop) traverses the list and prints out the values. The answer is C. ⏎

Chapter 3. Java Features, Part 2

3.1.   Classes

A Java program consists of classes. The term *class* refers to a class of objects.

You should know the following concepts and terms:

class	
object	*encapsulation* and *information hiding*
instance of a class	*static* methods and fields
constructor	*public static final* fields (constants)
new operator	*accessor*
instance variables (*fields*)	*modifier*
private and *public* fields and methods	*client* of a class

An object that belongs to a particular class is also called an *instance* of that class, and the process of creating an object is called *instantiation*.

A class definition includes *constructors*, *methods*, and data fields. The constructors describe how objects of the class can be created; the methods describe what an object of this class can do; the data fields (a.k.a. *instance variables* or simply *fields*) describe the object's attributes — the current state of an object.

Constructors

Constructors describe ways to create an object of a class and initialize the object's instance variables.

> **All constructors have the same name as the class. Constructors do not have any return data type, not even `void`.**

A constructor may take parameters that help define a new object. A constructor that takes no parameters is called a "no-args" constructor.

> **The term *parameter* is often interchangeable with the term *argument* (as in *function argument* in math), especially when it refers to the actual values passed to a constructor or method.**

Hence such usage as "no-args" constructor, `IllegalArgumentException`, or `main(String[] args)`. The *Course Description* seems to favor "parameter," and so do we.

A new object is created using the `new` operator. For example, suppose you have defined a class `School`:

```
public class School
{
  // constructor
  public School(String name, int numStudents) { < code not shown > }
  ...
}
```

Then you can create a `School` object in a *client class* (a class that uses `School` objects), declare a variable of the type `School`, and set it equal to a reference to the newly created object. For example:

```
School sch1 = new School("Gifted and Talented Magnet", 1200);
```

If a class has instance variables `name` and `numStudents` —

```
public class School
{
  ...
  private String name;
  private int numStudents;
}
```

— the constructor can set them to the values of the parameters passed to it:

```
public School(String nm, int num)
{
  name = nm;
  numStudents = num;
}
```

(Objects that are no longer accessible in the program, that is, no longer referred to by any variable, are automatically destroyed and the memory they occupy is recycled. This mechanism is called *garbage collection*.)

<hr>

`public` *and* `private`

<hr>

Data fields (static and instance variables) and methods may be *public* or *private*.

Private fields and methods can be referred to only within the source code of the class they are defined in.

Public fields and methods are accessible anywhere in the code.

> **The concept of "privacy" applies to the source code of <u>the class as a whole</u> and not to individual objects. Different objects of the same class <u>have full access</u> to each other's fields and methods, and can even modify the values of each other's fields.**

In the AP subset, constructors are always public.

> **It is a common practice in OOP (and a requirement on the AP exam) to make <u>all instance variables private</u>.**

Private fields and methods hide the implementation details of a class from other classes, its clients. This concept is known as *encapsulation*. A *client* class uses your class by invoking constructors and calling public methods of your class. In general, it is a good idea to supply as little information to client classes as possible. This concept is known as *information hiding*. For example, if a method is used only internally within a class, it should be made <u>private</u>.

Accessors and modifiers

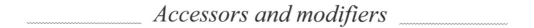

Since all instance variables are private, they are not directly accessible in client classes. It is common to provide special public methods, called *accessors*, that return the values of instance variables. For example:

```
public class School
{
  ...
  public String getName()
  {
    return name;
  }
  ...
}
```

Accessors' names often start with a "get." Accessors can have any name, but starting with "get" makes their purpose easier to remember. Accessors do not change the state of the object.

A public method that sets a new value of an instance variable is called a *modifier*. Modifiers' names often start with a "set." For example:

```
public class School
{
  ...
  public void setName(String nm)
  {
    name = nm;
  }
  ...
}
```

The "accessor" and "modifier" designations are somewhat informal — a class may have a method that sets an instance variable to a new value and at the same time returns, say, the old value.

Consider the following class:

```
public class Clock
{
  private int hours;
  private int mins;

  public Clock(int h, int m)
  {
    hours = h;
    mins = m;
  }

  // moves this clock one minute forward
  public void move()
  {
    < missing code >
  }

  public void set(int h, int m)
  {
    hours = h;
    mins = m;
    normalize();
  }

  private void normalize()
  {
    while (mins >= 60)
    {
      mins -= 60;
      hours++;
    }
    hours %= 12;
  }
}
```

Which of the following could replace *< missing code >* in the move method?

I. `this = new Clock(hours, mins + 1);`

II.
```
mins++;
normalize();
```

III. `set(hours, mins + 1);`

(A) I only
(B) II only
(C) I and II only
(D) II and III only
(E) I, II, and III

☞ Option I is wrong: it attempts to replace `this` with a new object instead of changing this one, which results in a syntax error. The other two options are acceptable: it is okay to access private instance variables and call private and public methods inside the same class. The answer is D.

(Note that it would be better to add a call to `normalize` in `Clock`'s constructor, too, just to make sure the clock is set correctly, even if $mins \geq 60$. Alternatively, the constructor could throw an `IllegalArgumentException` if its parameters didn't make sense.) ☟

3.2. Static Variables and Methods

Sometimes an attribute belongs to a class as a whole, not to individual objects (instances) of that class. Such an attribute is represented by a variable called a *static variable* (a.k.a. *class variable*), which is declared with the keyword `static`.

Static variables are used to keep track of a property or quantity shared by all objects of the class. For example,

```
public class School
{
  private static int numSchools = 0; // = 0 is optional: initialized to 0
                                      // by default
  private static int[] totalNationalEnrollmentByGrade;
  ...
}
```

A static variable can be also used to define a public symbolic constant. In that case, the keyword `final` is used in their declaration. For example:

```
public class School
{
  public static final int HIGHEST_GRADE = 12;
  ...
}
```

A class may also have static methods — methods that do not involve any particular instances of a class. For example,

```
public class School
{
  public static final int HIGHEST_GRADE = 12;
  private static int numSchools;
  private static int[] totalNationalEnrollmentByGrade;
  ...
  public static void initializeStatistics()
  {
    numSchools = 0;
    totalNationalEnrollmentByGrade = new int[HIGHEST_GRADE + 1];
                  // +1 for kindergarten
  }
  ...
}
```

> **Static methods cannot access or modify any instance variables and cannot refer to `this` (a reference to a particular object), because `this` is undefined when a static method is running.**

Static variables can be initialized in a class constructor and they can be accessed and modified in instance methods. For example:

```java
public class School
{
  // Static variables:
  public static final int HIGHEST_GRADE = 12;
  private static int numSchools;
  private static int[] totalNationalEnrollmentByGrade;

  // Static methods:
  public static int getNationalEnrollment(int grade)
  {
    return totalNationalEnrollmentByGrade[grade];
  }

  ...

  // Instance variables:
  private int[] enrollmentByGrade;
  ...

  // Constructor:
  public School(int[] numStudents)
  {
    numSchools++;

    enrollmentByGrade = new int[HIGHEST_GRADE + 1];

    for (int grade = 0; grade <= HIGHEST_GRADE; grade++)
    {
      enrollmentByGrade[grade] = numStudents[grade];
      totalNationalEnrollmentByGrade[grade] += numStudents[grade];
    }
    ...
  }

  // Instance methods:
  public void enrollOneStudent(int grade)
  {
    enrollmentByGrade[grade]++;
    totalNationalEnrollmentByGrade[grade]++;
  }

  ...
}
```

17

Consider a class with the following fields:

```
public class TestPow2
{
  private static int[] powersOfTwo = {1, 2, 4, 8, 16};
  private int num;
  ...
}
```

Which of the following methods inside the TestPow2 class will compile with no errors?

I.
```
public int pow2()
{
  return powersOfTwo[num];
}
```

II.
```
public static int pow2(int x)
{
  return powersOfTwo[x];
}
```

III.
```
public static int pow2()
{
  return powersOfTwo[num];
}
```

(A) I only
(B) II only
(C) I and II only
(D) II and III only
(E) I, II, and III

☞ The code in Option I would compile, because here an instance (non-static) method pow2 can work with both the instance variable num and the static variable powersOfTwo. The code in Option II would compile, too, because here a static method pow2 works only with its own parameter and the static variable powersOfTwo. The code in Option III would cause a syntax error, because a static method pow2 attempts to access the instance variable num. The answer is C. ↵

Java library class `Math` has static methods `abs`, `sqrt`, `pow`, `random`. For your convenience, it also includes the `public static final` "variables" `Math.PI`, which represents π, the ratio of a circle's circumference to its diameter, and `Math.E`, which represents *e*, the base of the natural logarithm. It might be useful (but not required) for you to know that `Math` also has static methods `min` and `max`, which return the smaller and the larger, respectively, of two numbers (`int`s or `double`s).

Outside the class, public static methods are called and public static constants are accessed using the dot notation, with the class's name as the prefix. For example:

```
double volume = 4.0 / 3.0 * Math.PI * Math.pow(r, 3);
```

3.3. Method Calls

In Java, all methods belong to classes.

> **It is universal Java style that all method names start with a lowercase letter.**

An *instance* method is called for a particular object; then the object's name and a dot are used as a prefix in a call, as in `obj.someMethod(...)`. If an object's method calls another method of <u>the same object</u>, the prefix is not needed and you write simply `otherMethod(...)`, which is the same as `this.otherMethod(...)`.

Class (*static*) methods belong to the class as a whole and are called using the class's name with a dot as a prefix. For example: `Math.max(x, y)` or `School.getNationalEnrollment(...)`.

A method takes a specific number of parameters of specific data types. (Starting with Java 5.0, a method can be defined with a variable number of parameters, as in `System.out.printf`; however, this feature is not in the AP subset.) Some methods take no parameters, such as `List`'s `size()` or `String`'s `length()`. A method call may include a whole expression as a parameter; then the expression is evaluated first and the result is passed to the method. An expression may include calls to other methods. For example:

```
double x, y;
...
x = Math.sqrt(Math.abs(2*y - 1));
```

A method usually returns a value of the specified data type, but a `void` method does not return any value. The return type is specified in the method's signature. The return <u>value</u> is specified in the `return` statement.

> It is considered a serious error (1 point deduction) to read the new values for a method's parameters from `System.in` inside the method. It is also a serious error to print the return value to `System.out` inside a method (when it is not requested) and another serious error to omit a `return` statement in a non-`void` method.

For example:

```
// Returns the sum of all integers from 1 to n.
// Precondition: n >= 1
public int addNumbers(int n)
{
   int sum = 0;

   n = System.in.read();

   for (int k = 1; k <= n; k++)
   {
      sum += k;
   }

   System.out.println(sum);

   return sum;
}
```

Error: n *is passed to this method from* main *or from another calling method*

Error: Not specified in the method description

18

`Math`'s static method `min` returns the value of the smaller of two integers. If a, b, c, and m are integer variables, which of the following best describes the behavior of a program with the following statement?

```
m = Math.min(Math.min(a, c), Math.min(b, c));
```

(A)   The statement has a syntax error and will not compile.

(B)   The program will run but go into an infinite loop.

(C)   a will get the smaller value of a and c; b will get the smaller value of b and c; m will get the smallest value of a, b, and c.

(D)   m will be assigned the smallest of the values a, b, and c.

(E)   None of the above

 Any expression of the appropriate data type, including a method call that returns a value of the appropriate data type, may be used in a larger expression or as a parameter to a method. The code above is basically equivalent to:

```
int temp1 = Math.min(a, c);
int temp2 = Math.min(b, c);
m = Math.min(temp1, temp2);
```

So m gets the smallest of the three values. The answer is D.

Parameters of primitive data types

> **In Java, all parameters of primitive data types are passed to methods "by value."**

When a parameter is passed by value, the method works with a <u>copy</u> of the variable passed to it, so it has no way of changing the value of the original.

19

Consider the following method:

```
public void fun(int a, int b)
{
  a += b;
  b += a;
}
```

What is the output from the following code?

```
int x = 3, y = 5;
fun(x, y);
System.out.println(x + " " + y);
```

(A) 3 5
(B) 3 8
(C) 3 13
(D) 8 8
(E) 8 13

x and y are ints, so they are passed to fun by value. fun works with copies of x and y, named a and b. What is happening inside fun is irrelevant here because x and y do not change after the method call. The answer is A.

Objects passed to methods

> **All objects are passed to methods as references. A method receives a <u>copy</u> of a reference to (the address of) the object.**

When a variable gets an "object" as a value, what it actually holds is a reference to (the address of) that object. Likewise, when an object is passed to a method, the method receives a copy of the object's address, and therefore it potentially <u>can</u> change the original object. Usually all instance variables of an object are private, so to change the object, the method would have to call one of the object's *modifier* methods.

But note that the `String`, `Integer`, and `Double` classes represent *immutable* objects, that is, objects without modifier methods. Even though these objects are passed to methods as references, no method can change them. For example, there is no way in Java to write a method

```
// Converts s to upper case
public void toUpperCase(String s)
{
  ...
}
```

because the method has no way of changing the string passed to it. For immutable objects, the method has to create and return a new object with the desired properties:

```
// Returns s converted to upper case
public String toUpperCase(String s)
{
  ...
}
```

Arrays passed to methods

A one- or two-dimensional array is passed to a method as a copy of a reference to the array. So an array is treated like an object.

> **A method can change the values of the elements of an array passed to it as a parameter, but cannot change the size of the array.**

(A method can change the size of an `ArrayList` passed to it as a parameter.)

| 20 |

Consider the following method:

```
public void accumulate(int[] a, int n)
{
  while (n < a.length)
  {
    a[n] += a[n-1];
    n++;
  }
}
```

What is the output from the following code?

```
int[] a = {1, 2, 3, 4, 5};
int n = 1;
accumulate(a, n);
for (int k = 0; k < a.length; k++)
  System.out.println(a[k] + " ");
System.out.println(n);
```

(A) 1 2 3 4 5 1
(B) 1 2 3 4 5 5
(C) 1 3 5 7 9 1
(D) 1 3 5 7 9 5
(E) 1 3 6 10 15 1

☞ n is passed to `accumulate` by value, so `accumulate` cannot change it. This rules out Choices B and D. (Inside `accumulate`, n acts like a local variable.) a is passed to `accumulate` as a reference, so `accumulate` can change its values. Starting at n = 1, it adds the value of the previous element to the current one. As the name of the method implies, this sets a[k] to the sum of all the elements up to and including a[k] in the original array. The answer is E. ☜

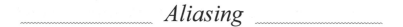

Aliasing

A more complicated concept is *aliasing*. It is good to understand in general, but it is <u>very unlikely</u> to come up on the exam. The following explanation is for a more inquisitive reader.

Suppose a class `Point` represents a point on the plane. Consider a method:

```
// point2 receives coordinates of point1 rotated 90 degrees
// counterclockwise around the origin
public void rotate90(Point point1, Point point2)
{
  point2.setY(point1.getX());
  point2.setX(-point1.getY());
}
```

In this example, `rotate90` takes two `Point` objects as parameters. Like all objects, these are passed to the method as references. Note that a `Point` object here is not immutable because it has the `setX` and `setY` methods. The code looks pretty harmless: it sets `point2`'s coordinates to the new values obtained from `point1`'s coordinates. However, suppose you call `rotate90(point, point)` hoping to change the coordinates of `point` appropriately. The compiler will not prevent you from doing that, but the result will be not what you expected. Inside the method, `point1` and `point2` actually both refer to `point`. The first statement will set `point`'s y equal to x, and the original value of y will be lost. If `point`'s coordinates are, say, x = 3, y = 5, instead of getting x = –5, y = 3, as intended, you will get x = –3, y = 3. This type of error is called an *aliasing* error.

In Java, aliasing may happen only when parameters are objects and they are mutable, or when parameters are arrays and the method moves values from one array to another. In the above example, it would be safer to make `rotate90` return a new value, as in

```
public Point rotate90(Point point)
{
  return new Point(-point.getY(), point.getX());
}
```

‾‾‾‾‾‾‾‾‾‾‾‾‾‾‾‾‾‾‾‾ `return` ‾‾‾‾‾‾‾‾‾‾‾‾

A method that is not `void` must return a value of the designated type using the `return` statement. `return` works with any expression, not just variables. For example:

```
return (-b + Math.sqrt(b*b - 4*a*c)) / (2*a);
```

An often overlooked fact is that a `boolean` method can return the value of a Boolean expression. For example, you can write simply

```
return x >= a && x <= b;
```

as opposed to the redundant and verbose

```
if (x >= a && x <= b)
  return true;
else
  return false;
```

A `void` method can use a `return` (within `if` or `else`) to quit early, but there is no need for a `return` at the end of the method. It is OK to have multiple `return` statements in a method, and often advisable. For example, the following recursive method is well-written:

```
// Returns the index of target in a sorted array
// among a[i], ..., a[j] or -1 if not found
public static int binarySearch(int[] a, int i, int j, int target)
{
  if (i > j)
    return -1;

  int m = (i + j) / 2;
  if (a[m] == target)
    return m;

  if (a[m] < target)
    return binarySearch(a, i, m-1, target);
  else
    return binarySearch(a, m+1, j, target);
}
```

Returning objects

A method's return type can be a class, and a method can return an object of that class. Often a new object is created in the method and then returned from the method. For example:

```
public String getFullName(String firstName, String lastName)
{
  return firstName + " " + lastName;
}
```

Or:

```
public Location adjacentSouth(Location loc)
{
  int r = loc.getRow(), c = loc.getCol();
  return new Location(r+1, c);
}
```

A method whose return type is a class can also return a `null` (a reference with a zero value, which indicates that it does not refer to any valid object). For example:

```java
/** Precondition: listOfNames and listOfAddresses (instance variables
 *  of this class) hold valid data
 */
public String getAddress(String name)
{
  for (int i = 0; i < listOfNames.length; i++)
  {
    if (listOfNames[i].equals(name))
      return listOfAddresses[i];
  }
  return null; // not found
}
```

If a method returns an `ArrayList`, write the full `ArrayList` type, including its elements' type in angle brackets, as the method's return type. For example:

```java
public ArrayList<Integer> getCourseNumbers()
{
  ArrayList<Integer> courseNumbers = new ArrayList<Integer>();
  ...
  return courseNumbers;
}
```

Overloaded methods

Methods of the same class with the same name but different numbers or types of parameters are called _overloaded_ methods. (The order of different types of parameters is important, too.)

> **The compiler treats overloaded methods as different methods. It figures out which one to call depending on the number, the types, and the order of the parameters.**

The `String` class, for example, has two forms of the `substring` method:

```java
String substring(int from)
String substring(int from, int to)
```

If you call `"Happy".substring(2)`, then the first overloaded method will be called, but if you call `"Happy".substring(1, 3)` then the second overloaded method will be called. Another example of overloading is `Math.abs(x)`, which has different versions of the static method `abs`, including `abs(int)` and `abs(double)`. `System.out.print(x)` has overloaded versions for all primitive data types as well as for `String` and `Object`.

The `ArrayList` class has two overloaded `add` methods: `add(obj)`, which adds an object `obj` at the end of the list, and `add(index, obj)`, which inserts `obj` at a specified index.

Overloading methods is basically a stylistic device. You could instead give different names to different forms of a method, but it would be hard to remember them. Overloaded methods do not have to have the same return type, but often they do, because they perform similar tasks. The return type alone cannot distinguish between overloaded methods.

> **All constructors of a class have the same name, so they are overloaded by definition and must differ from each other in the number and/or types of their parameters.**

21

Consider the following class declaration:

```
public class Date
{
  public Date()
  { < implementation not shown > }

  public Date(String monthName, int day, int year)
  { < implementation not shown > }

  public void setDate(int month, int day, int year)
  { < implementation not shown > }

    < fields and other constructors and methods not shown >
}
```

Consider modifying the `Date` class to make it possible to initialize variables of the type `Date` with month (given as a month name or number), day, and year information when they are declared, as well as to set their values later using the method `setDate`. For example, the following code segment should define and initialize three `Date` variables:

```
Date d1 = new Date();
d1.setDate("May", 11, 2006);
Date d2 = new Date("June", 30, 2010);
Date d3 = new Date(6, 30, 2010);
```

Which of the following best describes the additional features that should be present?

(A)   An overloaded version of `setDate` with three `int` parameters
(B)   An overloaded version of `setDate` with one `String` and two `int` parameters
(C)   A constructor with three `int` parameters
(D)   Both an overloaded version of `setDate` with three `int` parameters and a constructor with three `int` parameters
(E)   Both an overloaded version of `setDate` with one `String` and two `int` parameters and a constructor with three `int` parameters

☞   This is a wordy but simple question. Just match the declarations against the provided class features:

```
Date d1 = new Date();            ——————————  ✓ Date()

Date d2 = new Date("June", 30, 2010);   ——  ✓ Date(String, int, int)

Date d3 = new Date(6, 30, 2010);    ———————  Date(int, int, int)

d1.setDate("May", 11, 2004);     ——————————  void setDate(String, int, int)

         not used                ——————————  ✓ void setDate(int, int, int)
```

As we can see, what's missing in the class definition is a constructor with three `int` parameters and a version of `setDate` with one `String` and two `int` parameters. The answer is E. ☜

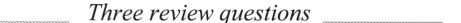

Three review questions

Questions 22-24 refer to the following partial class definition:

```java
public class TicketSales
{
  private String name;
  private double[] sales;
        /** sales[0], ..., sales[51] hold sales totals for 52 weeks */

  public TicketSales(String movieName) { < implementation not shown > }

  /** Sets box office receipts for a given week.
   *  Precondition: 1 <= week <= 52
   */
  public void setWeekSales(int week, double dollars)
  { < implementation not shown > }

  /** Finds and returns the week with best sales
   */
  private int findBestWeek() { < implementation not shown > }

  < Other methods not shown >
}
```

22

The method `findBestWeek` is declared `private` because

(A)   `findBestWeek` is not intended to be used by clients of the class.
(B)   `findBestWeek` is intended to be used only by clients of the class.
(C)   Methods that work with private instance variables of the `array` type cannot be public.
(D)   Methods that have a loop in their code cannot be public.
(E)   Methods that return a value cannot be public.

☞   In this question only the first two choices deserve any consideration — the other three are fillers. You might get confused for a moment about what a "client" means, but common sense helps: a client is anyone who is not yourself, so if a client needs to use something of yours, you have to make it public. Private things are for your class, not for clients. The answer is A. ☜

23

The constructor for the `TicketSales` class initializes the `sales` array to hold 52 values. Which of the following statements will do that?

(A)   `double sales[52];`
(B)   `double sales = new double[52];`
(C)   `double[] sales = new double[52];`
(D)   `sales = new double[52];`
(E)   `sales.setSize(52);`

☞   This is a syntax question. Choice A has invalid syntax. Choice E is absurd: an array does not have a `setSize` method (or any other methods). Choice B assigns an array to a `double` variable — a syntax error. Both Choices C and D appear syntactically plausible and in fact either one will compile with no errors. But C, instead of initializing an instance variable `sales`, will declare and initialize a local variable with the same name. This is a very common nasty bug in Java programs. The answer is D. ☜

24

Given the declaration

```
TicketSales movie = new TicketSales("Monsters, Inc.");
```

which of the following statements sets the third week sales for that movie to 245,000?

(A) `movie = TicketSales(3, 245000.00);`
(B) `setWeekSales(movie, 3, 245000.00);`
(C) `movie.setWeekSales(3, 245000.00);`
(D) `movie(setWeekSales, 3, 245000.00);`
(E) `setWeekSales(3, 245000.00);`

This is another syntax question. The variable `movie` of the type `TicketSales` is defined outside the class, in a client of the class. The key word in this question is "sets." It indicates that a method, a modifier, is called, and the way to call a method from a client class is with dot notation. (Besides, Choice A assumes that there is a constructor with two parameters; Choices B and D look like calls to non-existing methods; Choice E forgets to mention `movie` altogether.) The answer is C.

3.4.   Random Numbers

Random numbers simulate chance in computer programs. For example, if you want to simulate a roll of a die, you need to obtain a random number from 1 to 6 (with any one of these values appearing with the same probability). "Random" numbers are not truly random — their sequence is generated using a certain formula — but they are good enough for many applications.

One way to get random numbers in a Java program is to call the static method `random` of the `Math` class. It returns a random `double` from 0 (inclusive) to 1 (exclusive). To get a random integer from 1 to *n* use:

```
int r =  (int)(n * Math.random()) + 1;
```

25

Which of the following is a list of all possible outputs of the following code segment?

```
String memo = "MEMO";
System.out.print("[" +
    memo.substring((int)(3 * Math.random()),
                            (int)(3 * Math.random()) + 2) +
            "]");
```

(A)   [ME], [EM]

(B)   [ME], [EM], [MO]

(C)   [EM], [MO], [O], []

(D)   [], [M], [ME], [EM], [MO]

(E)   [], [M], [E], [ME], [EM], [MO], [MEM], [EMO], [MEMO]

☞ The two calls to `Math.random()` look the same, but they return different values — two successive values in the random number sequence. The "from" parameter of `memo.substring` can be 0, 1, or 2, and the "to" parameter can be 2, 3, or 4. Any combination of these from/to values results in a valid substring (including `substring(2,2)`, which returns an empty string). The answer is E. ⮧

> **Another way to get random numbers relies on the `java.util.Random` class, but it is not in the AP subset.**

3.5.   Input and Output

The AP subset does not include any classes or methods for data input. In particular, the `Scanner` class is not in the AP subset. If a question involves user input it may be stated as follows:

```
double x = < call to a method that reads a floating-point number >
```
or
```
int x = IO.readInt();   // Reads user input
```

Output is limited to `System.out.print` and `System.out.println` calls.

You do not have to worry about formatting numbers. Java converts an `int` or a `double` value passed to `System.out.print` or `System.out.println` into a string using default formatting. Starting with Java 5.0, `System.out.printf`, a new method with a variable number of parameters, can be used for more precisely formatted output of one or several numbers and strings. `printf` is <u>not</u> in the AP subset.

You can pass any object to `System.out.print`, `System.out.println`. These methods handle an object by calling its `toString` method. Both `Integer` and `Double` classes have reasonable `toString` methods defined. If you are designing a class, it is a good idea to supply a reasonable `toString` method for it. For example:

```
public class Fraction
{
  ...
  public String toString()
  {
    return num + "/" + denom;
  }
}
```

Otherwise, your class inherits a generic `toString` method from `Object`, which returns the object's class name followed by the object's address.

> **The `System.out.print` and `System.out.println` methods take only <u>one</u> parameter.**

If you need to print several things, use the + operator for concatenating strings. You can also concatenate a string and an `int` or a `double`: the latter will be converted into a string. For example:

```
System.out.println(3 + " hours " + 15 + " minutes.");
```

The displayed result will be

```
3 hours 15 minutes.
```

You can also concatenate a string and an object: the object's `toString` method will be called to convert it into a string. For example:

```
int n = 3, d = 4;
Fraction f = new Fraction(n, d);
System.out.println(f + " = " + (double)n / (double)d);
```

The displayed result will be

```
3/4 = 0.75
```

Just be careful not to apply a + operator to two numbers or two objects other than strings: in the former case the numbers will be added rather than concatenated; the latter will cause a syntax error.

3.6. Exceptions

An exception is a <u>run-time</u> event that signals an abnormal condition in the program. Some run-time errors, such as invalid user input or an attempt to read past the end of a file, are considered fixable. The `try-catch-finally` syntax allows the programmer to catch and process the exception and have the program recover. This type of exception is called a *checked exception*.

> **Checked exceptions and the `try-catch` statements are <u>not</u> in the AP subset.**

Other errors, such as an array index out of bounds or an attempt to call a method of a non-existing object (null reference) are considered fatal: the program displays an error message with information about where the error occurred, then quits. This type of exception is called an *unchecked exception*.

In Java, an exception is an object of one of Java exception classes. The Java library implements many types of exceptions, and, if necessary, you can derive your own exception class from one of the library classes. For an AP CS exam, you are expected to understand what `ArithmeticException`, `IndexOutOfBoundsException`, `ArrayIndexOutOfBoundsException`, `NullPointerException`, `IllegalArgumentException`, and `ClassCastException` mean.

We say that a program "throws" an exception. An `ArithmeticException` is thrown in case of an arithmetic error, such as integer division by zero. (You would expect `Math.sqrt(x)` to throw an `ArithmeticException` for a negative x, but it doesn't — it returns NaN, "not a number" instead. Java exception handling is inconsistent at times.)

`ArrayIndexOutOfBoundsException` is self-explanatory: it is thrown at run time when an array index is negative or is greater than `array.length-1`. `ArrayList` methods throw a similar `IndexOutOfBoundsException`.

`NullPointerException` is thrown when you forget to initialize an object-type instance variable or an element of an array and then try to call its method. For example:

```
public class MyClass
{
  private String name;  // name is set to null
  ...
    // the following statement is inside a method:
    int n = name.length();   // if name has not been initialized
                             // by MyClass's constructor, this statement
                             // will throw a NullPointerException
  ...
}
```

Another example:

```
        Integer[] a = new Integer[10];
        int x = a[0].intValue();      // a[0] is null -- Java interpreter
                                      // throws a NullPointerException
```

A third example:

```
public class DeckOfCards
{
  private Card[] cards;

  public DeckOfCards()
  {
    cards = new Card[52];    // all elements set to null
         // Forgot to initialize each element
  }

  public Card getCard(int k) { return cards[k]; }
}
```

In a client class,

```
        DeckOfCards deck = new DeckOfCards();
        int r = deck.getCard(0).getRank();
```

will throw a `NullPointerException`, because `deck.getCard(0)` returns `null`.

A `ClassCastException` is thrown when you are trying to cast an object into a class type to which it does not belong. For example:

```
        ArrayList<Object> list = new ArrayList<Object>();
        list.add("123.456");
        Double x = (Double)list.get(0);  // ClassCastException: trying to cast
                                         //   a string "123.456" into a Double
```

Throwing your own exceptions

Occasionally you need to "throw" your own exception. For example, you are implementing the `remove` method for a queue data structure. What is your method to do when the queue is empty? Throw a `NoSuchElementException`.

`throw` is a Java reserved word. The syntax for using it is

```
throw < exception >;
```

For example:

```
if (items.size() == 0)
   throw new NoSuchElementException();
```

Throw an `IllegalStateException` if an object is not ready for a particular method call. For example:

```
public void stop()
{
  if (!isMoving())
    throw new IllegalStateException();  // displays a message
                                        //   and quits
  speed = 0;
  ...
}
```

Throw an `IllegalArgumentException` if a constructor or method receives an unacceptable parameter. For example:

```
public Clock(int hours, int mins)
{
  if (hours < 0 || hours >= 24 || mins < 0 || mins >= 60)
    throw new IllegalArgumentException();
  ...
}
```

Your code does not need to explicitly throw an `ArithmeticException`, `NullPointerException` , `ClassCastException`, or `ArrayIndexOutOfBoundsException` — Java does it automatically when a triggering condition occurs.

26

Consider the following class:

```
public class TestSample
{
  private ArrayList<Integer> samples;

  public TestSample(int n)
  {
    for (int k = 0; k < n; k++)
    {
      samples.add(k);
    }
  }

  public double getBestRatio()
  {
    double maxRatio = samples.get(1).intValue() /
                              samples.get(0).intValue();

    for (int k = 1; k < samples.size() - 1; k++)
    {
      double ratio = samples.get(k+1).intValue() /
                              samples.get(k).intValue();
      if (ratio > maxRatio)
      {
        maxRatio = ratio;
      }
    }
    return maxRatio;
  }
}
```

What is the result of the following code segment?

```
TestSample t = new TestSample(1);
System.out.println(t.getBestRatio());
```

(A) NullPointerException
(B) ArithmeticException
(C) IndexOutOfBoundsException
(D) ClassCastException
(E) Infinity

☞ Luckily we don't have to look at the `getBestRatio` method. The programmer has forgotten to initialize `samples` and calls its `add` method in the constructor. The answer is A.

Now suppose we added

```
samples = new ArrayList<Integer>();
```

at the top of the constructor. What would happen then? `getBestRatio` would call `samples.get(1)`, but we would have added only one value to `samples`. The answer would be C, `IndexOutOfBoundsException`.

Now suppose we changed

```
TestSample t = new TestSample(1);
```

to

```
TestSample t = new TestSample(2);
```

What would happen then? The answer would be B, `ArithmeticException`, because we would have an integer division by 0.

Actually, the programmer probably meant to write

```
double maxRatio = (double)samples.get(1).intValue() /
                         samples.get(0).intValue();
```

What would happen if we added this cast to a `double`? We would still expect an `ArithmeticException` for floating-point division by 0, but Java actually prints "Infinity." The answer would be E (but you do not have to know that).

Note that the numbers and objects *are* cast correctly into `Integer`s automatically where necessary due to autoboxing, so `ClassCastException` does not occur. ↵

Chapter 4. Program Design and OOP Concepts

4.1. Computer Systems

You are probably aware by now that a typical computer system's *hardware* has at least one *processor*, (a.k.a. CPU), some *RAM* (*random-access memory*), secondary storage devices (such as magnetic disks, CD-ROM drives, etc.) and *peripherals* (printers, sound cards and speakers, mice or other pointing devices, wireless network adapters, etc.).

Chances are you also have worked with an *operating system*, a piece of *software* that controls the computer system and interacts with a user. Linux, Windows, and Mac OS, are examples of operating systems. A *compiler* is also a piece of software. It checks syntax in programs written in a high-level programming language and translates them into machine code. In Java, a compiler translates the *source code* (program's text, stored in a file with the extension `.java`) into machine-independent *bytecode* (stored in a file with the extension `.class`). Bytecode constitutes instructions for the *Java Virtual Machine* (*JVM*) that are independent of a particular computer model and operating system. Java *interpreter*, different for different computer models, reads bytecode and executes corresponding instructions on a particular computer. A *debugger* is a program that helps you run and test your program in a controlled way to find errors ("bugs") in it. The editor, compiler, interpreter, debugger, and other *software development tools* are combined in one package called an *IDE* (Integrated Development Environment), such as Eclipse or NetBeans. An IDE has a *GUI* (Graphical User Interface).

Issues of system reliability and security and the legal and ethical issues related to computer use are not precisely defined in the AP exam guidelines. Questions about these topics would have to be rather general.

4.2. Program Design and Development Methodology

Computer science courses try to emphasize problem solving, as opposed to just programming in a particular language or using specific hardware platforms. The exam topics related to general software design and development methodology emphasize *procedural* and *data abstraction*, *functional decomposition*, and the *reusability* of code. These topics are discussed in the context of *object-oriented* software design and development. Here is a very brief glossary of the relevant terms:

Specifications — a detailed description of what a piece of software should accomplish and how it should behave and interact with the user. Specifications may be given for a whole system, one module, or even one class or method.

Object-oriented programming (OOP) — a programming methodology based on designing the program as a world of interacting objects arranged in hierarchies of classes and using encapsulation and polymorphism.

Top-down design — a design methodology in which you first define the general structure of the program, laying out high-level classes and their interactions, and then refine the design of each class, identifying subtasks and smaller classes or methods. Then you refine the design of subtasks, individual methods, and so on.

Top-down development — similar to top-down design: you first lay out your code at a high level, defining general classes and methods. These methods may call lower-level methods, which are not yet implemented. You can compile and sometimes even test high-level pieces of your code by substituting "stubs" — empty or greatly simplified placeholders — for low-level methods that are still not implemented.

Data structure — a way of organizing data combined with methods of accessing and manipulating the data. For example, a two-dimensional array, together with methods or operators for accessing and modifying the values of its elements, is a data structure that may be useful for representing tables, grids, matrices, or images.

Encapsulation and information hiding — the practice of making all instance variables and helper methods that are used only inside the class private. The clients of a class can use such a class only through its public constructors and public methods.

Procedural abstraction — specifying and using procedures and functions (methods) without knowing the details of their implementation.

Reusable code — debugged and tested libraries, classes, or fragments of code that are somewhat general in nature and ready to be reused in other projects. Reusing code speeds up software development, no matter what methodology is being employed.

Team project development — object-oriented languages, such as Java, allow you to conveniently split a project into separate pieces and assign their development to different team members. Encapsulation and information hiding facilitate teamwork on a project by limiting the amount of interaction needed between developers.

User interface — the behavior of a program as it interacts with a user: screens, menus, commands, messages, graphics, sounds, and so on.

These are very general concepts, and it is not easy to come up with multiple-choice or free-response questions that test in-depth understanding of these concepts. In past exams, design and implementation questions have been limited to specific data structures and algorithms, which sometimes used these terms in their descriptions. An exam may include a free-response "design" question that asks you to design a small class, then implement and/or use some of its features (see Section 4.7).

4.3. Inheritance

Inheritance allows a programmer to state that one class *extends* another class, inheriting its features. In Java terminology, a *subclass* extends a *superclass*. extends is a Java reserved word. For example:

```
                    Subclass        Superclass
                      /               /
                     /               /
public class HighSchool extends School
{
   ...
}
```

Inheritance implements the IS-A relationship between objects: an object of a subclass type IS-A(n) object of the superclass. A high school is a kind of school. A HighSchool object IS-A (kind of) School object. Technically this means that in your program you can use an object of a subclass whenever an object of its superclass is expected. For example:

```
School sch = new HighSchool(...);
```

If a constructor or a method in a client class expects a School type of parameter to be passed to it, you can call it with a HighSchool type of parameter. Objects of a subclass inherit the data type of the superclass.

In Java, a class can directly extend only one superclass — there is no *multiple inheritance* for classes. But more than one subclass can be derived from the same superclass:

```
public class HighSchool extends School ...
public class ElementarySchool extends School ...
public class DrivingSchool extends School ...
```

The IS-A relationship of inheritance is not to be confused with the HAS-A relationship between objects. That *X* "has a" *Y* simply means that *Y* is a data field (an instance variable) in *X*. For example, you might say that a HighSchool HAS-A MarchingBand, but not that a HighSchool IS-A MarchingBand.

Subclass methods

A subclass inherits all the public methods of its superclass, and you can call an inherited method of the same object without any "dot prefix." For example, if `School` has a method

```
public String getName() { ... }
```

then `HighSchool`'s method `registerForAP` can call it directly:

```
public class HighSchool extends School
{
  ...
  public void registerForAP()
  {
    String registrationForm = getName() + ...;
    ...
  }
  ...
}
```

`HighSchool`'s clients can call `getName`, too, for any `HighSchool` object:

```
HighSchool hs = new HighSchool(...);
String name = hs.getName();
```

A subclass can add its own methods. It can also *override* (redefine) a method of the superclass by providing its own version with exactly the same *signature* (the same name, return type, and number, types, and order of parameters). For example, `School` may have a `toString` method, and `HighSchool`'s `toString` may override it.

Occasionally it may be necessary to make an explicit call to a superclass's public method from a subclass. This is accomplished by using the super-dot prefix. For example:

```
public class HighSchool extends School
{
  ...
  public String toString()
  {
    return super.toString() + collegeAcceptance() + ...;
  }
  ...
}
```

The superclass's <u>private</u> methods are not callable in the subclass.

Subclass constructors

> **Constructors are not inherited: a subclass has to provide its own or rely on the default no-args constructor.**

A subclass's constructors can explicitly call the superclass's constructors using the keyword `super`. For example:

```
public class School
{
  private String name;
  private int numStudents;

  public School(String nm, int num)
  {
    name = nm;
    numStudents = num;
  }
  ...
}

public class ElementarySchool extends School
{
  private int highestGrade;

  public ElementarySchool(String nm, int num, int grade)
  {
    super(nm, num); // calls School's constructor
    highestGrade = grade;
  }
  ...
}
```

If `super(...)` is used, it must be the <u>first</u> statement in the subclass's constructor (as in the above example). If `super` is not used, then superclass's no-args constructor is called by default, and it must exist, or the compiler will report an error.

Subclass's fields

A subclass inherits all the class (static) variables and instance variables of its superclass. However, the instance variables are usually declared private (always private in the AP subset) and so cannot be referenced directly in the subclass.

> **The superclass's private variables are <u>not</u> directly accessible in its subclass. So you must use public accessors and modifiers to get and set values instance variables declared in the superclass.**

Superclass's <u>public</u> constants (`public static final` variables) are accessible everywhere.

A subclass can add its own static or instance variables. For example, the class `ElementarySchool` above, a subclass of `School`, adds an instance variable

```
private int highestGrade;
```

Consider the following partial definitions:

```
public class MailingList
{
  private ArrayList<String> people;

  public MailingList() { people = new ArrayList<String>(); }
  public void add(String name) { people.add(name); }
  public ArrayList<String> getPeople() { return people; }

  < Other methods not shown >
}

public class Subscribers extends MailingList
{
  public Subscribers() { }  // Calls super() by default

  // Returns the number of names in people
  private int size()
  {
    return < expression >;
  }

  < Other methods not shown >
}
```

Which of the following should replace < *expression* > in the `size` method of the `Subscribers` class so that the method works as specified?

(A) `super.size();`
(B) `people.size();`
(C) `super.people.size();`
(D) `getPeople().size();`
(E) None of the above

The `MailingList` class HAS-A(n) `ArrayList<String> people` as an instance variable, but `MailingList` is not an `ArrayList`: it does not extend `ArrayList`. The programmer has not provided a `size` method for the `MailingList` class (a design mistake), so Choice A is wrong. Choices B or C might look plausible at first, but `people` is private in `MailingList`, so it is not directly accessible in `Subscribers`. But `MailingList` has a public method `getPeople`, and this method is inherited and accessible in the `Subscribers` class. `getPeople` returns an `ArrayList<String>`, which has a method `size` that returns the size of the list. The answer is D.

Also note that

```
return getPeople().size();
```

is equivalent to

```
ArrayList<String> temp = getPeople();
return temp.size();
```

4.4. Class Hierarchies

If you have a class, you can derive one or several subclasses from it. Each of these classes can in turn serve as a superclass for other subclasses. You can build a whole tree-like hierarchy of classes, in which each class has one superclass. For example:

In fact, in Java all classes belong to one big hierarchy; it starts at a class called `Object`. If you do not specify that your class extends any particular class, then it extends `Object` by default. Therefore, every object IS-A(n) `Object`. The `Object` class provides a few common methods, including `equals` and `toString`, but these methods are not very useful and usually get redefined in classes lower in the hierarchy.

Class hierarchies exist to allow reuse of code from higher classes in the lower classes without duplication and to promote a more logical design. A class lower in the hierarchy inherits the data types of all classes above it.

For example, if we have classes

```
public class Animal { ... }
public class Dog extends Animal { ... }
public class Spaniel extends Dog { ... }
```

all of the following declarations are legal:

```
Spaniel s = new Spaniel(...);
Dog d = new Spaniel(...);
Animal a = new Spaniel(...);
```

But if you also define

```
public class Horse extends Animal { ... }
```

then

```
Horse x = new Spaniel(...);
```

is an error, of course: `Spaniel` does not extend `Horse`.

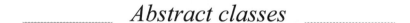

Abstract classes

Classes closer to the top of the hierarchy are more abstract — the properties and methods of their objects are more general. As you proceed down the hierarchy, the classes become more specific and the properties of their objects are more concretely spelled out. Java syntax allows you to define a class that is officially designated `abstract`. For example:

```
public abstract class Solid { ... }
```

An abstract class can have constructors and methods; however, some of its methods may be declared `abstract` and left without code. For example:

```
public abstract class Solid
{
  ...
  public abstract double getVolume();
  ...
}
```

This indicates that every `Solid` object has a method that returns its volume, but the actual implementation may depend on the specific type of solid. For example, the `Sphere` and `Cube` subclasses of `Solid` will define `getVolume` differently.

A class in which all the methods are defined is called *concrete*. Naturally, abstract classes appear near the top of the hierarchy and concrete classes sit below. You cannot instantiate an abstract class, but you can declare variables or arrays of its type. For example:

```
Solid s1 = new Sphere(radius);
Solid s2 = new Cube(side);
Solid[] solids = { new Sphere(100), new Cube(100) };
```

Questions 28-29 refer to the following partial class definitions:

```
public abstract class Account
{
  public Account() { ... }
}

public class BankAccount extends Account
{
  private double balance;

  public BankAccount(double amount)
  {
    super(); // optional: default
    balance = amount;
  }
}

public class CheckingAccount extends BankAccount
{
  private String customerName;

  public CheckingAccount(String name, double amount)
  {
    < missing statements >
  }
  ...
}
```

28

Which of the following is an acceptable replacement for < *missing statements* > in `CheckingAccount`'s constructor?

    I. `balance = amount;`
        `customerName = name;`

    II. `super(amount);`
        `customerName = name;`

    III. `super(name, amount);`

(A) I only
(B) II only
(C) I and II only
(D) II and III only
(E) I, II and III

`balance` is private in `BankAccount`; it is not accessible in `CheckingAccount`, so Option I cannot be right. `BankAccount` does not have a constructor with two parameters, so Option III cannot be right either. Option II is the way to go. The answer is B.

29

Which of the following declarations are valid?

    I. `Account acct = new BankAccount(10.00);`

    II. `CheckingAccount acct = new BankAccount(10.00);`

    III. `BankAccount acct = new CheckingAccount("Amy", 10.00);`

(A) I and II only
(B) II and III only
(C) I and III only
(D) I, II, and III
(E) None of the three

It may appear that Option I is wrong because an abstract class `Account` cannot be instantiated. But in fact we are not instantiating `Account` — we are instantiating `BankAccount` and assigning the newly created `BankAccount` object to an `Account` variable. Since a `BankAccount` IS-A(n) `Account`, we are okay. We only have to make sure that `BankAccount` has a constructor that takes one `double` parameter (which it does). Options II and III are clearly problematic as a pair: either a `BankAccount` IS-A `CheckingAccount` or a `CheckingAccount` IS-A `BankAccount`, but not both. Here `CheckingAccount` extends `BankAccount`, so Option III is okay (again, provided `CheckingAccount` has a constructor that takes a `String` and `double` parameters). The answer is C.

4.5. Polymorphism

Polymorphism is a mechanism that ensures that the correct method is called for an object disguised as a more generic type. In our "solids" example, if we write

```
double volume = solids[0].getVolume();
```

the compiler does not know whether `solids[0]` is a `Sphere` or a `Cube`. The decision of which `getVolume` method to call is postponed until run time. In Java implementation, each object holds a pointer to a table of entry points to its methods; thus the object itself "knows" what type of object it is. This technique is called *dynamic method binding* — which method to call is decided at run time, not compile time.

> **Polymorphism is a feature of Java and other object-oriented languages; all you have to do is understand it and use it correctly.**

One common situation when polymorphism comes into play occurs when different types of objects are mixed together in an array or list, as shown in the above example. This code

```
for (Solid solid : solids)
    totalVolume += solid.getVolume();
```

works no matter what `Solids` are stored in the `solids` array because the appropriate `getVolume` method is called for each element of the array. This is true even if several different types of `Solids` are in the `solids` array, such as `Sphere`, `Cube`, or `Pyramid`.

Another situation for polymorphism occurs when a method takes a more generic type of parameter and a client class passes a more specific type of parameter to the method. For example, one of the overloaded versions of `System.out`'s `print` method takes an `Object` type as a parameter. This method may be implemented as follows:

```
public void print(Object x)
{
  if (x != null)
    print(x.toString());
  else
    print("<null>");
}
```

This method works for any type of object `x` with a reasonable `toString` method defined (including `Integer`, `Double`, etc.). Polymorphism assures that the appropriate `toString` method is called for each type of `x`.

Given

```
public class Person
{
  private String name;

  public Person(String nm) { name = nm; }
  public String getName() { return name; }
  public String toString { return getName(); }
}

public class OldLady extends Person
{
  private int age;

  public OldLady(String nm, int yrs) { super(name); age = yrs; }
  public String getName() { return "Mrs. " + super.getName(); }
  public int getAge() { return age; }
}
```

what is the output of the following statements?

```
Person p = new OldLady("Robinson", 92);
System.out.println(p + ", " + ((OldLady)p).getAge());
```

(A) `Mrs. Robinson, 92`
(B) `Robinson, 92`
(C) `Robinson`
(D) `ClassCastException`
(E)   No output due to infinite recursion

☞ In this question we have to restore a somewhat convoluted sequence of events:

1.   The variable p is disguised as a `Person` type, but it is actually an `OldLady`.

2.   `p + ", "` calls p's `toString` method. `OldLady` inherits `toString` from `Person`, so `Person`'s `toString` is called.

3.   `toString` in turn calls `getName`. Which one? This is the trickiest part. Both `Person` and `OldLady` have a `getName` method, but, <u>due to polymorphism</u>, `OldLady`'s `getName` will be called (notwithstanding the fact that we call it from `Person`'s `toString` method).

4.   `OldLady`'s `getName` takes `"Mrs. "` and appends to it the result of `super.getName()`. The latter explicitly calls `Person`'s `getName`, which simply returns the name.

5.   Finally we cast p back to the `OldLady` type — we need this to call its `getAge` method. A `Person` does not have `getAge`, and the compiler does not keep track of what type we assigned to p. `getAge`'s result is appended to the output string.

Choice B tries to make you forget about polymorphism or suggests that polymorphism does not apply here. It does. Choice C is an awkward attempt to confuse you about p's data type. Deep inside, p is not just a `Person` but an `OldLady`, so it does have a `getAge` method once we cast it to `OldLady`. If p were only a `Person`, the cast to `OldLady` would cause a `ClassCastException`, as suggested in Choice D. Choice E hints that `getName` infinitely calls itself. This does not happen here: `OldLady`'s `getName` explicitly calls `Person`'s `getName` as indicated by the super-dot prefix. We would have infinite recursion only if we forgot the super-dot prefix. The answer is A. ⏎

4.6. Interfaces

In Java, an interface is even more "abstract" than an abstract class. An interface has no constructors or instance variables and no code at all — just headers for methods. All its methods are public and abstract. For example:

```
public interface Fillable
{
  void fill(int x);
  int getCurrentAmount();
  int getMaximumCapacity();
}
```

(No need to repeat "public abstract" for each method in an interface — it is understood.)

A class "implements" an interface by supplying code for all the interface methods. `implements` is a reserved word. For example:

```
public class Car implements Fillable
{
  private int fuelTankCapacity;
  private int fuelAmount;
  ...
  public void fill(int gallons) { fuelAmount += gallons; }
  public int getCurrentAmount() { return fuelAmount; }
  public int getMaximumCapacity() { return fuelTankCapacity; }
}

public class VendingMachine implements Fillable
{
  private int currentStock;
  ...
  public void fill(int qty) { currentStock += qty; }
  public int getCurrentAmount() { return currentStock; }
  public int getMaximumCapacity() { return 20; }
}
```

> **For a concrete class to implement an interface, it must define <u>all</u> the methods required by the interface. It must also explicitly state that it implements the interface. A class that claims it implements an interface but does not define some of the interface methods must be declared `abstract`.**

A class can extend only one class, but it can implement several interfaces. For example:

```
public class Car extends Vehicle implements Fillable, Sellable { ... }
```

Each interface adds a secondary data type to the objects of the class that implements it. If a class *C* implements interface *I*, objects of *C* can be disguised as type *I* objects and polymorphism applies (the same way as for subclasses). For example, we can have a method:

```
/** Fills all objects in the array a to capacity
 */
public void fillUp(Fillable[] a)
{
  for (Fillable f : a)
    f.fill(f.getMaximumCapacity() - f.getCurrentAmount());
}
```

The formula works polymorphically for different types of `Fillable` objects that might be stored in the array `a`.

> **If class *C* implements interface *I*, all subclasses of *C* automatically implement *I*.**

Interfaces help us write more general methods, facilitating code reuse.

The `Comparable<T>` *interface*

The library (built-in) interface `java.lang.Comparable<T>` is widely used for designating objects that can be compared in some way.

> **`Comparable<T>` is not in the AP subset, but it is better to understand what it is about, because `String`, `Integer`, and `Double` implement it and you are responsible for using their `compareTo` methods.**

We compare objects, for example, when we arrange them in order (sorting) or perform a binary search. Objects of a class that implements `Comparable` are said to have a *natural ordering* defined.

Starting with Java 5.0, the `Comparable<T>` interface is a "generic" interface, that is, it works with objects of a specific type. The `Comparable<T>` interface specifies only one method:

```
int compareTo(T other);
```

The method returns a positive integer if this object is "greater than" the other, zero if they are "equal," and a negative integer if this object is "less than" the other. (Sort of like `this` "minus" `other`.) It is up to the programmer to define what "smaller" and "greater" might mean when comparing objects of his class and whether the value returned by `compareTo` has any meaning besides telling which object is larger or smaller.

`compareTo` takes one parameter of the type T — and it is usually assumed that the parameter belongs to the same class that implements `Comparable<`T`>`. For example:

```
public class Flight implements Comparable<Flight>
{
   ...
  public int compareTo(Flight other)
  {
    return getDepartureTime() - other.getDepartureTime();
  }
}
```

`String`, `Integer`, and `Double` all implement `Comparable`, but, naturally, they do so in different ways. Strings are compared lexicographically. The comparison is case-sensitive, and all uppercase letters precede (are "smaller than") all lowercase letters. `Integer` and `Double` objects are compared as usual, based on their numeric values.

The `Comparable<`T`>` interface does not specify an `equals` method, and a class that implements `Comparable<`T`>` will compile without an `equals` method defined. But it is better to override the `equals` method inherited from `Object` and make it consistent with `compareTo`, to avoid possible errors later. For example:

```
public boolean equals(Object x)
{
  return x instanceof Flight && compareTo((Flight)x) == 0;
}
```

The Boolean operator `instanceof` is not in the AP subset, except in the context of the GridWorld case study.

Note that the parameter to your `equals` method should have the type `Object`, so that your `equals` indeed overrides `Object`'s `equals`.

Consider the following class:

```
public class Fraction implements Comparable<Fraction>
{
  private int num, denom;

  public int getNum() { return num; }
  public int getDenom() { return denom; }
  public double doubleValue() { return (double)num / denom; }

  < other constructors and methods not shown >
}
```

Which of the following would appropriately implement a `compareTo` method, required by the `Comparable<Fraction>` interface?

I.
```
public int compareTo(Object other)
{
  Fraction f = (Fraction)other;
  return getNum() * f.getDenom() -
         getDenom() * f.getNum();
}
```

II.
```
public int compareTo(Fraction other)
{
  double x = doubleValue();
  double y = other.doubleValue();
  if (x < y)
    return -1;
  else if (x > y)
    return 1;
  else
    return 0;
}
```

III.
```
public int compareTo(Fraction other)
{
  return (int)(doubleValue() - other.doubleValue());
}
```

(A) I only
(B) II only
(C) I and II only
(D) II and III only
(E) I, II, and III

☞   Option I would be problematic on an actual exam. First, it assumes that students know how to subtract fractions, which can't be taken for granted. Second, it is ambiguous with regard to possible arithmetic overflow: can we assume that the numerators and denominators of the fractions are small enough so that their products do not overflow the `int` range? Luckily we can eliminate this answer because the `compareTo` method is defined incorrectly: the parameter must be a `Fraction`, not an `Object`. If we put `Object` there, the compiler will display a cryptic error message "Fraction must be declared abstract" (because `compareTo(Fraction)` is not defined). Option II works, even though it provides a rather truncated result of the comparison: `compareTo` can return only 0, 1, or –1. Recall that only the sign of a comparison result really matters. Option III fulfills the formal requirements, but fractions that differ "by a small fraction" will be deemed equal. This is not in the spirit of `compareTo` for arithmetic objects. If a question like this happened to slip past exam editors, we'd say the answer was B.   ↵

32

What is the output from the following code segment?

```
Comparable<Integer> x = new Integer(123);     // Line 1
System.out.println(x.compareTo("123"));       // Line 2
```

(A)   0
(B)   A positive integer
(C)   A syntax error on Line 1
(D)   A syntax error on Line 2
(E)   `ClassCastException`

☞   There are three separate issues here. First, on Line 1, we are assigning an `Integer` object to a variable of the `Comparable<Integer>` type. Is this okay? Yes, because the `Integer` class implements `Comparable<Integer>`. Second, on Line 2 we are passing a string to x's `compareTo` method. Is this okay? No, because starting with Java 5.0, `compareTo`'s parameter has the type of the compared objects, in this case `Integer`. So the compiler won't allow a call to `compareTo` with a `String` parameter. The answer is D.   ↵

4.7. "Design" Question

The free-response section of the exam may include a "design" question, which asks you to design and write a short class — see, for example, free-response Question 2 in the 2010 AP CS exam and our solution (Chapter 7).

A design question may ask you to write a subclass of a given class, especially in the context of the GridWorld case study. For example, you might need to write a subclass of `Bug` or `Critter` — see the 2011 exam, Question 2, and the 2012 exam, Question 2, and our solutions (Chapter 7).

> **In writing a subclass of a given class avoid duplicating code of the superclass's constructors or methods —use `super(...)` or `super.someMethod(...)` calls whenever possible.**

In designing and writing your class, pay special attention to the following:

- Use reasonable and consistent style with proper indentation and generous spacing between statements.

- Do not include comments — they are not required and you will waste time.

- Choose meaningful names for your class, its methods and their parameters, and fields and local variables. A class name starts with an uppercase letter; the names of all methods, their parameters, and instance variables start with a lowercase letter. Make sure that all constructors have the same name as the class.

- <u>Make all instance variables private</u> and group them together at the top of the class.

- Make all methods public, unless there is a specific hint in the question that some of them are "helper" methods used only inside this class — then make them private.

- Specify appropriate return types for all methods. Recall that constructors do not have a return type, not even `void`.

- Provide public "accessor" methods if specified in the question. An accessor returns the value of the respective instance variable. Accessor names may start with "get." For example:

```
public double getBalance() { ... }
```

- Provide "modifier" methods if specified in the question. Modifiers set the values of one or several instance variables. Modifier names often start with "set". For example:

```
public void setPrice(double amount) { ... }
```

Part (b) may ask you to write a fragment of code from a client class that uses your class written in Part (a). In answering this part of the question, pay special attention to the following:

- Use constructors and call public methods of your Part (a) class with appropriate numbers, types, and order of parameters, consistent with what you wrote in Part (a). Use this opportunity to double-check the code you wrote in Part (a).

- Never refer directly to private instance variables of your Part (a) class in the client class; rather, call accessors or modifiers.

- It is allowed (and often desirable) to reuse in the client class the same names for variables as you used for similar formal parameters in methods in Part (a). For example, if in Part (a) you wrote

```
public void setPrice(double amount) { ... }
```

then in Part (b) you may write

```
double amount = ...;
...
item.setPrice(amount);
```

Chapter 5. Algorithms

5.1. Iterations

Most programming languages provide iteration control structures, such as the `while` and `for` loops in Java. Simple loops are good for iterating (repeating the same operation) over a range of numbers or over the elements of a one-dimensional array or a list.

A `for` loop is a convenient and idiomatic way to *traverse* a one-dimensional array:

```
for (int k = 0;  k < a.length;  k++)
{
  System.out.println(a[k]);       // ... or do whatever you need to do
                                  //      with each element
}
```

or

```
for (T x : a)
{
  System.out.println(x);
}
```

where T is the data type of the elements of a.

For working with two-dimensional arrays you usually need *nested* loops. The following code, for example, traverses a two-dimensional array m:

```
int nRows = m.length, nCols = m[0].length;

for (int r = 0;  r < nRows;  r++)
{
  for (int c = 0;  c < nCols;  c++)
  {
    System.out.println(m[r][c]);   // ... or do whatever...
  }
}
```

Note that braces are optional if the body of the loop has only one statement:

```
for (int i = 1;  i < n;  i++)
  for (int j = 0;  j < i;  j++)
    if (a[i] == a[j])
      count++;
```

In "triangular" nested loops, the outer loop may run, say, for i from 1 to $n-1$ and the inner loop may run for j from 0 to $i-1$. In the above example the inner loop runs i times for $i = 1, ..., n-1$, so the total number of comparisons is

$$1 + 2 + ... + (n-1) = \frac{n(n-1)}{2}$$

The "for each" loop makes it easy to traverse a `List`:

```
List<String> list = new ArrayList<String>();
...
for (String s : list)
{
    ...
}
```

Max and min

A common example of using loops is to find a maximum or a minimum value (or its position) in an array:

```
/** Returns maxValue such that maxValue >= a[k] for any 0 <= k <= n-1
 *   and maxValue = a[k] for some k.
 *   Precondition: array a holds values a[0], ..., a[n-1]; n >= 1
 */
public double max(double[] a, int n)
{
    double maxValue = a[0];

    for (int k = 1; k < n; k++)
    {
        if (a[k] > maxValue)
            maxValue = a[k];
    }
    return maxValue;
}
```

33

Consider the following method:

```java
public int mysteryMax(int[] a)
{
  int m = 0;

  for (int i = 0; i < a.length; i++)
  {
    int sum = 0;

    for (int k = i; k < a.length; k++)
    {
      sum += a[k];
      if (sum > m)
        m = sum;
    }
  }

  return m;
}
```

If a contains −1, −3, 2, −3, 2, 1, what value will be returned by `mysteryMax(a)`?

(A)   −2
(B)   −1
(C)   1
(D)   2
(E)   3

☞   The method returns the largest sum of several consecutive elements in a (or 0 if all the sums are negative). The answer is E. ↵

34

Consider the following method:

```
/** Returns the largest sum of any two elements.
 *  Precondition: n >= 2; a[0] ... a[n-1] are filled with values
 */
public double maxSum(double[] a, int n)
{
  < missing code >
}
```

Which of the following code segments can replace < *missing code* > so that the method works as specified?

I.
```
double max = a[0] + a[1];

for (int i = 1; i < n; i++)
  for (int j = 0; j < i; j++)
    if (a[i] + a[j] > max)
      max = a[i] + a[j];
return max;
```

II.
```
double max1 = a[0], max2 = a[0];

for (int i = 1; i < n; i++)
  if (a[i] > max1)
    max1 = a[i];

for (int i = 1; i < n; i++)
  if (a[i] != max1 && a[i] > max2)
    max2 = a[i];

return max1 + max2;
```

III.
```
double max1 = a[0], max2 = a[1];

if (a[1] > a[0])
{
  max1 = a[1];
  max2 = a[0];
}

for (int i = 2; i < n; i++)
{
  if (a[i] > max1)
  {
    max2 = max1;
    max1 = a[i];
  }
  else if (a[i] > max2)
    max2 = a[i];
}

return max1 + max2;
```

(A)   I only
(B)   II only
(C)   I and II only
(D)   I and III only
(E)   I, II, and III

☞   This is a lot of code for one question, so we need to focus on the key points. The code in Option I is inefficient but most straightforward: using triangular nested loops we generate sums for all the different pairs of elements and choose the largest of them. Option II is based on a different idea: finding the largest value and then the second largest value in two separate traversals of the array. But it has two problems. First, if the largest value happens to be `a[0]`, then the second `for` loop will never update `max2`. Second, it will fail if the largest value appears in the array more than once. The method description states that the method is looking for the largest sum of any two elements, but these can have the same value.

To work, Option II would need a couple of minor fixes:

```
int iMax1 = 0, iMax2 = 0;

for (int i = 1; i < n; i++)
  if (a[i] > a[iMax1])
    iMax1 = i;

if (iMax1 == 0)
  iMax2 = 1;

for (int i = 1; i < n; i++)
  if (i != iMax1 && a[i] > a[iMax2])
    iMax2 = i;

return a[iMax1] + a[iMax2];
```

In Option III we find both the largest and the second largest elements in one sweep. Note how the largest element becomes the second largest when we find another one with a greater value. It works fine. The answer is D. ↵

Insert in order

Many applications, including Insertion Sort, require you to insert a value into a sorted array while preserving the order:

```
/** Shifts values a[k], ..., a[n-1] appropriately into
 *  a[k+1], ..., a[n] and inserts newValue into a[k] so that the
 *  ascending order is preserved.
 *  Precondition:  a[0] <= a[1] <= ... <= a[n-1]; n < a.length
 */
public void insertInOrder(int[] a, int n, int newValue)
{
  // Shift values to the right by one until you find the
  //     place to insert:

  int k = n;               // Start at the end
  while (k > 0 && a[k-1] > newValue)
  {
    a[k] = a[k-1];
    k--;
  }
  a[k] = newValue;
}
```

In the above code, we shift the values in the array to the right by one to create a vacant slot and then insert the new value into the vacancy thus created. Note that the shifting has to proceed from the end, so that each shifted value is placed into a vacant slot and does not overwrite any data (Figure 5-1).

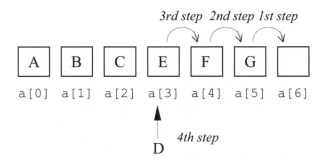

Figure 5-1. Inserting a new value in the middle of a sorted array

35

Consider an array a that contains n integer values sorted in ascending order
(n < a.length). Which of the following code segments correctly inserts
newValue into a, preserving the ascending order?

I.
```
for (int k = n; k > 0; k--)
{
  if (a[k-1] <= newValue)
  {
    a[k] = newValue;
    k = 0;
  }
  else
    a[k] = a[k-1];
}
```

II.
```
int k = n;
while (k > 0 && a[k-1] > newValue)
{
  a[k] = a[k-1];
  k--;
}
a[k] = newValue;
```

III.
```
int k = 0;

while (k < n && a[k] < newValue)
  k++;

for (int j = n-1; j >= k; j--)
{
  a[j+1] = a[j];
}
a[k] = newValue;
```

(A) I only
(B) II only
(C) III only
(D) I and II only
(E) II and III only

☞ When you have to decide whether such code is correct, check the boundary
conditions first: does it work if you have to insert the value at the very beginning or at
the very end of the array? The code in Option I, for example, looks good at first —
similar to the insertInOrder method described above. But if newValue is smaller
than all the values in the array, nothing is inserted. Option II is equivalent to the
insertInOrder code above. Option III uses a more step-wise approach: first find
the place to insert, then shift the values above that place, then insert. In Option III, it
is sufficient to check that this code works for newValue being the smallest and the
largest — that means there are no tricks. The answer is E. ⏎

Loop invariants

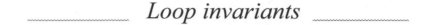

You might find useful the concept of a *loop invariant*. A loop invariant is an assertion about the loop that is relevant to the purpose of the loop and that holds true before and after each iteration through the loop. This assertion is usually expressed as a relation between the variables involved in the loop. Loop invariants are used to reason about programs formally and to prove their correctness without tracing all the iterations through a loop. If you can establish that an assertion is true before the first iteration, and also prove that for any iteration if the assertion is true before that iteration it will remain true after that iteration, then your assertion is a loop invariant. If you are familiar with mathematical induction, you can see how it works here. If not, you can still reason about loop invariants without too much trouble.

36

Consider the following code segment:

```
int count = 0;
int n = 41;
int k = 2;

while (k <= n)
{
  if (isPrime(k))
    count++;
  k++;
}
```

Which of the following statements are loop invariants for the above code?

 I. `k` is a prime
 II. 41 is a prime
 III. `count` is equal to the number of primes from 2 to `k-1`

(A) I only
(B) II only
(C) III only
(D) I and II only
(E) None of the three

☞ Statement I is not an invariant because it varies: k may or may not be a prime as we iterate through the loop. More precisely, k is a prime before the first iteration ($k = 2$) and before the second iteration ($k = 3$), but not after the second iteration ($k = 4$). This eliminates Choices A and D. Statement II is not an invariant for a different reason. Certainly 41 is a prime — so are 37, 43, 47, and an infinite number of other integers. Also, Washington, DC, is the capital of the United States. These facts, while true, do not help us reason about the purpose or correctness of the above code. But Statement III is a typical invariant: it links the values of the variables `count` and `k` and reflects the purpose of the loop, namely counting all the primes from 2 to n. The answer is C. ☜

5.2. Sequential Search and Binary Search

A typical application of a simple loop is *Sequential Search*:

```
/** Returns pos such that 0 <= pos < n and a[pos] == target,
 *  or -1 if target is not among a[0], ..., a[n-1].
 *  Precondition: array a holds values a[0], ..., a[n-1]
 */
public int sequentialSearch(int[] a, int n, int target)
{
  for (int k = 0; k < n; k++)
  {
    if (a[k] == target)
      return k;
  }
  return -1;
}
```

Sequential Search works for any array: the values in the array may be in random order. If an array is sorted (that is, if its elements are arranged in ascending or descending order), then Binary Search is a much more efficient searching method.

Binary Search is a "divide and conquer" method for quickly finding a target value in a sorted array. Suppose the array is sorted in ascending order. We take an element in the middle (or approximately in the middle) of the array and compare it to the target. If they are equal, we're done. If the target is greater, we continue the search in the right half of the array; if it's smaller, we continue in the left half.

For example:

```
/** Returns the position of the element equal to target or -1 if target
 *  is not in the array.
 *  Precondition: array a contains n values sorted in ascending order
 */
public int binarySearch(int[] a, int n, int target)
{
  int left = 0;
  int right = n - 1;

  while (left <= right)
  {
    int middle = (left + right) / 2;
    if (target == a[middle])
      return middle;
    else if (target < a[middle])
      right = middle - 1;      // continue search in the left half
    else
      left = middle + 1;       // continue search in the right half
  }
  return -1;
}
```

Binary Search in an array of $2^k - 1$ elements requires at most k iterations. In other words, Binary Search in an array of n elements requires $\log_2 n$ iterations. Thus in an array of 1,000,000 elements it would need at most 20 iterations. By comparison, Sequential Search in an array of n elements takes, on average, $n/2$ iterations, and in the worst case it may take n iterations.

| 37 |

Suppose that two programs, one using Binary Search and the other using Sequential Search, take (on average) the same amount of time to find a random target value in a sorted array of 30 elements. Roughly how much faster than the Sequential Search program will the Binary Search program run on an array of 1000 elements?

(A)   2 times faster
(B)   10 times faster
(C)   16 times faster
(D)   33 times faster
(E)   50 times faster

☞   Binary Search takes 5 iterations for 30 elements ($32 = 2^5$) and 10 iterations for 1000 elements ($1024 = 2^{10}$). So Binary Search will run roughly two times longer on a 1000-element array than on a 30-element array. Sequential search will run roughly 33 times longer ($1000 \approx 30 \cdot 33$). On 1000 elements, Binary Search will be $33/2 = 16.5$ faster. The answer is C. ☜

38

An e-mail address is a string made up of alphanumeric characters, one or several "dots," and one "@." The short substring after the last dot is called the domain name suffix. For example, in `jane.lee@math.bestacad.org`, "org" is the suffix. Which of the following methods can be used to find the beginning position of the suffix?

    I. A modified Sequential Search in which we scan through the whole array keeping track of the last occurrence of a given character

    II. A modified Sequential Search which proceeds backwards, starting at the end of the array

    III. A modified Binary Search in which each alphanumeric character is treated as '0' and a dot and @ are treated as '1'

(A) I only
(B) II only
(C) III only
(D) I and II only
(E) II and III only

☞ The task is basically to find the last dot in a string. Method I is not the most efficient, but it works:

```
for (int k = 0; k < email.length(); k++)
  if (email.charAt(k) == '.')
    dotPos = k;

// Characters, charAt, and char constants are not in the AP subset

return dotPos;
```

Method II works a bit faster:

```
for (int k = email.length() - 1; k >= 0; k--)
  if (email.charAt(k) == '.')
    return k;
```

The description of Method III tries to confuse you with a binary system which has no relation to Binary Search. The latter won't work here because the string is not sorted and dots are scattered among alphanumeric characters. The answer is D. ☜

5.3.   Selection and Insertion Sorts

Sorting means arranging a list of items in ascending or descending order, according to the values of the items or some key that is part of an item. Sorting algorithms are usually discussed for lists represented as arrays.

> **Selection Sort** and **Insertion Sort** are called *quadratic sorts* because they use two straightforward nested loops and the number of required comparisons is approximately proportional to n^2.

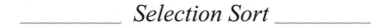
Selection Sort

In *Selection Sort* we iterate for *k* from *n* down to 2: we find the largest among the first *k* elements and swap it with the *k*-th element.

```
/** Sorts n values in array a in ascending order.
 * Precondition: array a contains a[0], ..., a[n-1] (n >= 1)
 */
public void selectionSort(int[] a, int n)
{
  for (int k = n; k >= 2; k--)
  {
    int maxPos = 0;
    for (int i = 1; i < k; i++)
    {
      if (a[i] > a[maxPos])
        maxPos = i;
    }
    // Swap a[maxPos], a[k-1]:
    int temp = a[maxPos]; a[maxPos] = a[k-1]; a[k-1] = temp;
  }
}
```

Or we can use a `while` loop:

```
public void selectionSort(int[] a, int n)
{
  while (n > 1)
  {
    int maxPos = 0;
    for (int i = 1; i < n; i++)
    {
      if (a[i] > a[maxPos])
        maxPos = i;
    }
    int temp = a[maxPos]; a[maxPos] = a[n-1]; a[n-1] = temp;
  }
  n--;
}
```

In another variation of *Selection Sort* we find the smallest among the elements a[k], ..., a[n-1] and swap it with a[k] (for $k = 0, ..., n-2$).

In *Selection Sort*, the inner loop runs $k-1$ times, for $k = n, n-1, ..., 2$.

The total number of comparisons in Selection Sort is always the same:

$$(n-1) + (n-2) + ... + 1 = \frac{n(n-1)}{2}$$

Insertion Sort

In *Insertion Sort*, we iterate for k from 1 up to *n-1*. We keep the first k elements — a[0], a[1], ..., a[k-1] — sorted and insert a[k] among them where it belongs:

```
/** Sorts n values in array a in ascending order
 *  Precondition: array a contains a[0], ..., a[n-1] (n >= 1)
 */
public void insertionSort(int[] a, int n)
{
  for (int k = 1; k < n; k++)
  {
    int temp = a[k];
    int i = k;
    while (i > 0 && a[i-1] > temp)
    {
      a[i] = a[i-1];
      i--;
    }
    a[i] = temp;
  }
}
```

In this version of Insertion Sort, if the array is already sorted, then the inner loop runs just one comparison and we immediately break out of it. Then the method needs a total of $n-1$ comparisons. This is the best case: instead of *quadratic* time, the method executes in *linear* time.

The worst case for this implementation of Insertion Sort is when the array is sorted in reverse order. Then the inner loop runs $k-1$ times and the whole method will need as many comparisons as Selection Sort:

$$1 + 2 + ... + (n-1) = \frac{n(n-1)}{2}$$

The average case is about half that number, still approximately proportional to n^2.

The methods above are just examples of how Selection Sort and Insertion Sort can be implemented. Other variations are possible.

39

Consider the task of sorting the elements of an array in ascending order. Which of the following statements are true?

    I.   Selection Sort always requires more comparisons than Insertion Sort.
    II. Insertion Sort always requires more moves than Selection Sort.
    III. Insertion Sort, on average, requires more moves than Selection Sort.

(A)   I only
(B)   II only
(C)   III only
(D)   I and II only
(E)   II and III only

☞ This question gives us a chance to review the properties of these two quadratic sorts. As we have seen, Statement I is false: although, on average, Selection Sort requires more comparisons, Insertion Sort in the worst case (an array sorted in reverse order) will take as many comparisons as Selection Sort. Statement II is false, too: in the best case, when the array is already sorted, Insertion Sort does not require any moves at all. (Selection Sort, too, with a slight modification, can avoid any moves when the array is already sorted.) Statement III is the vague part: what do we mean, "on average"? First, our array must be large enough to support some conclusions. Sorting an array of three elements will not be representative. Let's assume that we set up an experiment where we generate a fairly large array of random numbers, sort it using each of the two algorithms, and count the number of moves. Intuition tells us that Insertion Sort, on average, needs more moves. Indeed, the k-th iteration through the outer loop may require anywhere from 0 to k moves, $k/2$ moves on average. In Selection Sort, each iteration through the outer loop requires one swap, which can be counted as three moves. The answer is C. ⤶

5.4. Recursion

You may find recursion pleasant or difficult, depending on your taste. If you happen to hate it, you can still take a stab at the multiple-choice questions on recursion.

40

Consider the following method:

```
public void mystery(int n)
{
  if ( n <= 0)
    return;

  for (int i = 0; i < n; i++)
  {
    System.out.print("-");
  }

  for (int i = 0; i < n; i++)
  {
    System.out.print("+");
  }

  System.out.println();

  mystery(n-1);
}
```

What is the output when `mystery(4)` is called?

(A)
```
----++++
```

(B)
```
----++++
----++++
----++++
----++++
```

(C)
```
----+
----++
----+++
----++++
```

(D)
```
-+
--++
---+++
----++++
```

(E)
```
----++++
---+++
--++
-+
```

☞   This method calls itself — that's what recursion is. Note two things about it. First, if n <= 0, the method doesn't do anything. An exit from a recursive method, perhaps after some work but without recursive calls, is called the *base case* (or the *stopping case*). In this method the base case does nothing. Second, when the method calls itself, it calls itself with a parameter whose value is one less than the original. The parameter of a recursive call must be different from the parameter of the original call, usually decreased in some way in the direction of the base case, if the recursion is to terminate at some point.

Instead of trying to unwrap and trace all the recursive calls in this method, first try to reason more formally about its properties. The method prints some minuses followed by the same number of pluses. When called with *n* = 4, the method right away prints one line with 4 minuses and 4 pluses. But that is not all: after printing the first line, the method calls mystery(3), which must do the same thing as mystery(4) but on a smaller scale. The answer is E.   ☞

Now suppose we change the mystery method in the previous question, placing the recursive call <u>above</u> the for loops:

41

Consider the following method:

```
public void mystery(int n)
{
  if (n <= 0)
    return;

  mystery(n-1);

  for (int i = 0; i < n; i++)
  {
    System.out.print("-");
  }

  for (int i = 0; i < n; i++)
  {
    System.out.print("+");
  }

  System.out.println();
}
```

What is the output when mystery(4) is called?

< Same answer choices as in Question 40 >

☞ This question is a bit trickier, but D and E are still the only plausible answers:

(D)
```
-+
--++
---+++
----++++
```

(E)
```
----++++
---+++
--++
-+
```

We have to choose D because the last thing `mystery(4)` does is print `----++++`.

(If you are more mathematically inclined, you can reason as follows. `mystery(4)` prints a triangle pointing either up or down. Let's take a guess at this method's general behavior: say, "`mystery(n)` prints a triangle with *n* rows that points up." Suppose it's true for *n* = 3. Then `mystery(4)` first prints a triangle with 3 rows in the recursive call, then adds the longest fourth row. Our guess fits, so the answer should be D.) ↵

42

Consider the following method:

```
public void mysteryMix(String str)
{
  int len = str.length();
  if (len >= 3)
  {
    mysteryMix(str.substring(0, len / 3));
    System.out.print (str.substring(len / 3, 2*len / 3));
    mysteryMix(str.substring(2*len / 3));
  }
}
```

What is the output when `mysteryMix("la-la-la!")` is called?

(A) `la-la-la!`
(B) `ala-a`
(C) `ala-la-la-l`
(D) `lla-l`
(E) `a-la-a!`

☞   Many AP questions mix unrelated topics. This tough question tests both recursion and strings. We start with a string of nine characters, but immediately call `mysteryMix` recursively for a string of three characters. So it makes sense to see first what happens when we call, say, `mysteryMix("xyz")`. This call just prints the middle character, `"y"`, and does nothing else: when `len` is 3 the two recursive calls do nothing. Now back to the original string of nine characters. The two recursive calls print one character each and `System.out.print` prints three characters, so the output must have five characters. This eliminates Choices A, C, and E. The first character printed is the middle character in the first one-third of the string, which is `"a"`. The answer is B. ☜

Recursive implementation of Binary Search

The description of the Binary Search algorithm is recursive in nature, and it can be implemented recursively with ease.

43

Consider the following incomplete recursive implementation of Binary Search:

```
/** Returns the position of the element equal to target or -1,
 *  if target is not among the values a[left], ..., a[right].
 *  Precondition: array a contains values stored from a[left]
 *                to a[right], sorted in ascending order
 */
public int binarySearch(int[] a, int left, int right, int target)
{
  int targetPos = -1;

  < statement 1 >
  {
    int middle = (left + right) / 2;
    if (target == a[middle])
      < statement 2 >
    else if (target < a[middle])
      targetPos = binarySearch(a, left, middle - 1, target);
    else
      targetPos = binarySearch(a, middle + 1, right, target);
  }

  return targetPos;
}
```

Which of the following could be used to replace < *statement 1* > and < *statement 2* > so that the `binarySearch` method works as intended?

	< *statement 1* >	< *statement 2* >
(A)	`while (left <= right)`	`return targetPos;`
(B)	`while (left <= right)`	`return middle;`
(C)	`while (left < right)`	`targetPos = middle;`
(D)	`if (left <= right)`	`targetPos = middle;`
(E)	`if (left < right)`	`return middle;`

☞ In the choice between `while` and `if`, `if` wins, because this is a <u>recursive</u> solution and recursion <u>replaces</u> iterations. This eliminates A, B, and C. In D and E either choice works for Statement 2, but Statement 1 in E misses the case when `left == right`. The answer is D. ✑

5.5. Mergesort

Mergesort is a recursive sorting algorithm based on the "divide and conquer" principle. It takes, on average, $n \log n$ comparisons, as opposed to n^2 comparisons in quadratic sorts. This difference can be very significant for large arrays. For example, for 1024 elements, Mergesort may run 100 times faster than Selection Sort and Insertion Sort.

The idea of *Mergesort* is simple: divide the array into two approximately equal halves; sort (recursively) each half, then merge them together into one sorted array (Figure 5-2). Mergesort usually requires a temporary array for holding the two sorted halves before they are merged back into the original space.

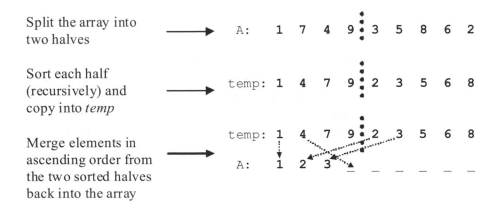

Figure 5-2. Mergesort

44

Consider the following implementation of Mergesort:

```
/** Sorts values a[n1], ..., a[n2] in ascending order.
 *  Precondition: 0 <= n1 <= n2 < a.length
 */
public void sort(int[] a, int n1, int n2)
{
  if (n1 == n2)
    return;

  int m = (n1 + n2) / 2;
  sort(a, n1, m);
  sort(a, m+1, n2);
  if (a[m] > a[m+1])          // Optional line
    merge(a, n1, m, n2);
}
```

Compare it with a more conventional version with the `if` statement on the "optional line" removed. Suppose `a` has 8 elements and `sort(a, 0, 7)` is called. For which of the following values in `a` will the version with `if` work faster than the version without?

I.   1 2 3 4 5 6 7 8
II. 5 6 7 8 2 1 4 3
III. 2 1 4 3 6 5 8 7

(A) I only
(B) I and II only
(C) I and III only
(D) I, II, and III
(E) None of the three

☞ A typical implementation of Mergesort doesn't skip the work even when the array is already sorted. The slight change proposed in this question allows Mergesort to skip all the merging and quickly establish that an array is already sorted, as in Option I. This version also avoids merging when the array is partially sorted, namely when all the values in the left half of the array are smaller than any value in the right half, as in Option III. In that case, after the two recursive calls to `sort` the array becomes sorted and the call to `merge` is skipped.

Since the algorithm is recursive, it will also save time when some portions of the array have these properties — are either sorted or partially sorted — even when the whole array isn't. In Option II, for example, the left half is sorted and the right half is partially sorted. The answer is D. ☜

5.6. Data Organization Questions

AP CS exam may contain multiple-choice questions on appropriate ways of representing data for specific tasks. Below are a few examples of such questions.

Consider designing a data structure that represents information about subscribers in an e-mail server system. Among other attributes, a subscriber has an ID and a number of unread new messages. Information about all subscribers who have unread mail will be stored in an array of `Subscriber` objects. Two possible implementations are being considered:

Method A: Store the array entries in arbitrary order.
Method B: Store the array entries in sorted order by subscriber ID.

Consider the following operations:

Operation 1:   Increment the number of messages for a subscriber with a specified ID.
Operation 2:   Add a new subscriber with a given number of messages to the list of subscribers.

Which of the following is true?

(A)   Both Operation 1 and Operation 2 can be implemented more efficiently using Method A than Method B.
(B)   Both Operation 1 and Operation 2 can be implemented more efficiently using Method B than Method A.
(C)   Operation 1 can be implemented more efficiently using Method A; Operation 2 can be implemented more efficiently using Method B.
(D)   Operation 1 can be implemented more efficiently using Method B; Operation 2 can be implemented more efficiently using Method A.
(E)   Operation 1 and Operation 2 can be implemented equally efficiently using either method.

☞ Such questions may test your reading comprehension skills, but in terms of real technical difficulty they don't go too far beyond common sense. It certainly helps if you have a good understanding of various data structures and their uses in different algorithms. Here, for example, we have to deal with finding an element with a given key (subscriber ID) in an array and inserting a new value into an array. The relevant ideas that come to mind are Sequential and Binary Search, inserting a value in order, and inserting at the end.

You may want to jot down a small table in order not to get confused in the Methods and Operations; then check the appropriate boxes (what works faster):

	A: random order	*B: sorted*
1. Increment # msgs — "find"		✓
2. Add a subscr — "insert".	✓	

Clearly, if you need to maintain the order, adding a subscriber to a sorted array will take more work than just slapping it on at the end of the array. This alone eliminates Choices B, C, and E. (Don't overcomplicate, thinking that you may need to reallocate and copy the array if it is not large enough. That is not what this question is about.)

Is it easier to find a value in a sorted array? Of course. If you remember that you can use Binary Search on a sorted array, that's great. But even if you don't, this would be a good guess. The fact that the array is sorted probably can't hurt the search operation. This eliminates Choice A. The answer is D. ↵

Questions 46-47 refer to the following information:

The College Board administers AP exams in N subjects ($N \geq 34$) over K days ($K \geq 14$). Each subject is offered only on one day. The subjects are represented by integers from 1 to N. Two different designs are being considered for an application that keeps track of the exam calendar:

Design 1:

The exam schedule information is held in a one-dimensional array of integers. For each of the K days there is one entry that represents the number of exams on that day, followed by a list of the subjects offered on that day. For example, if the first day has two exams, subjects 29 and 31, and the second day has no exams, the array will start with 2, 29, 31, 0, ...

Design 2:

The schedule is represented as two-dimensional array of Boolean values with N rows and K columns. The `true` value in the n-th row and k-th column indicates that the n-th subject is offered on the k-th day.

Which of the following statements about the space requirements of the implementation of the two designs in Java is true?

(A)   Design 1 will require less space.
(B)   Design 2 will require less space.
(C)   Which design will require more space depends on the value of N.
(D)   Which design will require more space depends on the value of K.
(E)   Which design will require more space depends on the number of bytes it takes to represent Boolean and integer values on a particular platform.

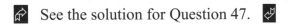   See the solution for Question 47.

47

Suppose that Design 2 is chosen and that the following method is implemented as efficiently as possible: given a subject number from 1 to N and a day number from 1 to K, the method returns `true` if the given subject is offered on the given day and `false` otherwise.

Which of the following statements is true?

(A)   The average time spent in the method is proportional to N.
(B)   The average time spent in the method is proportional to K.
(C)   The average time spent in the method is proportional to the total number of values in the array (N times K).
(D)   The average time spent in the method is proportional to the average number of exams per day.
(E)   The time spent in the method does not depend on N or K, nor on the distribution of exams by day.

👉👉   The above two questions compare space and time requirements for the same data represented as a list (Design 1) and as a *lookup table* (Design 2). You can answer these questions right away if you are familiar with lookup tables. In a lookup table, a data item (here a valid subject/day pair) is represented as a <u>location</u> in an array. Lookup tables usually take more space but provide instantaneous (constant time) access to data regardless of the size of the table.

If you've never heard the term *lookup table*, you can still figure it out.

In Question 46 the space requirement for Design 1 is $K + N$ integers: one for each day (representing the number of exams for that day) and one for each exam (each exam has to be listed under one of the days). The space requirement for Design 2 is $N \cdot K$ Boolean values. Recall that in Java, an integer always takes four bytes, regardless of the particular platform. A Boolean may vary, but even if it takes only one byte, still $4 \cdot (K + N) < N \cdot K$ for large enough N and K (recall that $N \geq 34$, $K \geq 14$). The answer is A. 👇

In Question 47, you must know that you can go directly to any element of a one-dimensional or two-dimensional array. This property is called *random access* and that's what arrays are all about.   The n-th subject is offered on the k-th day if `table[n-1][k-1]` is `true`. The answer is E. 👇

Chapter 6. GridWorld Case Study

6.1. Introduction

The GridWorld case study is a teaching and testing tool developed specifically for the AP Computer Science program. In the past, exams have had five multiple-choice questions and one free-response question on the case study.

The case study involves a fairly large program that manipulates various "actors" (bugs, critters, rocks, flowers) in a two-dimensional grid. The case study materials include a *Student Manual* (40 pages plus appendices); Java source code and class libraries; and *javadoc* documentation. All these materials are posted at the *College Board's* AP web site (`http://www.collegeboard.com/student/testing/ap/compsci_a/case.html?compscia`).

> **Only Parts 1 through 4 of the case study *Student Manual* are required for the exam. Part 5 used to be tested in the AB exam, and it is no longer required.**

The best way to prepare for the exam questions on the case study is to have the case study integrated into your course so you can work on the case study code and exercises as you go along. This chapter will help you review what you have learned. If you did not have the opportunity to work on the case study in your course, you can still answer case study questions successfully after studying the case study *Student Manual*, the required code, and this review.

> **Start by setting up the GridWorld project and running the `BugRunner` program, as described in Part 1 of the GridWorld *Student Manual*.**

The case study code includes Java files with `main` (such as `BugRunner.java` — the first project — or `BoxBugRunner.java`, `CritterRunner.java`, or `CrabRunner.java`) and the library file `gridworld.jar`. GridWorld projects are set up in the same manner as any other project in your IDE, but `gridworld.jar` must be added as a required library. The exact procedure depends on your IDE. See GridWorld Installation Guide or `www/skylit.com/javamethods/faqs` for more current information.

Figure 6-1 shows the "big picture" of the case study classes and interfaces.

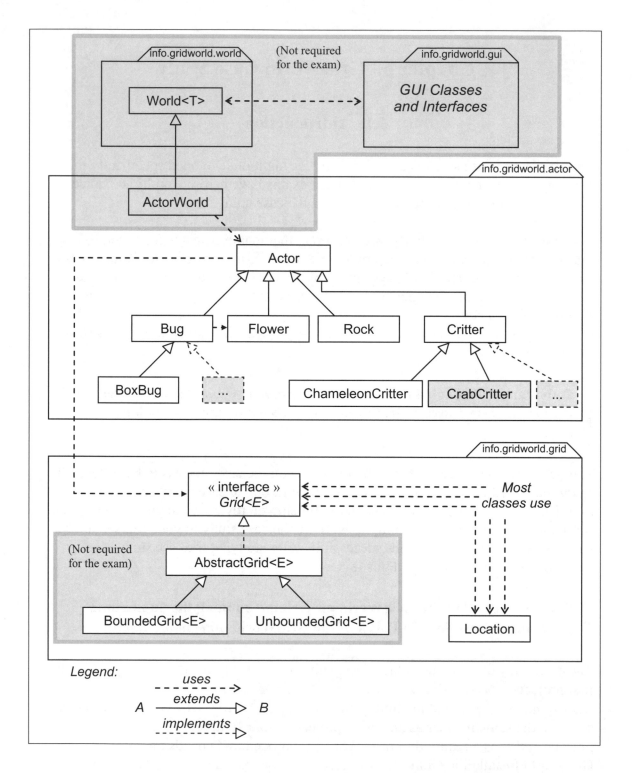

Figure 6-1. **GridWorld: the "Big Picture." The boxes with dotted-line borders indicate the natural places for extension.**

The code is organized into four packages: `gui`, `world`, `actor`, and `grid`. Of these four you are responsible for only two, `actor` and `grid`, and even these two you need to know to a limited extent.

> **You are not required to know what a package is or how the GridWorld classes are split into packages. However, to get practice projects to compile, you'll need to `import` classes from the correct packages.**

For example, if your class uses `Grid` and `Location`, you need

```
import info.gridworld.grid.Grid;
import info.gridworld.grid.Location;
```

If your class uses `ActorWorld`, `Actor`, or `Bug`, you need

```
import info.gridworld.actor.ActorWorld;
import info.gridworld.actor.Actor;
import info.gridworld.actor.Bug;
```

respectively.

Table 6-1 and Figure 6-2 summarize the classes and interfaces you need to learn. You need to be very comfortable with the code of four classes: `Bug`, `BoxBug`, `Critter`, and `ChameleonCritter`. You need to know only the API (Application Programming Interface, that is, specifications for using constructors and public methods) for the `Grid` interface, the `Location` class, and the `Actor`, `Flower`, and `Rock` classes.

API (documentation only)	Implementation (testable code)
Location Grid Actor Flower Rock	Bug BoxBug Critter ChameleonCritter

Table 6-1. GridWorld classes tested on the AP exam

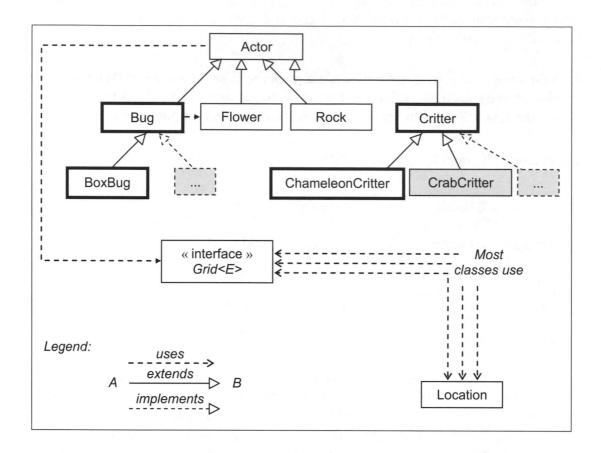

**Figure 6-2. GridWorld classes required for the AP exam. A bold
border indicates that the knowledge of the implementation
code is required; otherwise the API only is required. Grayed
classes are examples (not required but useful) and places for
likely extensions.**

The class `CrabCritter` is just an example of a subclass of `Critter` — it won't be
tested on the exam, but you should get familiar with it to know what to expect.

The case study also includes a few "runner" classes. A runner class configures the
grid and supplies a `main` method for a particular project.

The "runner" classes are not tested on the exam.

> **At the exam, you will receive a document called *Quick Reference*, which contains the required case study code and API.**

You or your teacher can find a copy of this document on the *AP Central* website. (You will actually receive two copies of *Quick Reference*: one with the multiple-choice questions and another with the free-response questions.)

The *Quick Reference* document contains Appendix B, Testable API, Appendix C, Testable Code, Appendix E, GridWorld Quick Reference, and Appendix G, Index for Source Code. Get used to referring to particular pages of this document while practicing.

6.2. The `Location` Class and the `Grid` Interface

———————— Location ————————

A `Location` object represents a (*row*, *col*) location (with integer coordinates) on a two-dimensional grid.

The `Location` class has one constructor —

```
public Location(int row, int col)
```

— and two accessor methods:

```
public int getRow()    //  Returns the row for this location
public int getCol()    //  Returns the column for this location
```

> **Location objects are *immutable*: once created, a `Location` object cannot change.**

`Location` implements `Comparable` and provides a `compareTo` method that compares locations first by row and then, if equal, by column. `Location` also overrides `Object`'s `equals` method in a manner consistent with `compareTo`.

Location's toString method converts a Location object into a String and returns the result:

```
public String toString()
{
  return "(" + getRow() + ", " + getCol() + ")";
}
```

The Location class also helps to handle directions on the grid. It defines eight public constants —

```
public static final int NORTH = 0;
public static final int NORTHEAST = 45;
public static final int EAST = 90;
public static final int SOUTHEAST = 135;
public static final int SOUTH = 180;
public static final int SOUTHWEST = 225;
public static final int WEST = 270;
public static final int NORTHWEST = 315;
```

— that represent compass directions (in degrees).

The row number increases in the direction from north to south. The column number increases from west to east.

Seven more constants represent turns:

```
public static final int LEFT = -90;
public static final int RIGHT = 90;
public static final int HALF_LEFT = -45;
public static final int HALF_RIGHT = 45;
public static final int FULL_CIRCLE = 360;
public static final int HALF_CIRCLE = 180;
public static final int AHEAD = 0;
```

In your code, you might find it easier to just use the numbers, 360, 180, 0, instead of Location.FULL_CIRCLE, Location.HALF_CIRCLE, Location.AHEAD.

Location's getAdjacentLocation(int dir) method returns the location that is adjacent to this location in the compass direction dir. Locations that touch in a corner are considered adjacent.

Location's getDirectionToward(Location other) method returns the compass direction (in degrees) from this location to other. For example,

```
Location loc1 = new Location(3, 7);
Location loc2 = loc1.getAdjacentLocation(Location.SOUTHWEST);
int dir = loc1.getDirectionToward(loc2);
```

sets loc2 to (4, 6) and dir to 225 (that is, Location.SOUTHWEST).

> **Note that getAdjacentLocation(int dir) and getDirectionToward(Location other) are methods of Location, <u>not</u> methods of Grid.**

-------- Grid --------

The Grid<E> interface represents a two-dimensional grid that can hold objects of the type E. GridWorld uses Grid<Actor> to hold objects that are Actors (that is objects of the class Actor or of any of the subclasses or descendants of Actor).

> **In GridWorld, only one actor can reside at a given location in the grid at any given time.**

The Grid interface isolates specific implementations of the grid from the rest of the GridWorld classes.

A grid can be implemented as a two-dimensional array (as in BoundedGrid), but it can be also implemented in other ways.

> **The particular implementations of the Grid interface are described in Part 5 of the case study and are <u>not</u> tested.**

The Grid<E> interface is shown in Figure 6-3. It has eleven methods that roughly fall into two groups: "general" grid methods and "local neighborhood" methods.

```
public interface Grid<E>
{
  // General grid methods:
  // =======================

    int numRows();                    // Returns the number of rows for a
                                      //   bounded grid; -1 for an unbounded
                                      //   grid

    int numCols();                    // Returns the number of columns for a
                                      //   bounded grid; -1 for an unbounded
                                      //   grid

    boolean isValid(Location loc);    // Returns true if loc is valid in this
                                      //   grid (always true for an
                                      //   unbounded grid)

    E get(Location loc);              // Returns the object at loc (or null
                                      //   if loc is empty)

    E put(Location loc, E obj);       // Puts obj at loc and returns the
                                      //   object previously at loc (or null
                                      //   if loc was empty)

    E remove(Location loc);           // Removes the object at loc and
                                      //   returns that object (or null
                                      //   if loc was empty)
    ArrayList<Location>
        getOccupiedLocations();       // Returns the list of all occupied
                                      //   locations in the grid


  // "Local neighborhood" methods:
  // =============================

  ArrayList<Location> getValidAdjacentLocations(Location loc);
                            // Returns a list of all valid locations
                            //   adjacent to loc

  ArrayList<Location> getEmptyAdjacentLocations(Location loc);
                            // Returns a list of all valid empty
                            //   locations adjacent to loc

  ArrayList<Location> getOccupiedAdjacentLocations(Location loc);
                            // Returns a list of all valid occupied
                            //   locations adjacent to loc

  ArrayList<E> getNeighbors(Location loc);
                            // Returns a list of all objects in the
                            //   occupied locations adjacent to loc
}
```

Figure 6-3. The Grid<E> interface

> All `Grid<E>` methods that take `Location loc` as a parameter, except `isValid`, assume that `loc` is a valid location in the grid. `isValid` assumes that `loc` is not `null`. The `put` method also assumes that `obj` is not `null`.

48

Consider the following method:

```
/** Returns true if loc1 and loc2 are neighbors in grid,
 *  false otherwise.
 *  Precondition: loc1 and loc2 are both valid locations in grid
 */
public boolean areNeighbors(Grid<Actor> grid, Location loc1,
                                                Location loc2)
{
  return < expression >;
}
```

Which of the following replacements for *< expression >* will make this method work as specified?

I. `loc1.getAdjacentLocation(loc1.getDirectionToward(loc2)) == loc2`

II. `loc1.getAdjacentLocation(loc1.getDirectionToward(loc2)).`
                                                `equals(loc2)`

III. `grid.getNeighbors(loc1).contains(loc2)`

(A) I only
(B) II only
(C) III only
(D) I and II only
(E) II and III only

☞ The idea in Options I and II is to first get the direction from `loc1` to `loc2`, then create a neighboring location from `loc1` in that direction and compare it to `loc2`. If `loc2` is a neighbor, these locations must be equal. But they won't be the same object! So Option II is correct while Option I is wrong, because == compares the addresses of objects. In Option III, `Grid`'s `getNeighbors` returns `ArrayList<Actor>`, a list of all <u>Actors</u> in neighboring locations, rather than `ArrayList<Location>`. (The `ArrayList` class does have a method `contains`, but it is not in the AP subset.) The answer is B. ☚

6.3.   The `Actor` Class

The `Actor` class serves as a base class for a hierarchy of classes that represent different kinds of "bugs," "flowers," "rocks," "critters," and so on. `Actor` is <u>not</u> an abstract class, so you can create an object of this class. However, an object of type `Actor` is not a very interesting object: when asked to "act" it just turns around 180 degrees.

An `Actor` object has four attributes: color, location, direction, and grid.

An actor can belong to one and only one grid at a time; its `grid` attribute refers to that grid, or it is `null` if the actor is currently not in any grid.

The `Actor` class has one constructor that takes no parameters. This constructor sets the actor's color to `Color.BLUE`, the actor's direction to 0 (`Location.NORTH`), and the actor's location and grid to `null`.

The `Actor` class has four accessors for its four attributes:

```
public Color getColor()
public Location getLocation()
public int getDirection()
public Grid<Actor> getGrid()
```

`Actor` has two modifiers:

```
public void setColor(Color newColor)
public void setDirection(int newDirection)
```

It also has a `toString` method:

```
public String toString()
```

The `grid` attribute is not set directly. `Actor`'s methods `putSelfInGrid` and `removeSelfFromGrid` are used instead, because the grid as well as the actor has to be notified of the change:

```
public void putSelfInGrid(Grid<Actor> gr, Location loc)
// Puts this actor at loc in grid.
// Precondition: the actor is not in grid;
//               loc is a valid location in grid

public void removeSelfFromGrid()
// Removes this actor from its grid.
// Precondition: the actor is in a grid
```

Actor's `moveTo` method —

```
public void moveTo(Location newLocation)
```

— sets the current location of the actor to `newLocation`, but it does more: it first removes the current occupant from `newLocation`, if any.

Finally, an actor has the method `act`. Actor's `act` method does something just to show some action: it turns the actor by 180 degrees.

Actor's `act` method is usually overridden in subclasses of `Actor`.

| 49 |

Which of the following code segments will move `Actor` andy south to the adjacent grid cell, assuming the new location is valid and empty?

I.
```
loc = andy.getLocation();
loc.setRow(loc.getRow() + 1);
```

II.
```
loc = andy.getLocation();
Location newLoc = new Location(loc.getRow() + 1, loc.getCol());
andy.setLocation(newLoc);
```

III.
```
loc = andy.getLocation();
andy.moveTo(loc.getAdjacentLocation(Location.SOUTH));
```

(A) I only
(B) II only
(C) III only
(D) I and II only
(E) II and III only

 Option I is nonsense because `Location` objects are immutable; a `Location` does not have a `setRow` method. Option II does not work because `Actor` has no method `setLocation`. When an actor changes its location in the grid, it has to inform the grid of the change, and possibly remove the current occupant of the new location. To emphasize that, the corresponding method is called `moveTo`, not `setLocation`. The statements

```
Location newLoc = new Location(loc.getRow() + 1, loc.getCol());
andy.moveTo(newLoc);
```

would work, but it is better to write

```
andy.moveTo(loc.getAdjacentLocation(Location.SOUTH));
```

because it is more abstract: it does not rely on the knowledge of how compass directions relate to rows and columns in the grid. The answer is C.

50

Suppose a class `CheckersPiece` is defined as follows:

```
public class CheckersPiece extends Actor
{
  public CheckersPiece(Color color)
  { setColor(color); }
}
```

Another class, `CheckersBoard`, implements `Grid<Actor>`. Consider the following method in a third class, `CheckersGame`:

```
/** If the piece at loc can "jump" a piece of the opposite color
 *  in the direction dir, then performs the jump and returns true;
 *  otherwise returns false.
 */
public boolean jump(CheckersBoard board, Location loc, int dir)
{
  if (!board.isValid(loc))
    return false;
  if (dir % 45 != 0 || dir % 90 == 0) // only diagonal jumps are allowed
    return false;

  Location loc2 = loc.getAdjacentLocation(dir);

  if (!board.isValid(loc2) || board.get(loc2) == null)
    return false;

  Location loc3 = loc2.getAdjacentLocation(dir);
  if (!board.isValid(loc3) || board.get(loc3) != null)
    return false;

  CheckersPiece piece1 = (CheckersPiece)board.get(loc);
  CheckersPiece piece2 = (CheckersPiece)board.get(loc2);
  if (piece1.getColor().equals(piece2.getColor()))
    return false;

  // loc2 is occupied by a piece of the opposite color; loc3 is empty;
  // piece1 is moved from loc to loc3; loc2 is emptied:

  < missing statements >

  return true;
}
```

Which of the following replacements for < *missing statements* > will make this method work as specified?

I.
```
piece1.moveTo(loc3);
board.remove(loc2);
```

II.
```
piece1.moveTo(loc3);
piece2.removeSelfFromGrid();
```

III.
```
board.remove(loc2);
board.remove(loc);
CheckersPiece piece3 = new CheckersPiece(piece1.getColor())
board.put(loc3, piece3);
```

(A) I only
(B) II only
(C) I and II only
(D) II and III only
(E) I, II and III

⤷ This question is a little too long for a typical multiple-choice exam question. We use it here for practice in reading GridWorld-type code and using low-level GridWorld classes. Note how general and reusable the GridWorld setup is: we can use it to play with critters or to program a game of checkers.

The code in Options I and II attempts to move `piece1` from `loc` to `loc3`, while the code in Option III tries to remove `piece1` and create an identical object in `loc3`. The latter approach could potentially work, but it is not in the spirit of GridWorld, and you would need to use `piece1.removeSelfFromGrid(...)` and `piece3.putSelfInGrid(...)`.

Option I incorrectly uses `board`'s `remove` method instead of `piece2.removeSelfFromGrid()`. Option III has the same problem: it uses `board`'s `put` and `remove`. The answer is B. ⤶

> **Grid's `put` and `remove` methods should never be used directly — use Actor's `putSelfInGrid` and `removeSelfFromGrid` instead.**

Otherwise, the actor won't know that it was put in the grid, or the actor will "think" it is still in the grid while it no longer is.

6.4.   Bugs, Flowers, and Rocks

The classes `Bug`, `Flower`, and `Rock` are subclasses of `Actor`.

The `Rock` class is the simplest of the three. It has two constructors: the no-args constructor creates a black rock, and the `Rock(Color color)` constructor creates a rock of a given color. `Rock`'s `act` method is empty — a rock just sits there.

The `Flower` class is similar to `Rock`, but its default color is `Color.PINK`, and its `act` method darkens the color of the flower. You don't need to worry about the implementation of this class — just remember how to call its constructors.

The `Bug` class is more interesting. It has two constructors, similar to `Rock`'s constructors and `Flower`'s constructors, but its default color is `Color.RED`. A `Bug` has three new methods: `canMove`, `move`, and `turn`. These methods are called from `Bug`'s `act` method, which looks like this:

```
public void act()
{
  if (canMove())
    move();
  else
    turn();
}
```

A `Bug` tries to move forward in its current direction. A `Bug` can move if the new location is valid and empty or contains a `Flower`:

```
public boolean canMove()
{
  Grid<Actor> gr = getGrid();
  if (gr == null)
    return false;

  Location loc = getLocation();
  Location next = loc.getAdjacentLocation(getDirection());
  if (!gr.isValid(next))
    return false;

  Actor neighbor = gr.get(next);
  return (neighbor == null) || (neighbor instanceof Flower);
  // OK to move into empty location or onto Flower
  // not OK to move onto any other actor
}
```

This method uses the Java `instanceof` operator, which is not part of the AP subset but is explained in the case study *Student Manual* and may be required on the AP exam in the context of GridWorld only.

The `move` method moves this `Bug` and places a `Flower` (of the same color as the bug) at its old location:

```
public void move()
{
  Grid<Actor> gr = getGrid();
  if (gr == null)
    return;

  Location loc = getLocation();
  Location next = loc.getAdjacentLocation(getDirection());

  if (gr.isValid(next))
    moveTo(next);
  else  // never happens, unless called interactively
        // from the pop-up menu of methods
    removeSelfFromGrid();

  Flower flower = new Flower(getColor());
  flower.putSelfInGrid(gr, loc);
}
```

The `turn` method turns this `Bug` clockwise by 45 degrees:

```
public void turn()
{
  setDirection(getDirection() + Location.HALF_RIGHT);
}
```

The purpose of the `Bug` class is to give an example of an `Actor` that does something "interesting" and to provide a base class for extensions and variations (and possible AP exam questions).

`BoxBug` is one such extension. Study its code carefully. Also do all the exercises on Page 12 in Part 2 of the case study *Student Manual*: `CircleBug`, `SpiralBug`, `ZBug`, and `DancingBug`.

51

A `Bug` is not allowed to move to a location occupied by another `Bug`. Suppose we want to define a new class `PredatorBug` as a subclass of `Bug`. A `PredatorBug` can move to a location occupied by another `Bug` and "eat" it. Otherwise, a `PredatorBug` acts like a regular `Bug`. Which methods should be redefined in `PredatorBug`?

(A) `act` only
(B) `canMove` only
(C) `move` only
(D) `act` and `move`
(E) `canMove` and `move`

Recall that when an actor moves to a new location (that is, its `moveTo` method is called) the current occupant is removed from that location. All we have to do is allow a `PredatorBug` to move to a location occupied by another `Bug`:

```
public boolean canMove()
{
  ...
  return (neighbor == null) || (neighbor instanceof Flower)
                || (neighbor instanceof Bug);
}
```

The answer is B.

6.5. Critters

A `Critter` is an actor that can interact with other actors in a more sophisticated way. Critters are introduced in Part 4 of the case study *Student Manual*.

The `Critter` class is designed to serve as a base class for a hierarchy of critters. `Critter`'s `act` method involves five steps:

  1. Get a list of actors to interact with;
  2. Process actors from that list;
  3. Get a list of locations that are candidates for this critter's next move;
  4. Select a location to move to from the list obtained in Step 3;
  5. Move to the selected location.

Each of these steps is accomplished in a separate method, so a critter's `act` method calls five methods, which we will call "service" methods. It looks like this:

```
public void act()
{
  if (getGrid() == null)
    return;

  // Step 1:
  ArrayList<Actor> actors = getActors();

  // Step 2:
  processActors(actors);

  // Step 3:
  ArrayList<Location> moveLocs = getMoveLocations();

  // Step 4:
  Location loc = selectMoveLocation(moveLocs);

  // Step 5:
  makeMove(loc);
}
```

In the `Critter` class itself, the service methods `getActors`, `processActors`, `getMoveLocations`, `selectMoveLocation`, and `makeMove` are pretty simple:

- `getActors` returns a list of all actors in the eight <u>neighboring locations</u> of this critter;

- `processActors` "eats" (removes from the grid) all actors from that list, except rocks and other critters;

- `getMoveLocations` returns the list of all <u>empty</u> neighboring locations (including the ones just emptied by `processActors`);

- if the list returned by `getMoveLocations` is not empty, `selectMoveLocation` selects a <u>random location</u> from that list; otherwise it returns this `Critter`'s current location;

- `makeMove` moves this `Critter` to the selected location by calling its `moveTo` method.

> **AP exam questions may ask you to reason about or to write a subclass of `Critter`.**

A critter is an actor that <u>first</u> processes some other actors, <u>then</u> moves. The case study *Student Manual* states: "It is usually not a good idea to override the `act` method in a `Critter` subclass."

> **Do not override the `act` method in subclasses of `Critter`. Override one or more of the five service methods instead.**

`Critter`'s `act` method will call the correct service method(s) of a `Critter`'s subclass due to polymorphism.

`Critter`'s setup is very flexible, and you can implement many different behaviors by overriding one or more of the five service methods. You should call the superclass's methods, where appropriate, to avoid duplicating code.

> **Pay attention to the postconditions specified in `Critter`'s service methods. When writing a subclass of `Critter` and overriding some of `Critter`'s methods, make sure these postconditions are satisfied.**

In particular, `getActors`, `getMoveLocations`, and `selectMoveLocation` must leave the state of all actors unchanged; `processActors` can only change the state of this critter and the actors in the given list, and it must leave the location of this critter unchanged; `makeMove` can change only the state of this critter and the actor in the new location (if any). Note that `selectMoveLocation` can return only a location from a given list, a `null`, or this critter's current location. `makeMove(Location loc)` must move this critter to `loc`, if `loc` is not `null`, or remove this critter from the grid by calling `removeSelfFromGrid` or `super.makeMove(loc)` if `loc` is `null`.

A `Bee` is an actor that acts as follows. First the `Bee` makes all the `Flower`s in adjacent locations brighten their color. After that, the `Bee` moves to a randomly picked adjacent location that contains a `Flower` or, if no adjacent `Flower`s have been found, to a randomly picked empty adjacent location. If there is nowhere to move, the `Bee` stays in its current location. If the `Bee` moves onto a `Flower`, it saves that `Flower` and restores the same `Flower` when it moves away from that location. Which of the following is the best approach to implementing the `Bee` class?

(A)   Implement `Bee` as a subclass of `Actor`, overriding the `act` method
(B)   Implement `Bee` as a subclass of `Bug`, overriding the `act` and `moveTo` methods
(C)   Implement `Bee` as a subclass of `Critter`, overriding the `act` and `moveTo` methods
(D)   Implement `Bee` as a subclass of `Critter`, overriding the `processActors`, `getMoveLocations` and `makeMove` methods
(E)   Implement `Bee` as a subclass of `Critter`, overriding the `getActors`, `processActors`, `getMoveLocations`, `selectMoveLocation`, and `makeMove` methods

A Bee first does something to some other actors, then moves, so it falls into the general category of "critters." It is of course possible to derive Bee directly from Actor (Choice A), but why duplicate code, when the Critter class already exists? It is also possible to derive Bee from Bug (Choice B), but that would damage the neat hierarchy of GridWorld actors. A Bug moves in a particular way, and it is better to leave it alone. We wouldn't be able to reuse any of Bug's code by deriving Bee from Bug.

We are left with the three "critter" choices. Choice C is totally unacceptable: we never override Actor's low-level moveTo method, and we never override Critter's act method. The question remains: Will overriding processActors, getMoveLocations, and makeMove (Choice D) be sufficient to achieve Bee's functionality, or do we need to override all five of Critter's service methods (Choice E)? Note that Critter's getActors method returns a list of <u>all</u> actors in neighboring locations, then processActors decides which ones to "eat." A Bee can work in a similar way: it can use Critter's getActors and let its processActors test which neighbors are Flowers and brighten their color.

getMoveLocations can return a list of all neighboring Flowers or, if there are no flowers among the neighbors, return a list of all empty neighboring locations. No need to change Critter's selectMoveLocation, which simply selects a random location from the list. Bee's makeMove method can handle saving and/or restoring the Flower the Bee "landed on," if necessary, and call super.makeMove() to move. So Choice E is overkill. The answer is D.

Subclasses of Critter

The case study gives two examples of subclasses of Critter: ChameleonCritter and CrabCritter. The code for ChameleonCritter may be tested on the AP exam. CrabCritter is just an example, but we recommend that you study it very carefully.

The ChameleonCritter class has no constructors defined — it relies on the default no-args constructor, which calls Critter's no-args constructor. ChameleonCritter overrides two of Critter's five service methods: processActors and makeMove. processActors chooses a random neighbor and assigns its color to this ChameleonCritter:

```
public void processActors(ArrayList<Actor> actors)
{
  int n = actors.size();
  if (n == 0)
    return;

  int r = (int)(Math.random() * n);

  Actor other = actors.get(r);
  setColor(other.getColor());
}
```

Note the idiom for choosing a random object from a list:

```
int n = list.size();
if (n == 0)
    return;
int r = (int)(Math.random() * n);
Object x = list.get(r);
```

ChameleonCritter's makeMove method sets the direction of this ChameleonCritter to the direction of the move, then moves like a regular Critter:

```
public void makeMove(Location loc)
{
  setDirection(getLocation().getDirectionToward(loc));
  super.makeMove(loc);
}
```

53

Suppose we want to create a critter Butterfly that acts like a ChameleonCritter but changes color to the color of a Flower in a neighboring location. If there are several Flowers around, the Butterfly picks any one of them at random; if there are no Flowers around, the Butterfly does nothing. Which of the following is the best way to implement Butterfly?

(A) Derive Butterfly from Critter and redefine its act and makeMove methods.
(B) Derive Butterfly from Critter and redefine the processActors and makeMove methods.
(C) Derive Butterfly from ChameleonCritter and redefine the act method.
(D) Derive Butterfly from ChameleonCritter and redefine the getActors method.
(E) Derive Butterfly from ChameleonCritter and redefine the getActors and processActors methods.

Since a `Butterfly` acts in a manner similar to a `ChameleonCritter`, it makes sense to derive the `Butterfly` class from `ChameleonCritter`. `Butterfly` can override `ChameleonCritter`'s `getActors` method to include only `Flowers` in the returned list. Alternatively, `Butterfly` can override `ChameleonCritter`'s `processActors` method to select a random neighbor only among `Flowers`. There is no need to override both, though. The answer is D.

6.6. Tips for the Case Study Questions

To answer GridWorld case study questions successfully, you need to be familiar with both the relevant code and the concepts behind it. Look very carefully at the code for the `Bug`, `BoxBug`, `Critter`, `ChameleonCritter`, and `CrabCritter` classes. Also take a look at the `Flower` and `Rock` classes. Make sure you are very comfortable with the `Location`, `Grid`, and `Actor` APIs. Do all the exercises for Part 2 and Part 4 of the case study *Student Manual*.

Several multiple-choice questions are likely to focus on concepts: why certain design decisions were made, what the alternatives and tradeoffs are, what certain methods do, how inheritance and polymorphism work in the case study, and so on. Don't panic; most of it is common sense, especially if you have read the case study *Student Manual*.

The free-response questions will ask you to write variations on the case-study code. The key here is to find a similar code segment in the case study booklet and adapt it. Do not improvise your code from scratch. Pay attention to the following:

- Do <u>not</u> write any `import` statements.

- `equals` vs. `==`: Use `equals` for comparing `Location` objects; use `==` for comparing directions and any object to `null`.

- `ArrayLists` vs. arrays: `Grid` methods `getOccupiedLocations`, `getValidAdjacentLocations`, `getEmptyAdjacentLocations`, `getOccupiedAdjacentLocations` return an `ArrayList<Location>`; `getNeighbors` returns an `ArrayList<Actor>`. Use `.get(i)`, not `[i]`, on these lists.

- Call methods of the correct class. For example, `getAdjacentLocation(int direction)` and `getDirectionToward(Location target)` are in `Location`, <u>not</u> in `Grid`; `getValidAdjacentLocations(Location loc)` is in `Grid`.

- Use an actor's `getLocation` and `getGrid` methods to get hold of its location and grid, respectively.

- Use an actor's `putSelfInGrid` method to assign the actor to a given location in a given grid. Use an actor's `removeSelfFromGrid` method to remove the actor from the grid.

- To change an actor's direction, use:

  ```
  setDirection(getDirection() + ...);
  ```

  For example, to reverse the direction, write:

  ```
  setDirection(getDirection() + 180);
  ```

- `private`: it is an error to access private instance fields <u>of another class</u>. Use accessor methods instead. For example:

  ```
  Grid<Actor> gr = getGrid();
  Location loc = getLocation();
  ...
  Flower flower = new Flower(getColor());
  flower.putSelfInGrid(gr, loc);
  ```

  Note that neither `Bug` nor `Critter` has instance variables, except those inherited from `Actor` (which are private in `Actor`).

- In addition to hands-on computer work, do some paper-and-pencil exercises while practicing for the case study questions. Use appendices in the case study *Student Manual* or in *Quick Reference* to get used to the format: the materials you will receive on the exam will be the same.

Chapter 7. Annotated Solutions to Past Free-Response Questions

The material for this chapter is on our web site:

`www.skylit.com/beprepared/fr.html`

That page includes links to free-response questions from recent years, an annotated solution for each question, and executable files for all questions.

Practice Exams

Multiple-Choice answer form is available at

www.skylit.com/beprepared/MCAnswerForm.pdf

Practice Exam #1

SECTION I

Time — 1 hour and 15 minutes
Number of questions — 40
Percent of total grade — 50

1. What is printed when the following statement is executed?

    ```
    System.out.println(17 / 5 % 3 + 17 * 5 % 3);
    ```

    (A) 1
    (B) 4
    (C) 9
    (D) 42
    (E) 42.5

2. Consider the following method.

    ```
    public void process(String s)
    {
      s = s.substring(2, 3) + s.substring(1, 2) +
                                    s.substring(0, 1);
    }
    ```

    What is printed as a result of executing the following statements (in a method in the same class)?

    ```
    String s = "ABCD";
    process(s);
    System.out.println(s);
    ```

    (A) ABCD
    (B) CBA
    (C) CDBCA
    (D) CDBCAB
    (E) IndexOutOfBoundsException

3.   Suppose m is a two-dimensional array of size 4 by 4, with all its elements initialized to
     zeroes. What will be the values stored in m after fill(m) is called? The method fill
     is defined as follows:

```
public void fill(int[][] m)
{
  int n = m.length;
  for (int i = 1; i < n - 1; i++)
  {
    for (int j = 1; j < n - 1; j++)
      m[i][j] = 1;
  }
}
```

   (A)   0000
         0000
         0000
         0000

   (B)   1100
         1100
         0000
         0000

   (C)   0000
         0110
         0110
         0000

   (D)   1110
         1110
         1110
         0000

   (E)   1111
         1111
         1111
         1111

4.   Which of the following statements will result in a syntax error?

   (A)   String x = "123";
   (B)   Integer x = "123";
   (C)   Object x = "123";
   (D)   String[] x = {"123"};
   (E)   All of the above will compile with no errors.

5. What is printed as a result of executing the following statements?

```
double x = 2.5, y = 1.99;
System.out.println((int)(x/y) + (int)(x*y));
```

(A) 0
(B) 3
(C) 4
(D) 4.0
(E) 5

6. Which of the following expressions is `true` if and only if NOT all three variables a, b, and c have the same value?

(A) `a != b && b != c`
(B) `a != b || b != c`
(C) `a >= b && b >= c && c >= a`
(D) `a > b || b > c || a > c`
(E) `!(a == b || b == c || a == c)`

7. What is the result when the following code segment is compiled and executed?

```
int m = 4, n = 5;
double d = Math.sqrt((m + n)/2);
System.out.println(d);
```

(A) Syntax error "sqrt(double) in java.lang.Math cannot be applied to int"
(B) `1.5` is displayed
(C) `2.0` is displayed
(D) `2.1213203435596424` is displayed
(E) `ClassCastException`

8. For which of the following pairs of values a and b does the expression

```
(a > 20 && a < b) || (a > 10 && a > b)
```

evaluate to `true`?

(A) 5 and 0
(B) 5 and 10
(C) 15 and 10
(D) 15 and 20
(E) None of the above

9.   What is printed as a result of executing the following code segment?

```
List<Integer> lst = new ArrayList<Integer>();
for (int k = 1; k <= 6; k++)
  lst.add(new Integer(k));
for (int k = 0; k < 3; k++)
{
    Integer i = lst.remove(k);
    lst.add(i);
}
for (Integer i : lst)
  System.out.print(i);
```

(A)   123456
(B)   456123
(C)   456321
(D)   246135
(E)   IndexOutOfBoundsException

10.   Which of the following methods are equivalent (always return the same value for the same values of input parameters)?

I.
```
public boolean fun(int a, int b, int c)
{
  if (a >= b)
    if (b >= c)
      return true;
    else
      return false;
  else
    return false;
}
```

II.
```
public boolean fun(int a, int b, int c)
{
  if (a >= b && b >= c)
    return true;
  else
    return false;
}
```

III.
```
public boolean fun(int a, int b, int c)
{
  return a >= b || b >= c;
}
```

(A)   I and II only
(B)   I and III only
(C)   II and III only
(D)   All three are equivalent
(E)   All three are different

11. Consider the following class.

```
public class Matrix
{
  private int[][] m;

  /** Initializes m to a square n by n array with all
   *   the elements on the diagonal m[k][k] equal to 0 and
   *   all other elements equal to 1
   */
  public Matrix(int n)
  {
    m = new int[n][n];

    < missing code >
  }

  < other constructors and methods not shown >
}
```

Which of the following could replace < *missing code* > in `Matrix`'s constructor, so that it compiles with no errors and works as specified?

I.
```
        for (int r = 0; r < n; r++)
           for (int c = 0; c < n; c++)
             m[r][c] = 1;
        for (int k = 0; k < n; k++)
           m[k][k] = 0;
```

II.
```
        for (int k = 0; k < n; k++)
           m[k][k] = 0;
        for (int r = 0; r < n; r++)
           for (int c = 0; c < n; c++)
             if (r != c)
               m[r][c] = 1;
```

III.
```
        for (int c = 0; c < n; c++)
           for (int r = 0; r < n; r++)
             if (r == c)
                m[r][c] = 0;
             else
                m[r][c] = 1;
```

(A)   I only
(B)   II only
(C)   I and II only
(D)   II and III only
(E)   I, II, and III

12. Which of the following statements about developing a Java program is FALSE?

    (A) The main purpose of testing a Java program is to make sure it doesn't generate run-time exceptions.
    (B) `Hello.class`, a Java class file obtained by compiling `Hello.java` under a Windows operating system can be executed on a Mac computer.
    (C) The size of an `int` variable in Java is four bytes, the same under any operating system and computer model.
    (D) At run time, `int` values are represented in the computer memory in the binary number system.
    (E) Division of an integer value by zero in a Java program will cause a run-time `ArithmeticException`.

13. Amelia and Pat are working on a programming project for a restaurant. They are considering a hierarchy of classes that includes, among other classes, `MenuItem`, `FoodItem`, and `Dessert`. Pat, who likes to eat his dessert first, is proposing to make both `FoodItem` and `Dessert` direct subclasses of `MenuItem`; Amelia's proposal is to make `FoodItem` a subclass of `MenuItem` and `Dessert` a subclass of `FoodItem`.

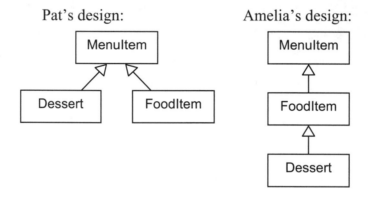

Which of the following is an advantage of Pat's design as compared to Amelia's?

    I.   Both `FoodItem` and `Dessert` can reuse public methods of `MenuItem`.

    II. Both `FoodItem` and `Dessert` type of object can be passed to a method that accepts a `MenuItem` as a parameter.

    III. Pat's design better reflects the IS-A relationships between the three classes.

    (A) None of the three
    (B) I only
    (C) II only
    (D) I and II only
    (E) I, II, and III

14. Consider the following two implementations of the method
`getValue(double[] c, int n, double x)` that computes and returns the value of
$c_0 + c_1 x + c_2 x^2 + ... + c_n x^n$.

Implementation 1

```
double getValue(double[] c, int n, double x)
{
  double value = 0.0, powx = 1.0;
  for (int k = 0; k <= n; k++)
  {
    value += powx * c[k];
    powx *= x;
  }
  return value;
}
```

Implementation 2

```
public static double getValue(double[] c, int n, double x)
{
  double value = c[n];
  for (int k = n-1; k >= 0; k--)
  {
    value = value * x + c[k];
  }
  return value;
}
```

What is the total number of arithmetic operations on floating-point numbers (additions and multiplications combined) that are performed within the `for` loop in Implementation 1 and Implementation 2, when $n = 5$?

	Implementation 1	Implementation 2
(A)	10	5
(B)	12	6
(C)	15	10
(D)	18	10
(E)	18	12

15. Consider the following code segment.

```
int[] nums = new int [51];

for (int k = 0; k < nums.length; k++)
  nums[k] = 1;

for (int k = 3; k <= 50; k += 3)
  nums[k] = 0;

for (int k = 5; k <= 50; k += 5)
  nums[k] = 0;
```

How many elements in the array `nums` have the value 0 after this code has been executed?

(A)   23
(B)   25
(C)   26
(D)   27
(E)   28

16. Consider the following method.

```
public int countSomething(int[] p)
{
  int count = 0;
  for (int i = 0; i < p.length; i++)
  {
    count++;
    int j = p[i];
    while (j != i)
    {
      j = p[j];
      count++;
    }
  }
  return count;
}
```

Given

```
int[] arr = {0, 2, 3, 1};
```

what will `countSomething(arr)` return?

(A)   2
(B)   3
(C)   5
(D)   10
(E)   13

17. Classes `Salsa` and `Swing` implement an interface `Dance`. If both calls

```
perform(new Salsa());
perform(new Swing());
```

are valid, which of the following headers of the `perform` method(s) in a class `Dancer` will compile successfully?

    I.   Two methods:

```
public void perform(Salsa dance)
public void perform(Swing dance)
```

    II.   `public void perform(Dance dance)`

    III.   `public void perform(Object dance)`

(A)   I only
(B)   II only
(C)   I and II only
(D)   II and III only
(E)   I, II, and III

18. What are the contents of the array `nums` after the following code segment has been executed?

```
int[] nums = new int[8];
nums[0] = 0;
int n = 1;
while (n < nums.length)
{
  int k;
  for (k = n; k < 2*n; k++)
    nums[k] = nums[k-n] + 1;
  n = k;
}
```

(A)   0 1 1 1 1 1 1 1
(B)   0 1 0 1 0 1 0 1
(C)   0 1 1 2 1 2 2 3
(D)   0 1 2 3 1 2 3 4
(E)   0 1 2 3 4 5 6 7

Questions 19-20 refer to the following classes.

```
public class Point
{
  private int x, y;

  public Point(int _x, int _y) { x = _x; y = _y; }
  public int getX() { return x; }
  public int getY() { return y; }
  public void move(int dx, int dy) { x += dx; y += dy; }
}

public class Polygon
{
  private ArrayList<Point> vertices;

  public Polygon() { vertices = new ArrayList<Point>(); }
  public void add(Point p) { vertices.add(p); }

  /** Returns the x-coordinate of the k-th vertex
   *  (counting from 0)
   */
  public int getX(int k)
  { return < missing expression >; }

  /** Moves every vertex of the polygon horizontally by dx
   *  and vertically by dy
   */
  public void move(int dx, int dy)
  { < missing code > }
}
```

19. Which of the following could replace *< missing expression >* in the `getX` method of the `Polygon` class?

    (A) `vertices[k].x`
    (B) `vertices.getX(k)`
    (C) `vertices.get(k).x`
    (D) `vertices.get(k).getX()`
    (E) `vertices.get(k+1).getX()`

20. Which of the following could replace < *missing code* > in `Polygon`'s `move` method for it to work as specified?

I.
```
for (int k = 0; k < vertices.size(); k++)
{
  Point p = vertices.get(k);
  p.x += dx;
  p.y += dy;
}
```

II.
```
for (int k = 0; k < vertices.size(); k++)
  vertices.get(k).move(dx, dy);
```

III.
```
for (Point p : vertices)
  p.move(dx, dy);
```

(A) I only
(B) II only
(C) I and II only
(D) II and III only
(E) I, II, and III

21. Suppose class `C` has a private `int` data field `value`:

```
public class C
{
  private int value;

  < other fields, constructors, and methods not shown >
}
```

Suppose we have a method

```
public static int compare(C x, C y)
{
  return x.value - y.value;
}
```

and we need to find a "home" for it: place it into some class. Where can we place this method so that it compiles with no errors?

(A) Only into `C`
(B) Only into `C` or any subclass of `C`
(C) Only into `C` or any superclass of `C`
(D) Into any class
(E) This method will always cause a syntax error, no matter what class we place it in.

22. Consider the following method.

```
/** Rearranges the elements in words according to
 *  the values stored in an integer array indices,
 *  so that the element of words at index indices[k]
 *  is moved to the element at index k.
 *  Precondition: words.size() == indices.length
 */
public void permute(List<String> words, int[] indices)
{
  ArrayList<String> temp = new ArrayList<String>();
  < missing code >
}
```

For example, after executing the code segment

```
List<String> words = new ArrayList<String>();
words.add("I");
words.add("am");
words.add("Sam");
int[] indices = {2, 0, 1};
permute(words, indices);
```

words will become the list `["Sam", "I", "am"]`. Which of the following code segments could replace < *missing code* > in the permute method?

I.
```
for (String word : words)
  temp.add(word);
for (int k = 0; k < indices.length; k++)
  words.set(k, temp.get(indices[k]));
```

II.
```
for (int j : indices)
  temp.add(words.get(j));
for (int k = 0; k < indices.length; k++)
  words.set(k, temp.get(k));
```

III.
```
while (words.size() > 0)
  temp.add(words.remove(0));
for (int j : indices)
  words.add(temp.get(j));
```

(A)   I only
(B)   II only
(C)   I and II only
(D)   II and III only
(E)   I, II, and III

23. What is printed as a result of executing the following code segment?

```
ArrayList<String> digits = new ArrayList<String>();
for (int k = 0; k <= 9; k++)
  digits.add("" + k);

for (int k = 0; k <= 4; k++)
{
  String d1 = digits.remove(k);
  String d2 = digits.remove(k);
  digits.add(k, d1 + "+" + d2);
}
System.out.println(digits);
```

(A) [0+1, 1+2, 2+3, 3+4, 4+5]
(B) [0+1, 2+3, 4+5, 6+7, 8+9]
(C) [0+1, 1+2, 2+3, 3+4, 5, 6, 7, 8, 9]
(D) [0+1, 1+2, 2+3, 3+4, 4+5, 6, 7, 8, 9]
(E) [0+0, 1+1, 2+2, 3+3, 4+4, 5, 6, 7, 8, 9]

24. Consider the following method.

```
/** Returns the number of zeroes in s.
 *  Precondition: s.length() = 31; s holds several
 *                0's followed by several 1's
 *                (s can also be all 0's or all 1's)
 */
public int countZeroes(String s)
{
  int i = 0, j = 30;
  while (i <= j)
  {
    int k = (i + j) / 2;
    if (s.substring(k, k+1).equals("0"))
      i = k + 1;
    else
      j = k - 1;
  }
  return i;
}
```

How many iterations through the `while` loop will be made in the best and the worst case?

	Best case	Worst case
(A)	1	5
(B)	1	15
(C)	4	5
(D)	4	15
(E)	5	5

25. Given two arrays of `double` values, sorted in ascending order, one with 100 elements, the other with 10 elements, how many comparisons will it take in an optimal algorithm to merge these arrays into one sorted array, in the best case and in the worst case?

	Best case	Worst case
(A)	10	109
(B)	50	110
(C)	100	110
(D)	109	999
(E)	100	1000

26. Consider the following method.

```
public void printSomething(String s)
{
  int n = s.length();
  if (n < 1)
    return;
  String s1 = s.substring(1, n);
  printSomething(s1);
  System.out.println(s);
  printSomething(s1);
}
```

How many letters 'A' and how many letters total will be printed as a result of calling `printSomething("ABCD")`?

	A's	Total
(A)	1	10
(B)	4	10
(C)	1	26
(D)	4	26
(E)	15	26

27. The statement

```
System.out.println(Integer.MAX_VALUE);
```

prints `2147483647`, which is equal to $2^{31} - 1$. What does the following statement print?

```
System.out.println(Integer.MAX_VALUE + 2);
```

(A)   0
(B)   2147483649
(C)   2147483647.0
(D)   -2147483647
(E)   Nothing: it causes a `ClassCastException`

28. Brad has derived his class from the library class `JPanel`. `JPanel`'s `paintComponent` method displays a blank picture in a panel. Brad has redefined `JPanel`'s `paintComponent` to display his own picture. Brad's class compiles with no errors, but when he runs the program, only a blank background is displayed. Which of the following hypotheses CANNOT be true in this situation?

   (A)   Brad misspelled "paintComponent" in his method's name.
   (B)   Brad specified an incorrect return type for his `paintComponent` method.
   (C)   Brad chose the wrong type for a parameter in his `paintComponent` method.
   (D)   Brad specified two parameters for his `paintComponent` method, while `JPanel`'s `paintComponent` takes only one parameter.
   (E)   Brad has a logic error in his `paintComponent` code that prevents it from generating the picture.

29. Consider the following method.

```
public int countSomething(int[] arr)
{
   int m = arr[0];
   int count = 1;
   for (int k = 1; k < arr.length; k++)
   {
      int a = arr[k];
      if (a > m)
      {
         m = a;
         count = 1;
      }
      else if (m == a)
         count++;
   }
   return count;
}
```

   For which of the following arrays `countSomething` will return 3?

   (A)   `int[] arr = {0, 1, 1, 1, 1};`
   (B)   `int[] arr = {1, 6, 5, 4, 0};`
   (C)   `int[] arr = {1, 0, 5, 6, 1};`
   (D)   `int[] arr = {3, 2, 1, 0, 5};`
   (E)   None of the above

Questions 30-34 refer to the code from the GridWorld case study. Reference materials are provided in the appendices.

30. Assuming that `loc1` and `loc2` are `Location` objects that represent valid locations in a grid, which of the following conditions verifies that `loc2` lies to the north of `loc1`?

    (A)   `Grid.getDirection(loc1, loc2).equals(Location.NORTH)`
    (B)   `loc1.getAdjacentLocation(Location.NORTH).equals(loc2)`
    (C)   `loc1.getDirectionToward(loc2) == Location.NORTH`
    (D)   `loc1.getDirectionToward(loc2).equals(Location.NORTH)`
    (E)   `loc1.getDirection(loc2).equals(new Location(Location.NORTH, 0))`

31. The diagram below shows the relationships between some of the GridWorld classes and interfaces.

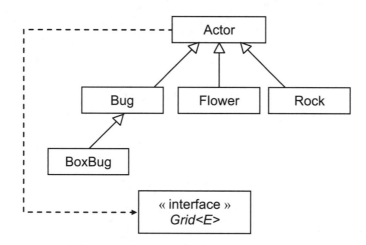

An ⎯▷ arrow from *B* to *A* indicates that *B* extends *A*. An --→ arrow from *A* to *B* indicates that *A* uses *B*, that is, *A* refers to variables of the type *B*. Two "uses" arrows can be added to the diagram to make it more accurate. Which ones?

    (A)   `Bug` uses `Grid` and `Bug` uses `Flower`
    (B)   `Bug` uses `Flower` and `Bug` uses `Rock`
    (C)   `Bug` uses `Grid` and `Flower` uses `Grid`
    (D)   `Bug` uses `Grid` and `BoxBug` uses `Grid`
    (E)   `Bug` uses `Grid` and `BoxBug` uses `Flower`

32. `ZipBug` is a subclass of `Bug`. Each time its `act` method is called, a `ZipBug` moves forward up to five times, while it can, leaving a `Flower` in each cell in its wake. If it can't move at all from its starting location, the `ZipBug` turns, like a regular `Bug`. Which of the following approaches will implement `ZipBug`, as specified?

I. Override only `Bug`'s `act` method, as follows:

```
public void act()
{
  for (int count = 1; count <= 5; count++)
    super.act();
}
```

II. Override only `Bug`'s `act` method, as follows:

```
public void act()
{
  int count;
  for (count = 0; count < 5 && canMove(); count++)
    move();
  if (count == 0)
    turn();
}
```

III. Override only `Bug`'s `move` method, as follows:

```
public void move()
{
  for (int count = 1; count <= 5; count++)
  {
    if (!canMove())
      return;
    super.move();
  }
}
```

(A)   I only
(B)   II only
(C)   I and II only
(D)   II and III only
(E)   I, II, and III

33. A `Caterpillar` actor has some features of `Bug` and some of `Critter`. A `Caterpillar` first "eats" all the flowers in the adjacent locations (except the one just behind it), then, if possible, moves ahead to the adjacent location and leaves a flower in its wake. If the location in front is occupied, the `Caterpillar` stays in place and turns 45 degrees to the right. `Caterpillar` has two constructors similar to `Bug`'s constructors. `Caterpillar` can be implemented as a subclass of `Bug` or as a subclass of `Critter`. Approximately how many lines of code would each of these two implementations require (not counting braces, comments, and `import` statements)?

	extends Bug	extends Critter
(A)	10	10
(B)	10	30
(C)	20	30
(D)	30	50
(E)	50	50

34. `RockJumpingCritter` is a subclass of `Critter`. A `RockJumpingCritter` acts exactly like a `Critter`, with one exception: it is allowed to jump from its current location over one `Rock` into a valid empty location. The `RockJumpingCritter` is implemented by overriding <u>only one</u> method of the `Critter` class, in such a way that that method's postcondition remains the same. Which method can be overridden?

(A) Only `processActors`
(B) Only `getMoveLocations`
(C) Only `selectMoveLocation`
(D) Either `processActors` or `getMoveLocations`
(E) Either `getMoveLocations` or `selectMoveLocation`

35. The statement

```
Animal a = new Mammal("Elephant");
```

compiles with no errors. Which of the following situations will permit that?

(A) `Mammal` is a class with a constructor that takes one parameter of the `String` type, and `Animal` is its subclass.
(B) `Animal` is a class with a constructor that takes one parameter of the `String` type, `Mammal` is its subclass that has no constructors defined.
(C) `Mammal` is a class with a constructor that takes one parameter of the `String` type, `Animal` is an interface, and `Mammal` implements `Animal`.
(D) `Animal` has a public static data field `String Mammal`.
(E) None of the above

36. What is printed when the following code segment is executed?

```
String[] xy = {"X", "Y"};
String[] yx = xy;
yx[0] = xy[1];
yx[1] = xy[0];
System.out.println(xy[0] + xy[1] + yx[0] + yx[1]);
```

(A) XXXX
(B) XYYX
(C) XYXY
(D) XYYY
(E) YYYY

37. Consider the following interface TV and class MyTV.

```
public interface TV
{
  void tuneTo(String channel);
}

public class MyTV implements TV
{
  private ArrayList<String> myFavoriteChannels;

  public MyTV(ArrayList<String> channels)
  { /* implementation not shown */ }

  public void tuneTo(int k)
  { /* implementation not shown */ }

  public void tuneTo(int k, String name)
  { /* implementation not shown */ }
}
```

One of them has one or more errors and won't compile properly. Which of the following best describes the compiler errors reported for the code that is shown?

(A) In the TV interface, the tuneTo method header is missing the keyword public
(B) MyTV should be declared abstract; it does not define tuneTo(String)
(C) tuneTo is defined more than once in MyTV
(D) Cannot convert int to String in the tuneTo method in MyTV
(E) Two errors: (1) tuneTo is defined more than once and (2) cannot convert int to String in the tuneTo(int) method in MyTV

Questions 38-39 refer to the following class Game and the incomplete class ChessGame.

```java
public class Game
{
  private String gameName;
  private List<String> players;

  public Game(String name)
  {
    gameName = name;
    players = new ArrayList<String>();
  }

  public Game(String name, String[] people)
  {
    gameName = name;
    players = new ArrayList<String>();
    for (String nm : people)
      players.add(nm);
  }

  public void addPlayer(String name) { players.add(name); }

  public String getPlayer(int k)
  {
    return players.get(k - 1);
  }

  public String toString()
  {
    return gameName + " game " + players.toString();
  }
}


public class ChessGame extends Game
{
  public ChessGame(String white, String black)
  {
    < missing code >
  }
}
```

38. Consider the following code segment in a `Game`'s client class.

```
String[] players = {"Annette", "Bertrand",
                               "Claude", "Danielle"};
Game game = new Game("Bauernschnapsen", players);
System.out.println( < missing expression >);
```

Which of the following can replace < *missing expression*> so that the code results in printing `"Annette"`?

(A) `game.getPlayer(0)`
(B) `game.getPlayer(1)`
(C) `game.players.get(0)`
(D) `game.players.get(1)`
(E) `game.getPlayers().get(0)`

39. Which of the following can replace < *missing code* > in `ChessGame`'s constructor so that the statement

```
System.out.println(new ChessGame("Deep Blue",
                                      "Kasparov"));
```

prints

```
Chess game [Deep Blue, Kasparov]
```

    I.   `super("Chess", white, black);`

    II.   `super("Chess");`
                `super.addPlayer(white);`
                `super.addPlayer(black);`

    III.   `String[] players = {black, white};`
                `super("Chess", players);`

(A) I only
(B) II only
(C) I and II only
(D) II and III only
(E) I, II, and III

40. Consider the following two recursive versions of the method `choose(n, k)`.

Version 1

```
public static int choose(int n, int k)
{
  if (k == 0)
    return 1;
  else
    return choose(n, k-1) * (n-k+1)/k;
}
```

Version 2

```
public static int choose(int n, int k)
{
  if (k < 0 || k > n)
    return 0;
  else if (n == 0)
    return 1;
  else
    return choose(n-1, k-1) + choose(n-1, k);
}
```

When `choose(4, 2)` is called, how many times total, including the original call, will `choose` be called in each version?

	Version 1	Version 2
(A)	2	7
(B)	2	19
(C)	3	7
(D)	3	19
(E)	3	27

Practice Exam #1

SECTION II

Time — 1 hour and 45 minutes
Number of questions — 4
Percent of total grade — 50

1. Any reasonable word processor or text editor offers a global replace operation and an "undo" operation that restores the original text. In this question you will implement three static methods of the `GlobalReplace` class, which help support these operations. To receive full credit, you may use `String` methods `length`, `indexOf`, and `substring`, but no other `String` methods.

   (a) Write the `replaceOne` method. `replaceOne(text, i, n, sub)` replaces a segment of `text` of length `n` that starts at index `i` with the replacement string `sub`. (The length of `sub` is not necessarily the same as the length `n` of the segment to be replaced). `replaceOne` returns the modified text. Complete the method `replaceOne` below.

   ```
   /** Replaces several characters in a given text string,
    *   starting at a given index, with a new substring.
    *   @param text string to be modified,
    *   @param i starting index of replacement
    *   @param n number of characters to be replaced
    *   @param sub replacement string
    *   @return modified text
    *   Precondition: i + n <= text.length()
    */
   public static String replaceOne(String text, int i,
                                             int n, String sub)
   ```

167

(b)   Write `replaceAll` and `undoReplaceAll` methods.

The `GlobalReplace` class has a static variable `savedText` shown below.

```
public class GlobalReplace
{
    /** Holds saved text strings from successive calls
        to replaceAll */
    private static List<String> savedText =
                        new ArrayList<String>();

    ...
}
```

`replaceAll(text, what, sub)` saves `text` in the `savedText` list, then replaces all occurrences of `what` in `text` with `sub` and returns modified text. Do not duplicate code from Part (a) — assume that `replaceOne` works as specified, regardless of what you wrote in Part (a). Do not use any `String` methods other than `length` and `indexOf`. You may not receive full credit if you duplicate code from Part (a) or use any `String` methods other than `length` and `indexOf`.

Note that `replaceAll` proceeds from the beginning of `text` and replaces the occurrences of `what` in `text` in the order in which they are encountered. For example, `replaceAll("AAAA", "AA", "B")` should return `"BB"`, and `replaceAll("AAAA", "AAA", "B")` should return `"BA"`.

`undoReplaceAll` returns the original text from the last call to `replaceAll`. If there is no saved text, `undoReplaceAll` returns `null`.

Complete the methods `replaceAll` and `undoReplaceAll` below.

```
/** Saves the original text in savedText, replaces all
 *  occurrences of what in text with sub (in order of
 *  occurrence); returns modified text.
 *  @param text string to be modified
 *  @param what substring to be replaced
 *  @param sub replacement substring
 *  @return modified text
 */
public static String replaceAll(String text,
                            String what, String sub)



/** Returns the text saved by the last call to replaceAll;
 *  if there is no saved text, returns null
 */
public static String undoReplaceAll()
```

2.   Simply Bagels bakery relies on a Java application for handling its orders. The designer
     of the application started the project by defining an interface `OrderItem`, shown below.

```
public interface OrderItem
{
  /** Returns the price of this item */
  double getPrice();

  /** Returns the number of units ordered */
  int getQuantity();

  /** Returns the total cost for this order item */
  double getCost();
}
```

She then wrote a class `BagelsOrderItem`, which implements the `OrderItem` interface,
and a class `BakersDozen`, a subclass of `BagelsOrderItem`. This arrangement is
summarized in the class diagram below.

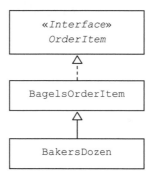

In this question you will write the `BagelsOrderItem` and `BakersDozen` classes.

(a)   Write a class `BagelsOrderItem` that implements the `OrderItem` interface.
      Implement your class in accordance with the encapsulation principle. Provide one
      constructor that takes two parameters: `double price` and `int quantity`.
      Provide accessor methods that return the item's price and quantity.
      `BagelsOrderItem`'s `getCost` method should return price times quantity. Write
      the entire `BagelsOrderItem` class, including all necessary instance variables and
      methods.

(b) Write a class `BakersDozen`, a subclass of `BagelsOrderItem`. A `BakersDozen` object represents an order of 13 bagels, which includes one free bagel.[*] Provide one constructor that takes one parameter, `double price` (the quantity is known: it is 13). Override `BagelsOrderItem`'s `getCost` method to reflect one free bagel. Do not duplicate the instance variables of `BagelsOrderItem` class in `BakersDozen`. Write class `BakersDozen` below.

For additional practice, write the class `ShoppingCart`. Your class should <u>extend</u> `ArrayList<OrderItem>`. Add only one method, `totalDue`, which returns the sum of the costs of all the items in the list. `ShoppingCart` does not have any explicitly defined constructors or instance variables. Note that a `ShoppingCart` can contain `BagelsOrderItem` objects, `BakersDozen` objects, perhaps other kinds of `OrderItem` objects. For example, the segment of code

```
ShoppingCart cart = new ShoppingCart();
cart.add(new BagelsOrderItem(0.25, 3));
cart.add(new BakersDozen(0.35););
    System.out.printf("Total due: $%.02f", cart.totalDue());
```

should display `Total due: $4.95`.

---

[*] According to Wikipedia, the oldest known source for the expression "baker's dozen" dates to the 13th century in one of the earliest English statutes, instituted during the reign of Henry III (1216–1272), called the Assize of Bread and Ale. Bakers who were found to have shortchanged customers (some variations say that they would sell hollow bread) could be subject to severe punishment including judicial amputation of a hand. To guard against losing a hand to an axe, a baker would give 13 for the price of 12 in order to be certain of not being called a cheat.

3. This question involves reasoning about the GridWorld case study. Reference materials
    are provided in the appendices.

    `Twister` is a subclass of `Actor`. A `Twister` always stays in the same row in which it
    was created: on each step it moves to an adjacent location, choosing randomly between
    east or west, with equal probabilities. If the location of the intended move contains
    another actor, that actor is removed from the grid. If the location of the intended move is
    invalid, the `Twister` removes itself from the grid. Before moving, a `Twister` destroys
    all the actors in its column that are below (to the south of) the `Twister`. For example:

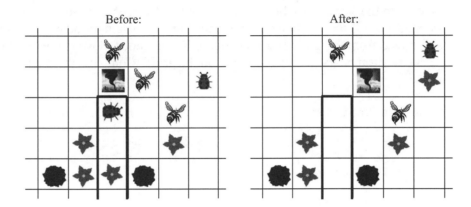

    A partial definition of the `Twister` class is shown below.

```
public class Twister extends Actor
{
    public Twister()
    {
        setColor(Color.GRAY);
    }

    public void act()
    {
        destroy();
        move();
    }

    /** Removes from the grid all the actors in its column
     *  that are below (to the south of) this Twister
     */
    public void destroy()
    { /* to be implemented in part (a) */ }

    /** Moves this Twister east or west, with equal probabilities;
     *  if the location of the intended move contains another
     *  actor, that actor is removed from the grid; if the location
     *  of the intended move is invalid, this Twister removes
     *  itself from the grid
     */
    public void move()
    { /* to be implemented in part (b) */ }
}
```

(a)   Write the `destroy` method of the `Twister` class. The method removes from the grid all the actors that are in the same column as this `Twister` to the south of it. Complete the method `destroy` below.

```
/** Removes from the grid all the actors in this Twister's
 *  column that are below (to the south of) this Twister
 */
public void destroy()
```

(b)   Write the `move` method of the `Twister` class. A `Twister` moves to an adjacent location in the same row, choosing randomly between east or west, with equal probabilities. If the location of the intended move contains another actor, that actor is removed from the grid. If the location of the intended move is invalid, the `Twister` disappears (removes itself from the grid). Complete the method `move` below.

```
/** Moves this Twister east or west, with equal probabilities;
 *  if the location of the intended move contains another
 *  actor, that actor is removed from the grid; if the location
 *  of the intended move is invalid, this Twister removes
 *  itself from the grid
 */
public void move()
```

4. In a traffic modeling application, a segment of a highway is represented as a two-dimensional array of integers, in which each row represents one lane and each column represents a multi-lane cross-section at a given position. A value of 1 signifies a car is present and a value of 0 signifies an empty slot. All cars move in the same direction. Cars can also make lateral moves ("switch lanes"). For example, the stretch of highway below has 4 lanes.

```
00000000
00010010
01001000
00100000
```

Direction of traffic

To simulate continuous traffic in a stretch of highway in the model, a car that goes out of bounds on the right reappears in the back of the same lane on the left.

The model is implemented with the help of the class `Highway`. A partial definition of this class is shown below. You will write two methods of this class.

For additional practice, write the other methods of the `Highway` class whose code is not shown.

```java
public class Highway
{
    /** hwy[lane][x] = 1 if there is a car at position x
     *  in lane; hwy[lane][x] = 0 if there is no car */
    private int[][] hwy;

    /** Constructs an empty Highway with a given number of
     *  lanes and a given length
     */
    public Highway(int lanes, int length)
    {
        hwy = new int[lanes][length]; // all values in hwy
                         // are initialized to 0 by default
    }

    /** Places a car in a given lane at a given position */
    public void addCar(int lane, int x)
    {
        hwy[lane][x] = 1;
    }

    /** A car can switch to an adjacent lane if that lane is within
     *  the hwy bounds and there are no cars at the same position
     *  in other lanes in the direction of the lateral move.
     *  @param lane current lane
     *  @param dir direction of the move: -1 (up, the row index
     *             is decreased) or 1, down, the row index is
     *             increased
     *  @param x position on hwy
     *  @return true if can switch lanes in the given lateral
     *  direction; otherwise false
     */
    public boolean canSwitchLane(int lane, int dir, int x)
    { /* to be implemented in part (a) */ }

    /** All cars in hwy attempt to switch lanes: with
     *  the probability 0.1 up and the same probability
     *  down; all cars that can make such a lateral move,
     *  do so.  The probability of a car not attempting
     *  to change lanes is 0.8.
     */
    public void moveAllSideways()
    { /* implementation not shown */ }

    /** Moves all cars in all lanes forward by one position;
     *  a car in the last (rightmost) position moves into the
     *  first position (position 0) in the same lane
     */
    public void moveAllForward()
    { /* to be implemented in part (b) */ }
}
```

(a) Write the `boolean` method `canSwitchLane` of the `Highway` class. A car at
`hwy[lane][x]` can move in direction –1 (up) if `lane-1` exists and there are no
cars at position `x` in any lanes above the current lane (lanes `lane-1`, `lane-2`, etc.).
A car can move in direction +1 (down) if `lane+1` exists and there are no cars at
position `x` in any lane below (lanes `lane+1`, `lane+2`, etc.). In the example below,
the cars that can change lanes are shown in bold.

Can move up ↑
dir = -1

Can move down ↓
dir = 1

01000010	01000010
000**1**0010	000100**1**0
0100**1**000	0**1**001000
00**111**000	00111000

Complete the method `canSwitchLane` below.

```
/** A car can switch to an adjacent lane if that lane is within
 *   the hwy bounds and there are no cars at the same position
 *   in other lanes in the direction of the lateral move.
 *   @param lane current lane
 *   @param dir direction of the move: -1 (up, the row index
 *              is decreased) or 1, down, the row index is
 *              increased
 *   @param x position on hwy
 *   @return true if can switch lanes in the given lateral
 *   direction; otherwise false
 */
public boolean canSwitchLane(int lane, int dir, int x)
```

(b) Write the method `moveAllForward` of the `Highway` class. In this simplified version of the model, each car moves forward by one position. A car in the last position (rightmost column) is placed into the same lane in the leftmost position (column 0). <u>You may not use any temporary arrays or lists</u>. If a temporary array or list is used, your solution may not receive full credit. Complete the method `moveAllForward` below.

```
/** Moves all cars in all lanes forward by one position;
 *   a car in the last (rightmost) position moves into the
 *   first position (position 0) in the same lane
 */
public void moveAllForward()
```

For additional practice, implement a more sophisticated version of `moveAllForward` in which each car moves halfway toward the current position of the next car in the same lane. (For the last car in the lane, the "next" car will be the first car in that lane). Do not use any temporary arrays or lists.

Practice Exam #2

SECTION I

Time — 1 hour and 15 minutes
Number of questions — 40
Percent of total grade — 50

1. What is the output of the following program segment?

    ```
    int num = 5;
    while (num >= 0)
    {
      num -= 2;
    }
    System.out.print(num);
    ```

    (A) -2
    (B) -1
    (C) 0
    (D) 2
    (E) 21

2. What is the output from

    ```
    int n = 12;
    System.out.print(goFigure(n));
    System.out.print(" " + n);
    ```

    where the method goFigure is defined as follows:

    ```
    public double goFigure(int n)
    {
      n %= 7;
      return (double)(12 / n);
    }
    ```

    (A) 2.4 12
    (B) 2.4 6
    (C) 2.4 5
    (D) 2.0 12
    (E) 2.0 5

3. Which of the following expressions will evaluate to `true` when `x` and `y` are `boolean` variables with different values?

    I.   `(x || y) && (!x || !y)`
    II. `(x || y) && !(x && y)`
    III. `(x && !y) || (!x && y)`

    (A) I only
    (B) II only
    (C) I and II only
    (D) II and III only
    (E) I, II, and III

4. Recall that the value of `Integer.MIN_VALUE` is -2^{31}. What is printed as a result of executing the following statement?

    ```
    System.out.println((Integer.MIN_VALUE + 1) /
                                      (1024*1024*1024));
    ```

    (A) `0`
    (B) `1`
    (C) `2`
    (D) `-1`
    (E) `1024`

5. Consider the following code segment.

    ```
    int x = < integer value >, y = < another integer value >;
    while (x > y && x % y != 0)
    {
       x -= y;
    }
    ```

    Which of the following conditions will be always `true` after the `while` loop, regardless of the initial values of `x` and `y`?

    (A) `x < y`
    (B) `x < y || x % y != 0`
    (C) `x <= y && x % y != 0`
    (D) `x >= y && x % y == 0`
    (E) `x <= y || x % y == 0`

Questions 6-7 refer to the following method.

```
public void printVals(String[] items, int k)
{
  if (k > 1)
  {
    printVals(items, k - 1);
    System.out.print(items[k] + " ");
    printVals(items, k - 2);
  }
}
```

Suppose the following code segment has been executed.

```
String[] names = {"Pat", "Joe", "Ann", "Cal", "Amy"};
printVals(names, names.length - 1);
```

6.   What is the output?

    (A)   Ann Cal Amy Ann
    (B)   Ann Cal Amy Cal Ann
    (C)   Ann Cal Joe Amy Joe Ann
    (D)   Joe Ann Cal Joe Amy Joe Ann
    (E)   Joe Ann Pat Cal Joe Amy Joe Ann Pat

7.   How many calls to printVals have been made, including the original call?

    (A)   3
    (B)   5
    (C)   7
    (D)   8
    (E)   9

8.   In OOP, programmers often arrange classes into inheritance hierarchies instead of implementing isolated classes. Which of the following is NOT a valid reason for doing so?

    (A)   Abstract classes at the top of the hierarchy can be extended in the project or reused in other projects.
    (B)   Methods from a superclass can often be reused in its subclasses without duplication of code.
    (C)   Objects from different subclasses can be passed as parameters to a method designed to accept objects of the superclass.
    (D)   Objects from different subclasses can be stored in the same array.
    (E)   All of the above are valid reasons for using inheritance hierarchies.

9. At the county fair, prizes are awarded to the five heaviest cows. More than 2000 cows are entered, and their records are stored in an array. Which of the following algorithms provides the most efficient way of finding the records of the five heaviest cows?

    (A) Selection Sort
    (B) Selection Sort terminated after the first five iterations
    (C) Insertion Sort
    (D) Insertion Sort terminated after the first five iterations
    (E) Mergesort

10. Which of the following recommendations for testing software is NOT good advice?

    (A) Test a program with all possible values of input data.
    (B) When testing a large program, test the smaller pieces individually before testing the entire program.
    (C) If possible, use automated testing procedures or read test data from files so that you can re-run the tests after corrections have been made.
    (D) Design test data that exercises as many different paths through the code as is practical.
    (E) Test on data that is at the boundary of program conditionals to check for "off by one" errors.

11. Consider the following method of the class `Test`.

```
public static List<String> doNothing(List<String> list)
{
  return list;
}
```

    Which of the following program segments in a `Test`'s client class will compile with no errors?

    I.   ```
          ArrayList<String> nums = new ArrayList<String>();
          nums = Test.doNothing(nums);
          ```

    II.   ```
          List<String> nums = new ArrayList<String>();
          nums = Test.doNothing(nums);
          ```

    III. ```
          ArrayList<String> nums1 = new ArrayList<String>();
          List<String> nums2 = Test.doNothing(nums1);
          ```

    (A)  I only
    (B)  II only
    (C)  I and II only
    (D)  II and III only
    (E)  I, II, and III
          ```

Questions 12-13 refer to the following method.

```
private int product(int n)
{
  if (n <= 1)
    return 1;
  else
    return n * product(n-2);
}
```

12. What is the output when `product(6)` is called?

(A) 1
(B) 8
(C) 12
(D) 48
(E) 720

13. `product(25)` returns -1181211311, a negative number. Which of the following accounts for this result?

(A) Integer arithmetic overflow
(B) Logic error that shows up for odd values of n
(C) Stack overflow error in recursive calls
(D) Small range of integers in the Java Virtual Machine installed on your computer
(E) A loss of precision in calculations

14. What will array `arr` contain after the following code segment has been executed?

```
int[] arr = {4, 3, 2, 1, 0};
for (int k = 1; k < arr.length; k++)
{
  arr[k-1] += arr[k];
}
```

(A) 4, 7, 5, 3, 1
(B) 4, 7, 9, 10, 10
(C) 7, 3, 2, 1, 0
(D) 7, 5, 3, 1, 0
(E) 10, 6, 3, 1, 0

15. The two versions of the `search` method shown below are both intended to return `true` if `ArrayList<Object> list` contains the target value; otherwise they are supposed to return `false`.

Version 1

```
public boolean search(ArrayList<Object> list, Object target)
{
  for (Object x : list)
  {
    if (target.equals(x))
      return true;
  }
  return false;
}
```

Version 2

```
public boolean search(ArrayList<Object> list, Object target)
{
  boolean found = false;

  for (Object x : list)
  {
    if (target.equals(x))
      found = true;
  }
  return found;
}
```

Which of the following statements about the two versions of `search` is true?

(A) Only Version 1 works as intended.
(B) Only Version 2 works as intended.
(C) Both versions work as intended; Version 1 is often more efficient than Version 2.
(D) Both versions work as intended; Version 2 is often more efficient than Version 1.
(E) Both versions work as intended; the two versions are always equally efficient.

16. Consider the following class.

```
public class BuddyList
{
  /** Contains the names of buddies */
  private ArrayList<String> buddies;

  < constructors and other methods and variables not shown >

  public ArrayList<String> getBuddies()
  {
    return buddies;
  }
}
```

If `BuddyList myFriends` is declared and initialized in some other class, a client of `BuddyList`, which of the following correctly assigns to `name` the name of the first buddy in the `myFriends` list?

    I.   `String name = myFriends.buddies[0];`

    II. `String name = myFriends.buddies.get(0);`

   III. `String name = myFriends.getBuddies().get(0);`

(A)   I only
(B)   II only
(C)   III only
(D)   I and II only
(E)   II and III only

17. Consider the following class.

```
public class Counter
{
  private int count = 0;

  public Counter() { count = 0; }
  public Counter(int x) { count = x; }         // Line 1
  public int getCount() { return count; }      // Line 2
  public void setCount(int c) { int count = c; }  // Line 3
  public void increment() { count++; }         // Line 4
  public String toString() { return "" + count; } // Line 5
}
```

The test code

```
    Counter c = new Counter();
    c.setCount(3);
    c.increment();
    System.out.println(c.getCount());
```

is supposed to print 4, but the class has an error. What is actually printed, and which line in the class definition should be changed to get the correct output, 4?

(A)   0, Line 1
(B)   1, Line 3
(C)   0, Line 4
(D)   3, Line 4
(E)   36, Line 5

18. Which of the following code segments correctly traverses row by row a rectangular two-dimensional `int` array `m`?

(A)
```
for (int x : m)
{
    ...
}
```

(B)
```
for (int r : m)
{
    for (int c = 0; c < m.length; c++)
    {
        int x = m[r][c];
        ...
    }
}
```

(C)
```
for (int c = 0; c < m.length; c++)
{
    for (int r = 0; r < m[c].length; r++)
    {
        int x = m[r][c];
        ...
    }
}
```

(D)
```
for (int r = 0; r < m.length; r++)
{
    for (int c = 0; c < m[0].length; c++)
    {
        int x = m[r][c];
        ...
    }
}
```

(E)
```
for (int r = 0; r < m[0].length; r++)
{
    for (int c = 0; c < m.length; c++)
    {
        int x = m[r][c];
        ...
    }
}
```

19. Consider the following method.

```
public void change(double[] nums, int n)
{
  for (int k = 0; k < n; k++)
  {
    nums[k] = 5.4;
  }
  n = 2;
}
```

What will be stored in `samples` and `len` after the following statements are executed?

```
double[] samples = {1.0, 2.1, 3.2, 4.3};
int len = samples.length;
change(samples, len);
```

(A)   `samples` contains `5.4, 5.4, 5.4, 5.4`; `len` is 4
(B)   `samples` contains `5.4, 5.4, 5.4, 5.4`; `len` is 2
(C)   `samples` contains `1.0, 2.1, 3.2, 4.3`; `len` is 4
(D)   `samples` contains `5.4, 5.4`; `len` is 2
(E)   `samples` contains `1.0, 2.1`; `len` is 2

20. What is the output of the following code segment?

```
List<Integer> list = new ArrayList<Integer>();

for (int i = 1; i <= 8; i++)
{
  list.add(new Integer(i));
}

for (int i = 0; i < list.size(); i++)
{
  list.remove(i);
}

for (Integer x : list)
{
  System.out.print(x + " ");
}
```

(A)   `IndexOutOfBoundsException`
(B)   No output because the resulting list is empty
(C)   `1 3 5 7`
(D)   `2 4 6 8`
(E)   `1 2 3 4 5 6 7 8`

21. Suppose `mat` is declared as

```
int[][] mat = new int[3][4];
```

If `mat` initially contains

```
2 1 3 4
9 7 2 1
0 2 5 6
```

what is the output of the following code segment?

```
for (int r = 1; r < mat.length; r++)
{
  for (int c = 1; c < mat[0].length; c++)
  {
    if ((r + c) % 2 == 0)
      mat[r][c] = 2 * mat[r - 1][c - 1] + c;
  }
}
System.out.println(mat[2][2]);
```

(A)   5
(B)   11
(C)   12
(D)   15
(E)   16

22. Consider the following code segment.

```
List<String> list = new ArrayList<String>();
list.add("A");
list.add("B");
list.add("C");
for (String s : list)
{
  String t = list.get(list.size() - 1);
  list.set(list.size() - 1, s);
  s = t;
}
```

What will `list` contain after the above code segment has been executed?

(A)   ["A", "B", "C"]
(B)   ["A", "B", "B"]
(C)   ["C", "B", "A"]
(D)   ["C", "A", "B"]
(E)   ["C", "C", "C"]

23. The following incomplete method `cutToAverage` first finds the average `avg` of the values in an array, then replaces every element that exceeds `avg` with `avg`. `cutToAverage` returns `avg`.

```
public double cutToAverage(double[] amps)
{
  double avg = 0.0;
  < missing code >
  return avg;
}
```

Which of the following could replace < *missing code* > so that `cutToAverage` works as specified?

I.
```
for (double x : amps)
    avg += x;
avg /= amps.length;
for (double x : amps)
  if (x > avg)
     x = avg;
```

II.
```
for (int k = 0; k < amps.length; k++)
    avg += amps[k];
avg /= amps.length;
for (int k = 0; k < amps.length; k++)
  if (amps[k] > avg)
     amps[k] = avg;
```

III.
```
for (double x : amps)
    avg += x;
avg /= amps.length;
for (int k = amps.length - 1; k >= 0; k--)
  if (amps[k] > avg)
     amps[k] = avg;
```

(A) I only
(B) II only
(C) I and II only
(D) II and III only
(E) I, II, and III

24. Suppose it takes about 18 milliseconds to sort an array of 80,000 random numbers using Mergesort. Suppose for an array of 160,000 numbers, Mergesort runs for 40 milliseconds. Approximately how much time will Mergesort run on an array of 320,000 numbers? Choose the closest estimate.

(A) 80 milliseconds
(B) 88 milliseconds
(C) 96 milliseconds
(D) 126 milliseconds
(E) 160 milliseconds

25. Consider the following class `Athlete`.

```
public class Athlete implements Comparable<Athlete>
{
  private int numMedals;

  public int getRank() { return numMedals; }

  public int compareTo(Athlete other)
  {
    // return numMedals - other.numMedals;
    return getRank() - other.getRank();
  }

  < constructors and other methods not shown >
}
```

As you can see, the programmer has commented out direct references to `Athlete`'s instance variable `numMedals` in the `compareTo` method and replaced them with calls to the `getRank` method. What is the most compelling reason for doing this?

(A)   To correct a syntax error: being private, neither `numMedals` nor `other.numMedals` are directly accessible in the method's code

(B)   To correct a syntax error: being private, `other.numMedals` is not directly accessible in the method's code (`numMedals` is replaced with `getRank()` for consistency)

(C)   To avoid possible problems later: if `other` happens to be an object of a subclass of `Athlete` in which `numMedals` is not used in calculating the rank, the original code would fail

(D)   To improve run-time efficiency

(E)   To achieve better encapsulation of the `Athlete` class

Questions 26-30 refer to the code from the GridWorld case study. Reference materials are provided in the appendices.

26. How does a `Bug` act if it is located in the northeast corner of a bounded grid and is facing north?

    (A)   The `Bug` turns west
    (B)   The `Bug` turns south
    (C)   The `Bug` turns northeast
    (D)   The `Bug` turns northwest
    (E)   The `Bug` is removed from the grid

27. Consider the following method.

```
/** Moves bug to the neighboring location to the west,
 *   leaving bug's current location empty and bug's
 *   direction unchanged.
 *   Precondition: (1) this actor is in a grid
 *                 (2) adjacent location to the west is valid
 *                     and empty in the grid of this bug
 */
public void moveWest(Bug bug)
{
  Location loc = bug.getLocation();
  Location next = loc.getAdjacentLocation(Location.WEST);
  < missing code >
}
```

Which of the following code segments could replace < *missing code* > for the method to work as specified?

    I.   `bug.moveTo(next);`

    II.
```
Grid<Actor> gr = bug.getGrid();
bug.removeSelfFromGrid();
bug.putSelfInGrid(gr, next);
```

    III.
```
int dir = bug.getDirection();
bug.setDirection(Location.WEST);
bug.move();
bug.setDirection(dir);
```

    (A)   I only
    (B)   II only
    (C)   I and II only
    (D)   II and III only
    (E)   I, II, and III

28. Which of the following code segments sets n equal to the number of occupied locations adjacent to the `Location loc` in the `Grid<Actor> gr`?

I.
```
ArrayList<Location> neighbors =
        gr.getOccupiedAdjacentLocations(loc);
int n = neighbors.size();
```

II.
```
ArrayList<Actor> neighbors = gr.getNeighbors(loc);
int n = neighbors.size();
```

III.
```
ArrayList<Location> neighbors =
        gr.getValidAdjacentLocations(loc);
ArrayList<Location> emptyNeighbors =
        gr.getEmptyAdjacentLocations(loc);
int n = neighbors.size() - emptyNeighbors.size();
```

(A) I only
(B) II only
(C) I and II only
(D) II and III only
(E) I, II, and III

29. In the GridWorld design, why is the `Actor` class not made abstract, with the `act` method abstract?

(A) To enable polymorphism for instances of `Actor`
(B) To be able to override the `act` method in `Actor`'s subclasses
(C) To avoid duplication of code in constructors of `Actor`'s subclasses
(D) To avoid duplication of the `setColor` method in `Actor`'s subclasses
(E) To be able to create `Actor` objects in GridWorld applications and explore their attributes and behavior

30. Suppose we modify the `act` and `makeMove` methods in `Critter`. We place the calls to `getMoveLocations` and `selectMoveLocation` into `makeMove`, rather than into `act`, as follows:

```
public void act()
{
  if (getGrid() == null)
    return;
  ArrayList<Actor> actors = getActors();
  processActors(actors);
  makeMove();
}

public void makeMove()
{
  ArrayList<Location> moveLocs = getMoveLocations();
  Location loc = selectMoveLocation(moveLocs);

  if (loc == null)
    removeSelfFromGrid();
  else
    moveTo(loc);
}
```

Then all subclasses of `Critter` that override `makeMove` will need to be modified, too. Which other subclasses of `Critter` will need to be modified?

(A) None
(B) All subclasses that override `getMoveLocations`
(C) All subclasses that override `selectMoveLocation`
(D) All subclasses that override both `getMoveLocations` and `selectMoveLocation`
(E) All subclasses that override either `getMoveLocations` or `selectMoveLocation` (or both)

31. Consider the following method.

```
public int locate(String str, String oneLetter)
{
  int j = 0;
  while (j < str.length() &&
         str.substring(j, j+1).compareTo(oneLetter) < 0)
  {
    j++;
  }
  return j;
}
```

Which of the following must be true when the `while` loop terminates?

(A) `j == str.length()`

(B) `str.substring(j, j+1) >= 0`

(C) `j <= str.length() ||`
       `str.substring(j, j+1).compareTo(oneLetter) > 0`

(D) `j == str.length() ||`
       `str.substring(j, j+1).compareTo(oneLetter) >= 0`

(E) `j == str.length() &&`
       `str.substring(j, j+1).compareTo(oneLetter) >= 0`

32. Suppose an array `arr` contains 127 different random values arranged in ascending order, and the most efficient searching algorithm is used to find a target value. How many elements of the array will be examined when the target equals `arr[39]`?

(A) 4

(B) 5

(C) 7

(D) 63

(E) 64

33. Suppose a class `Particle` has the following variables defined.

```
public class Particle
{
  public static final int START_POS = 100;
  private double velocity;

  private boolean canMove()
  { /* implementation not shown */ }

  < constructors, other variables and methods not shown >
}
```

Which of the following is true?

(A)   Java syntax rules wouldn't allow us to use the name `startPos` instead of `START_POS`.

(B)   Java syntax rules wouldn't allow us to make `velocity` public.

(C)   Both `velocity` and `START_POS` can be changed by one of `Particle`'s methods.

(D)   A statement

```
double pos = START_POS + velocity;
```

in `Particle`'s `canMove` method would result in a syntax error.

(E)   All of the above statements are false.

34. What is the value of `product` after the following code segment is executed?

```
int[] factors = {2, 3, 4, 7, 2, 5};
int product = 1;

for (int i = 1; i < factors.length; i += 2)
{
  product *= (factors[i] % factors[i - 1]);
}
```

(A)   0
(B)   1
(C)   2
(D)   3
(E)   5

Questions 35-38 refer to the following classes.

```
public class Party
{
  private List<String> theGuests;

  public Party() { theGuests = null; }

  public Party(List<String> guests) { theGuests = guests; }

  public void setGuests(List<String> guests)
  { theGuests = guests; }

  public String toString()
  { /* implementation not shown */ }
}

public class BDayParty extends Party
{
  private String theName;

  public BDayParty(String name, List<String> guests)
  { /* implementation not shown */ }

  public String getName() { return theName; }

  < other methods not shown >
}
```

35. Given

```
List<String> guests = new ArrayList<String>();
guests.add("Alice");
guests.add("Ben");
guests.add("Candy");
```

which of the following declarations is NOT valid?

(A) `Party[] celebrations = new Party[2];`

(B) `Party[] celebrations =`
       `{new Party(guests), new Party()};`

(C) `BDayParty[] celebrations =`
       `{new BDayParty("Malika", guests), new Party(guests)};`

(D) `BDayParty[] celebrations =`
       `{new BDayParty("Lee", guests),`
       ` new BDayParty("Henry", guests)};`

(E) All of the above are valid.

36. Which of the following statements can replace < *missing statement* > in the following `BDayParty` constructor?

```
public BDayParty(String name, List guests)
{
  < missing statement >
  theName = name;
}
```

   I.   `theGuests = guests;`

   II.   `super(guests);`

   III.   `setGuests(guests);`

(A)   I only
(B)   II only
(C)   I and II only
(D)   II and III only
(E)   I, II, and III

37. Suppose we have decided to make the `Party` class `abstract` and have added the following methods to it:

```
public abstract String getOccasion();
public String getMessage() { return "Happy"; }
public String greetings() { return getMessage() + " "
                                    + getOccasion(); }
```

Which of the following is the smallest set of `Party` methods that would have to be overridden in the `BDayParty` class to make

```
BDayParty birthday = new BDayParty("Aaron", guests);
System.out.println(birthday.greetings());
```

display

```
 Happy Birthday Aaron
```

(A)   None
(B)   `getOccasion`
(C)   `getMessage`
(D)   `getOccasion` and `getMessage`
(E)   `getOccasion`, `getMessage`, and `greetings`

38. `Party`'s `toString` method lists all the entries in the `theGuests` list. Should the programmer use a "for each" loop or the list's `get(i)` method within a loop to traverse the list?

    (A) `get(i)`, because it is always more efficient
    (B) `get(i)`, because "for each" loops work only for arrays
    (C) A "for each" loop, because `get(i)` may be not available in the implementation of `List` passed to the constructor
    (D) A "for each" loop, because it is more efficient when `theGuests` happens to be an `ArrayList`
    (E) Either method works and is equally efficient when the `List` passed to the constructor is an `ArrayList`.

39. Consider the following code segment with a missing statement.

```
String abc = "ABCDEFGHIJKLMNOPQRSTUVWXYZ";
< missing statement >
System.out.println(abc.substring(k, k+1));
```

    It is supposed to print a randomly chosen letter of the alphabet. Any of the 26 letters can be chosen with equal probability. Which of the following can replace
    < *missing statement* > for the code to work that way?

    (A) `int k = Math.random(25);`
    (B) `int k = Math.random(0, 25);`
    (C) `int k = Math.random(25) + 1;`
    (D) `int k = Math.random(26) - 1;`
    (E) `int k = (int)(26*Math.random());`

40. Consider the following interface and class.

```
public interface Student
{
  double getGPA();
  int getSemesterUnits();
}

public class FullTimeStudent implements Student
{
  < required methods go here >
}
```

What is the minimum set of methods that a developer must implement in order to successfully compile the FullTimeStudent class?

(A)   No methods would need to be implemented
(B)   getGPA(), getSemesterUnits()
(C)   getGPA(), getSemesterUnits(), equals(Object s)
(D)   getGPA(), getSemesterUnits(), equals(Object s), toString()
(E)   getGPA(), getSemesterUnits(), compareTo(Object s),
                                    equals(Object s), toString()

Practice Exam #2

SECTION II

Time — 1 hour and 45 minutes
Number of questions — 4
Percent of total grade — 50

1. Mancala is a board game for two players. A Mancala board has 12 small pits, called "houses," and two large pits, called "stores." At the beginning, the same number of "seeds" (for example, three) is placed in each house; the stores are left empty. Each player controls the six houses on her side of the board, and her store is to the right of her houses.

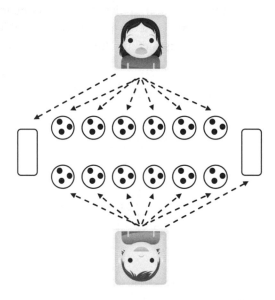

The Java class `Mancala` is used in the computer implementation of the game. In this question you are asked to write the constructor and one method of that class.

The board is represented as `int[] board` with 14 elements. The first player's houses are represented by the elements with indices from 1 to 6 and her store has index 7. The second player's houses are represented by the elements with indices from 8 to 13 and her store has index 0. The constants and instance variables of the `Mancala` class are shown below.

```
public class Mancala
{
  /** The total number of pits on the board */
  private static final int BOARD_SIZE = 14;

  /** The indices of the stores */
  private static final int store1 = BOARD_SIZE/2;
  private static final int store2 = 0;

  /** board[k] holds the numbers of seeds in the k-th pit */
  private int[] board;

  ...
}
```

Throughout your solution, use the three symbolic constants defined above, rather than literal constants (to make it easier to change the board size, if necessary).

(a)   Write a constructor for the `Mancala` class that takes one integer parameter n and initializes the board, "placing" n seeds in each house and leaving the stores empty. Complete the `Mancala`'s constructor below.

```
/** Initializes the board to hold BOARD_SIZE values;
 *   places n "seeds" into each "house"; leaves both
 *   "stores" empty.
 */
public Mancala(int n)
```

(b)   On each move, a player takes <u>all</u> the seeds from one of her houses and "sows" them, moving along the board counterclockwise and placing one seed in each pit, including her houses, her own store, and the opponent's houses, but <u>excluding the opponent's store</u>. For example:

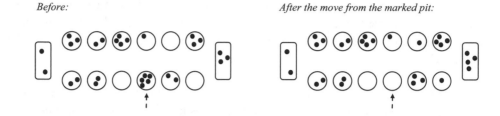

Before: *After the move from the marked pit:*

If the move ends in the player's own store, the player gets another turn. Write the method `move(int k)` that implements the move from the pit with index `k`. The method should return `true` if the move ends in the player's own store; otherwise it should return `false`. Complete the method `move` below.

```
/** Updates the board for the move from a given pit.
 *   @param k the index of the pit in the array board.
 *   @return true if the move ends in the player's
 *          own store; otherwise false.
 *   Precondition: k != store1 && k != store2
 */
public boolean move(int k)
```

In one variation of the game, if a player's move ends in one of that player's houses, and that house is empty, the player captures the last sown seed and all the seeds in the opponent's house directly opposite. All the captured seeds are placed into the player's store. For additional practice, implement this rule in the `move` method.

2.   This question involves reasoning about the GridWorld case study. Reference materials are provided in the appendices.

Your task is to write an entire class `Dahlia`, a subclass of `Flower`. A `Dahlia` at first acts like a regular `Flower`, but at some point, when mature, it produces seeds for new `Dahlias` and dies. Your implementation of the `Dahlia` class must be such that any change in the implementation of the `Flower` class (such as the default color or the formula for darkening the color) automatically applies to `Dahlia`, without changes to `Dahlia`'s code.

Provide two constructors, similar to `Flower`'s constructors. A `Dahlia` constructed with a "no-args" constructor (the constructor that takes no parameters) should get the same color as `Flower`'s default color. The constructor that takes one parameter of the type `Color` should set the initial color of this `Dahlia` to the given color. A `Dahlia` of a particular color produces seeds that later "grow" into `Dahlias` of the same color. Therefore, `Dahlia`'s constructors should save the initial color of the `Dahlia` in an instance variable to be used later for generating seeds.

A `Dahlia` keeps track of its age (the number of times the `act` method has been called). For the first five "weeks" (first five calls to `act`) a `Dahlia` acts like a regular `Flower`. On the sixth call, the `Dahlia` produces three seeds and attempts to place each of them into the grid. Then `Dahlia` dies (removes itself from the grid).

A Dahlia seed is represented by an object of the `DahliaSeed` class. Assume that the class `DahliaSeed` is provided and that it has one constructor, which takes a color as a parameter. The `Dahlia` should pass its own initial color to that constructor. A `Dahlia` attempts to place each of the three seeds into a location randomly chosen, with equal probabilities, from the valid adjacent locations. If the chosen location is occupied by any other actor (including a previously placed seed), the attempt is wasted, and the seed is not placed.

Write the entire `Dahlia` class, including all necessary instance variables, constructors, and methods.

For additional practice, write `DahliaSeed`, too. The seed's own color is `Color.GRAY`, but it has the original `Dahlia`'s color saved in an instance variable. When a seed matures (after three "weeks"), it turns into a new `Dahlia` of that color.

3. E*Theater recommends movies to customers based on their previous selections. Clearly some movie matching mechanism is employed. A movie is described by a set of predefined features, such as genre, rating, director, lead actress, lead actor, and so on. Each feature is coded by a three-letter code. For example, the genre of a movie may be COM for comedy, DRA for drama, ADV for adventure. The three-letter codes are concatenated to form one string `features`. The lengths of the `features` strings are the same for all movies, and that length is evenly divisible by 3. A particular feature may have different values for different movies, but its code always occurs at the same position in the respective `features` strings.

A movie is represented by an object of the following partially defined class `Movie`.

```
public class Movie
{
   /** Describes the features of this movie */
   private String features;

   /** Returns the likeness score between this movie and other
    *  Precondition: The length of the features string is the
    *                same in this and other; it is positive and
    *                evenly divisible by 3
    */
   public double likenessScore(Movie other)
   {  /* to be implemented in part (a) */  }

   < other variables, constructors, and methods not shown >
}
```

The likeness score of two movies is defined as the number of matching features, divided by the total number of features. For example:

movie1 features	"COMROMPALAFF_R_"
movie2 features	"DRAROMPALHOP_R_"
Total number of features	5
Number of matching features	3
Likeness score	3/5 = 0.6

(a)   Write the `likenessScore` method of the `Movie` class that returns the likeness score between this movie and another movie. Complete the method `likenessScore` below.

```
/** Returns the likeness score between this movie and other
 *  Precondition: The length of the features string is the
 *                same in this and other; it is positive and
 *                evenly divisible by 3
 */
public double likenessScore(Movie other)
```

(b)   Each subscriber to E*Theater services has a list of movies he has watched recently. Some of the movies in that list may not fit well with the rest (for example, a movie may have been ordered for a friend or a family member). E*Theater's marketing department wishes to detect and remove such "outliers" from each subscriber's movie list.

The method `getFitCoefficients` takes a list of movies and returns an array of values that measure how well each movie in the list fits with the rest. The size of the array returned by `getFitCoefficients` is the same as the size of the `movies` list. The k-th element in the returned array is equal to the fit coefficient for the k-th movie.

Your task is to write the method `removeOutliers`. This method (in the same class as `getFitCoefficients`) takes a list of movies, obtains an array of the fit coefficients for it, calculates their average, and uses half of that value as a threshold. It then removes all the elements from the list of movies whose fit coefficient is less than the threshold. (Hint: to simplify the code, traverse the movies list and the array of fit coefficients in reverse.) Complete the method `removeOutliers` below.

```
/** Obtains the fit coefficients for the movies in the
 *   given list, calculates their average, and removes
 *   from the movies list all the elements whose fit
 *   coefficient is less than half the average.
 *   Precondition: The size of the movies list is
 *                 not less than 2
 */
public static void removeOutliers(List<Movie> movies)
```

The implementation of the `getFitCoefficients` method is not shown — write it yourself for additional practice. The fit coefficient for a movie M is defined as the average of the likeness scores between M and all the other movies in the list. Make sure that the likeness score for any pair of movies from the list is computed only once but do not use a temporary two-dimensional array.

```
/** Returns an array of values that measure how well each
 *   movie in the movies list fits with the rest
 *   @return   an array whose size is equal to the size
 *             of the list movies; the value of the k-th
 *             element holds the average of the likeness
 *             scores between the k-th movie in movies
 *             and the rest of the movies in the list.
 *   Precondition:  The size of the list movies is
 *                  not less than 2
 *   Postcondition: the list movies remains unchanged
 */
private static double[] getFitCoefficients(List<Movie> movies)
{ /* implementation not shown */ }
```

4. Bill is planning a U.S. tour for the Bolshoi Ballet. He has made a list of cities where the Bolshoi will perform. His plan is to always proceed to the nearest city that has not been visited yet. The tour will begin in the "remotest" city; Bill defines the "remotest" city as the one for which the sum of distances to all other cities is the largest.

    Bill uses a distance chart to plan the trip. It is a square table with the cities listed horizontally and vertically in the same order; the intersection of the *i*-th row and *j*-th column shows the distance between the *i*-th and *j*-th cities. The table has zero values on the diagonal and is symmetrical with respect to the diagonal. For example:

	Atlanta	Boston	Cleveland	Dallas	Washington
Atlanta	0	936	550	719	540
Boston	936	0	554	1547	396
Cleveland	550	554	0	1018	309
Dallas	719	1547	1018	0	1181
Washington	540	396	309	1181	0

    In this example, Dallas is the remotest city, because for Dallas the sum of the distances to the other cities — 4465 miles — is greater than for any other city. So the tour would begin in Dallas and then proceed to Atlanta, then Washington, then Cleveland, then Boston.

    The distance chart is represented by the class `DistanceChart`, partially defined below.

```
public class DistanceChart
{
  /** The list of cities in the chart */
  private List<String> cityNames;

  /** The table of distances between cities */
  private int[][] distances;

  /** Returns the index of the city for which the sum of
   *  the distances to all other cities is the largest;
   *  (if there is more than one candidate, returns
   *  any one of them).
   *  Precondition: cityNames is not empty;
   *                distances[i][j] holds the distance
   *                between the i-th and the j-th cities
   */
  public int findRemotestCity()
  {  /* to be implemented in part (a) */  }


  /** Returns the index of the city from cityNames to be
   *  visited next, that is, the city nearest to the i-th
   *  city among those cities that have not been visited yet.
   *  @param i  the index of a given city, already visited
   *  @param visited  indicates which cities have been
   *                  visited: visited[j] == true if the
   *                  j-th city has been visited
   *  Precondition:  0 <= i < cityNames.size();
   *                 visited[i] == true;
   *                 not all cities have been visited
   *  Postcondition: visited remains unchanged
   */
  public int findNearestCity(int i, boolean[] visited)
  {  /* implementation not shown */  }


  /** Returns the itinerary (an ArrayList of city names)
   *  starting from the remotest city and going through
   *  all the cities in cityNames, always proceeding to the
   *  nearest city that has not been visited yet.
   *  Precondition: cityNames is not empty;
   *                distances[i][j] holds the distance
   *                between the i-th and the j-th cities
   */
  public List<String> makeItinerary()
  {  /* to be implemented in part (b) */  }

  /* Constructors and other methods not shown */
}
```

The implementation of method `findNearestCity` is not shown; write it yourself for additional practice.

(a) `findRemotestCity` returns the index of the city in `cityNames` that has the largest sum of distances to all other cities. If the same largest sum is found for more than one city, `findRemotestCity` can return the index of any one of them. Complete the method `findRemotestCity` below.

```
/** Returns the index of the city for which the sum of
 *  the distances to all other cities is the largest;
 *  (if there is more than one candidate, returns
 *  any one of them).
 *  Precondition: cityNames is not empty;
 *                distances[i][j] holds the distance
 *                between the i-th and the j-th cities
 */
public int findRemotestCity()
```

(b) Write the method `makeItinerary` that generates and returns a list of cities, starting with the remotest one and visiting each city in the `cityNames` list once. The itinerary proceeds from a city to the nearest one that has not been visited yet. Assume that the `findRemotestCity` works as specified, regardless of what you wrote in Part (a), and use `findNearestCity` as described above. Complete the method `makeItinerary` below.

```
/** Returns the itinerary (an ArrayList of city names)
 *  starting from the remotest city and going through
 *  all the cities in cityNames, always proceeding to the
 *  nearest city that has not been visited yet.
 *  Precondition: cityNames is not empty;
 *                distances[i][j] holds the distance
 *                between the i-th and the j-th cities
 */
public List<String> makeItinerary()
```

Practice Exam #3

SECTION I

Time — 1 hour and 15 minutes
Number of questions — 40
Percent of total grade — 50

1. Given the declarations

    ```
    int p = 5, q = 3;
    ```

    which of the following expressions evaluate to 7.5?

    I.   `(double)p * (double)q / 2;`
    II. `(double)p * (double)(q / 2);`
    III. `(double)(p * q / 2);`

    (A) I only
    (B) II only
    (C) I and II only
    (D) I, II, and III
    (E) None of them

2. Consider the following method.

    ```
    public void mystery(int a, int b)
    {
      System.out.print(a + " ");
      if (a <= b)
        mystery(a + 5, b - 1);
    }
    ```

    What is the output when `mystery(0, 16)` is called?

    (A) 0
    (B) 0 5
    (C) 0 5 10
    (D) 0 5 10 15
    (E) 0 5 10 15 20

3. Consider the following method `fun2`.

    ```
    public int fun2(int x, int y)
    {
      y -= x;
      return y;
    }
    ```

    What are the values of the variables `a` and `b` after the following code is executed?

    ```
    int a = 3, b = 7;
    b = fun2(a, b);
    a = fun2(b, a);
    ```

    (A)   -1 and 4
    (B)   -4 and 7
    (C)   -4 and 4
    (D)   3 and 7
    (E)   3 and 4

4. Assuming that `a` and `b` are `boolean` variables, when is the following expression true?

    ```
    !(!a || b) || (!a && b)
    ```

    (A)   If and only if `a` and `b` have different values
    (B)   If and only if `a` and `b` have the same value
    (C)   If and only if both `a` and `b` are true
    (D)   If and only if both `a` and `b` are false
    (E)   Never

5. A project needs two related classes, X and Y. A programmer has decided to provide an abstract class A and derive both X and Y from A rather than implementing X and Y completely independently of each other. Which of the following is NOT a valid rationale for this design decision?

    (A)   Being able to cast objects of type X into Y and vice-versa
    (B)   Being able to use some common code accessible in classes X and Y without duplication
    (C)   Being able to pass as a parameter an object of either type, X or Y, to the same constructor or method in place of a parameter of the type A
    (D)   Being able to place objects of both types, X and Y, into the same array of type `A[]`
    (E)   Making it easier in the future to implement another class that reuses some code from A

6. The method

```
private void transpose(int[][] m)
{
  < implementation not shown >
}
```

flips the elements of m symmetrically over the diagonal. For example:

```
1 2 3              1 4 7
4 5 6   transpose  2 5 8
7 8 9   ───────►   3 6 9
```

Which of the following implementations of transpose will work as specified?

I.
```
for (int r = 0; r < m.length; r++)
{
  for (int c = 0; c < m[0].length; c++)
  {
    int temp = m[r][c];
    m[r][c] = m[c][r];
    m[c][r] = temp;
  }
}
```

II.
```
for (int c = m[0].length - 1; c > 0; c--)
{
  for (int r = c-1; r >= 0; r--)
  {
    int temp = m[r][c];
    m[r][c] = m[c][r];
    m[c][r] = temp;
  }
}
```

III.
```
for (int c = 0; c < m[0].length - 1; c++)
{
  for (int r = c + 1; r < m.length; r++)
  {
    int temp = m[r][c];
    m[r][c] = m[c][r];
    m[c][r] = temp;
  }
}
```

(A) I only
(B) II only
(C) I and II only
(D) II and III only
(E) I, II, and III

7. What is the value of v[4] after the following code is executed?

```
int d = 1;
int[] v = {1, 1, 1, 1, 1};

for (int i = 0; i < v.length; i++)
{
  d *= 2;
  v[i] += d;
}
```

(A) 16
(B) 32
(C) 33
(D) 64
(E) 65

8. Which of the following is NOT a good reason to use comments in programs?

(A) To describe the parameters of a method
(B) To explain a convoluted piece of code
(C) To document which methods of a class are private
(D) To document requirements for correct operation of a method
(E) To document the names of the programmers and the date of the last change

9. What is printed when the following code segment is executed?

```
List<Integer> lst = new ArrayList<Integer>();
int k = 2;
while (lst.size() < 5)
{
  boolean found = false;
  for (Integer n : lst)
    if (k % n.intValue() == 0)
      found = true;
  if (!found)
    lst.add(new Integer(k));
  k++;
}
System.out.println(lst);
```

(A) [2, 3, 4, 5, 6]
(B) [2, 3, 5, 7, 11]
(C) [2, 3, 4, 5, 6, 7]
(D) [2, 3, 5, 7, 11, 13]
(E) Nothing is printed — the program goes into an infinite loop.

10. Suppose we have the following interface `Game`.

```
public interface Game
{
  void playWith(Fun other);
}
```

We have found a compiled Java class, `Fun.class`. We do not have its source code, but we have discovered that a statement

```
Fun fun = new Fun(100);
```

compiles with no errors. Which of the following statements, if it compiles correctly, will convince us that `Fun` implements `Game`?

   I.   `Game game = fun;`
   II. `System.out.print(fun.playWith(new Fun(99)));`
   III. `System.out.print(fun.playWith(fun));`

(A)   I only
(B)   II only
(C)   I and II only
(D)   II and III only
(E)   I, II, and III

11. What is the result from the following code segment?

```
List<String> xyz = new ArrayList<String>();
xyz.add("X");
xyz.add("Y");
xyz.add("Z");

int count = 0;
for (String s1 : xyz)
{
  for (String s2 : xyz)
  {
    if (s1.equals(s2))
    {
      count++;
    }
  }
}

System.out.print(count);
```

(A)   Syntax error
(B)   0 is displayed
(C)   1 is displayed
(D)   3 is displayed
(E)   `NullPointerException`

12. What are the smallest and the largest possible values of x after the following statement has been executed?

```
int x = (int)(Math.sqrt(4*Math.random()) + 0.5);
```

(A) 0 and 1
(B) 0 and 2
(C) 0 and 3
(D) 1 and 2
(E) 1 and 3

13. Which of the following statements about Java's platform independence are true?

   I. The value of the MAX_VALUE constant in the java.lang.Integer class is the same on any computer.

   II. Java source code is compiled into bytecode, which then may be run on any computer that has a Java Virtual Machine installed.

   III. Overflow in arithmetic operations occurs at the same values regardless of the platform on which the Java program is running.

(A) I only
(B) II only
(C) I and II only
(D) II and III only
(E) I, II, and III

14. What is the output of the following code segment?

```
String s = "ban";
ArrayList<String> words = new ArrayList<String>();
words.add(s);
words.add(s.substring(1));
words.add(s.substring(1, 2));
String total = "";
for (String w : words)
{
   total += w;
}
System.out.print(total.indexOf("an"));
```

(A) 1
(B) 2
(C) 3
(D) ana
(E) banana

Questions 15-16 refer to the method `smile` below.

```
public static void smile(int n)
{
  if (n == 0)
    return;
  for (int k = 1; k <= n; k++)
  {
    System.out.print("smile!");
  }
  smile(n-1);
}
```

15. What is the output when `smile(4)` is called?

    (A) smile!
    (B) smile!smile!
    (C) smile!smile!smile!
    (D) smile!smile!smile!smile!
    (E) smile!smile!smile!smile!smile!smile!smile!smile!smile!smile!

16. When `smile(4)` is called, how many times will `smile` actually be called, including the initial call?

    (A) 2
    (B) 3
    (C) 4
    (D) 5
    (E) 10

17. Consider the following code segment, intended to find the position of an integer `targetValue` in `int[] a`.

```
int i = 0;
while (a[i] != targetValue)
{
  i++;
}
int position = i;
```

When will this code work as intended?

    (A) Always
    (B) Only when `targetValue == a[0]`
    (C) Only when `0 <= targetValue < a.length`
    (D) Only when `targetValue` equals `a[i]` for some i, such that
         `0 <= i < a.length`
    (E) Only when `targetValue` is not equal to `a[i]` for any i, such that
         `0 <= i < a.length`

18. Given two initialized `String` variables, `str1` and `str2`, which of the following conditions correctly tests whether the value of `str1` is greater than or equal to the value of `str2` (in lexicographical order)?

(A)   `str1 >= str2`
(B)   `str1.compareTo(str2) >= 0`
(C)   `str1.compareTo(str2) == true`
(D)   `str1.length() > str2.length() || str1 >= str2`
(E)   `str1.equals(str2) || str1.compareTo(str2) == 1`

19. Consider the following method from `ClassX`.

```
private int modXY(int x, int y)
{
  r = x / y;
  return x % y;
}
```

If `ClassX` compiles with no errors, which of the following must be true?

    I.   r must have the type `double`.
   II.   r is not a local variable in the `modXY` method.
  III.   r must be a static variable in `ClassX`.

(A)   I only
(B)   II only
(D)   I and II only
(C)   II and III only
(E)   I, II, and III

20. What is the output from the following code segment?

```
double pi = 3.14159;
int r = 100;
int area = (int)(pi * Math.pow(r, 2));
System.out.println(area);
```

(A)   30000
(B)   31415
(C)   31416
(D)   314159
(E)   Depends on the particular computer system

21. Consider the following three code segments.

    I.
```
int  i = 1;
while (i <= 10)
{
   System.out.print(i);
   i += 2;
}
```

    II.
```
for (int i = 0; i < 5; i++)
{
   System.out.print(2*i + 1);
}
```

    III.
```
for (int i = 0; i < 10; i++)
{
   i++;
   System.out.print(i);
}
```

Which of the three segments produce the same output?

(A)   I and II only
(B)   II and III only
(C)   I and III only
(D)   I, II, and III
(E)   All three outputs are different.

22. Suppose a, b, and c are positive integers under 1000 and x satisfies the formula

$$\frac{a}{b} = \frac{c}{x}$$

The integer value d is obtained by truncating x to an integer. Which of the following code segments correctly calculates d?

    I.
```
d = c * b / a;
```

    II.
```
int temp = c * b;
d = temp / a;
```

    III.
```
int temp = b / a;
d = c * temp;
```

(A)   I only
(B)   II only
(C)   I and II only
(D)   II and III only
(E)   I, II, and III

23. Consider the following class.

```
public class Question
{
  private boolean answer;

  public void flip(Question q)
  {
    < missing statement >
  }

  < constructors and other methods not shown >

}
```

Which of the following could replace < *missing statement* > in the `flip` method so that it compiles with no errors?

    I.   `answer = !answer;`

    II.   `answer = !q.answer;`

    III.   `q.answer = !q.answer;`

(A) None
(B) I only
(C) II only
(D) I and II only
(E) All three

24. Which of the following statements will compile with no errors?

    I.   `ArrayList<Integer> nums = new ArrayList<Integer>();`
    II.   `List<Integer> nums = new ArrayList<Integer>();`
    III.   `ArrayList<Integer> nums = new List<Integer>();`

(A) I only
(B) II only
(C) I and II only
(D) II and III only
(E) I, II, and III

25. Consider the following method with two missing statements.

```
/** Returns the sum of all positive odd values
 *   among the first n elements of arr
 *   Precondition: 1 <= n <= arr.length
 */
public static int addPositiveOddValues(int[] arr, int n)
{
  int sum = 0;
  < statement 1 >
  {
    < statement 2 >
      sum += arr[i];
  }
  return sum;
}
```

Which of the following are appropriate replacements for < *statement 1* > and < *statement 2* > so that the method works as specified?

	< *statement 1* >	< *statement 2* >
(A)	`for (int i = 1; i < n; i += 2)`	`if (arr[i] > 0)`
(B)	`for (int i = 0; i < n; i++)`	`if (arr[i] > 0 && arr[i] % 2 != 0)`
(C)	`for (int i = 1; i <= n; i += 2)`	`if (arr[i] > 0)`
(D)	`for (int i = 0; i <= n; i++)`	`if (arr[i] % 2 != 0)`
(E)	None of the above	

26. Consider the following method.

```
public boolean isGood(String s)
{
  int n = s.length();
  return n < 2 ||
     (s.substring(1, n).indexOf(s.substring(0, 1)) < 0 &&
      isGood(s.substring(1, n)));
}
```

What do `isGood("ABCD")`, `isGood("AACD")`, and `isGood("ABCA")` return?

	`isGood("ABCD")`	`isGood("AACD")`	`isGood("ABCA")`
(A)	true	true	true
(B)	true	false	true
(C)	false	true	true
(D)	true	false	false
(E)	false	true	false

Questions 27-31 refer to the code from the GridWorld case study. Reference materials are provided in the appendices.

27. How does a `Bug` act if there is a `Flower` directly in front of it in the grid?

    (A)   The `Bug` is removed from the grid.
    (B)   The `Bug` remains in its current state — no action is taken.
    (C)   The `Flower` is removed, and the `Bug` moves forward, putting into its old location a new `Flower`.
    (D)   The `Bug` turns 180 degrees.
    (E)   The `Bug` turns 45 degrees to the right.

28. Consider the following method.

```
/** Returns true if location in front of bug contains
 *  a Rock; otherwise returns false.
 */
public boolean rockInFront(Bug bug)
{
  Grid<Actor> gr = bug.getGrid();
  if (gr == null)
    return false;
  Location loc = bug.getLocation();
  Location next = < expression 1 >;
  if (!gr.isValid(next))
    return false;
  return < expression 2 >;
}
```

Which of the following could replace < *expression 1* > and < *expression 2* > for the method to work as specified?

    (A)   < *expression 1* >   `loc.getAdjacentLocation(Location.AHEAD)`
           < *expression 2* >   `gr.get(next).equals(Rock)`

    (B)   < *expression 1* >   `loc.getLocationToward(Location.AHEAD)`
           < *expression 2* >   `gr.get(next).equals(Rock)`

    (C)   < *expression 1* >   `loc.getLocationToward(bug.getDirection())`
           < *expression 2* >   `gr.get(next).equals(Rock)`

    (D)   < *expression 1* >   `loc.getAdjacentLocation(Location.AHEAD)`
           < *expression 2* >   `gr.get(next) instanceof Rock`

    (E)   < *expression 1* >   `loc.getAdjacentLocation(bug.getDirection())`
           < *expression 2* >   `gr.get(next) instanceof Rock`

29. Suppose we replace the `act` method in `Actor` with an empty method (only braces and no code) and remove the `act` method from `Rock`. What effect will this have on the `BugRunner` program?

   (A)   The program will work as before with no changes.
   (B)   The program will work as before, except that `Actor` objects, if added to the grid, won't flip over.
   (C)   The `Rock` class won't compile.
   (D)   It will become possible for a `Bug` to move to a location occupied by a `Rock`.
   (E)   `Critter`'s `processActors` method will no longer work as specified.

30. Which of the following code segments will compile with no errors?

   I.
   ```
   Actor a = new Actor();
   a.setColor(Color.RED);
   ```

   II.
   ```
   Actor a = new Bug(Color.GREEN);
   ```

   III.
   ```
   Actor a = new Bug();
   a.setColor(Color.BLUE);
   ```

   (A)   I only
   (B)   II only
   (C)   I and II only
   (D)   II and III only
   (E)   I, II, and III

31. Let us change the design of the `Critter` class, moving the call to `getActors` from `act` to `processActors` —

```
public void act()
{
  if (getGrid() == null)
    return;
  processActors();
  ...
}

public void processActors()
{
  ArrayList<Actor> actors = getActors();
  for (Actor a : actors)
    ...
}
```

How does the new design compare to the original design?

(A)   The new design violates encapsulation.

(B)   The new design is less flexible than the original design, because some of the subclasses of `Critter` that overrode only `getActors` and `processActors` now will have to override `act`, too.

(C)   The new design is less flexible than the original design, because in the original design, a `Critter`'s subclass can override only the `getActors` method, while in the new design that is not possible.

(D)   The new design is less flexible than the original design, because in the original design, methods of `Critter`'s subclasses can call `super.getActors`, while in the new design that won't work.

(E)   The new design is as flexible as the original design and may be more economical, because it may eliminate the need to override `getActors` in some subclasses of `Critter`.

32. Which of the following best describes the return value for the method `propertyX` below?

```
/** Precondition: v.length >= 2
 */
public boolean propertyX(int[] v)
{
  boolean flag = false;

  for (int i = 0; i < v.length - 1; i++)
  {
    flag = flag || (v[i] == v[i+1]);
  }

  return flag;
}
```

(A)   Returns `true` if the elements of `v` are sorted in ascending order, `false` otherwise
(B)   Returns `true` if the elements of `v` are sorted in descending order, `false` otherwise
(C)   Returns `true` if `v` has two adjacent elements with the same value, `false` otherwise
(D)   Returns `true` if `v` has two elements with the same value, `false` otherwise
(E)   Returns `true` if all elements in `v` have different values, `false` otherwise

33. Consider the following classes.

```
public class A
{
  public A() { methodOne(); }

  public void methodOne() { System.out.print("A"); }
}

public class B extends A
{
  public B() { System.out.print("*"); }

  public void methodOne() { System.out.print("B"); }
}
```

What is the output when the following code statement is executed?

```
A obj = new B();
```

(A)   `*`
(B)   `*A`
(C)   `*B`
(D)   `A*`
(E)   `B*`

Questions 34-36 involve reasoning about classes and objects used in an implementation of a library catalog system.

An object of the class BookInfo represents information about a particular book, and an object of the class LibraryBook represents copies of a book on the library's shelves.

```java
public class BookInfo
{
  private String title;
  private String author;
  private int numPages;

  < constructors not shown >

  public String toString()
  {
    return title + " by " + author;
  }

  public String getTitle() { return title; }
  public int getNumPages() { return numPages; }
}

public class LibraryBook
{
  private BookInfo info;
  private int numCopies;    // Number of copies on shelf

  < constructors not shown >

  public int getNumCopies() { return numCopies; }
  public void setNumCopies(int num)
                            { numCopies = num; }
  public BookInfo getInfo() { return info; }

  /** If there are copies on shelf, decrements
   *  the number of copies left and returns true;
   *  otherwise returns false
   */
  public boolean checkOut() { /* implementation not shown */ }
}
```

34. If `catalog` is declared in a client class as

    ```
    LibraryBook[] catalog;
    ```

    which of the following statements will correctly display *title* by *author* of the third book in `catalog`?

    I.   `System.out.println(catalog[2]);`

    II. `System.out.println(catalog[2].getInfo());`

    III. `System.out.println(catalog[2].getInfo().toString());`

    (A) I only
    (B) II only
    (C) I and II only
    (D) II and III only
    (E) I, II, and III

35. Consider the following method from another class, a client of `LibraryBook`.

    ```
    /** Returns the total number of pages in all
     *  books in catalog that are on the shelves
     */
    public int totalPages(LibraryBook[] catalog)
    {
      int count = 0;

      for (LibraryBook bk : catalog)
      {
        < statement >
      }
      return count;
    }
    ```

    Which of the following replacements for < *statement* > completes the method as specified?

    (A) `count += bk.numCopies * bk.info.numPages;`
    (B) `count += bk.getNumCopies() * bk.getNumPages();`
    (C) `count += bk.(numCopies * info.getNumPages());`
    (D) `count += bk.getNumCopies() * bk.getInfo().getNumPages();`
    (E) None of the above

36. Which of the following code segments will correctly complete the `checkOut()` method of the `LibraryBook` class?

I.
```
if (getNumCopies() == 0)
{
  return false;
}
else
{
  setNumCopies(getNumCopies() - 1);
  return true;
}
```

II.
```
int n = getNumCopies();
if (n == 0)
{
  return false;
}
else
{
  setNumCopies(n - 1);
  return true;
}
```

III.
```
if (numCopies == 0)
{
  return false;
}
else
{
  numCopies--;
  return true;
}
```

(A)   I only
(B)   II only
(C)   I and II only
(D)   I and III only
(E)   I, II, and III

37. The following method is intended to remove from `List<Integer> list` all elements whose value is less than zero.

```
public void removeNegatives(List<Integer> list)
{
  int i = 0, n = list.size();

  while (i < n)
  {
    if (list.get(i) < 0)
    {
      list.remove(i);
      n--;
    }
    i++;
  }
}
```

For which lists of `Integer` values does this method work as intended?

(A)   Only an empty list
(B)   All lists that do not contain negative values in consecutive positions
(C)   All lists where all the negative values occur before all the positive values
(D)   All lists where all the positive values occur before all the negative values
(E)   All lists

38. Consider the following method.

```
/** Returns the location of the target value
 *   in the array a, or -1 if not found
 *   Precondition: a[0] ... a[a.length - 1] are
 *                 sorted in ascending order
 */
public static int search(int[] a, int target)
{
  int first = 0;
  int last = a.length - 1;

  while (first <= last)
  {
    int middle = (first + last) / 2;
    if (target == a[middle])
      return middle;
    else if (target < a[middle])
      last = middle;
    else
      first = middle;
  }
  return -1;
}
```

This method fails to work as expected under certain conditions. If the array has five elements with the values 3, 4, 35, 42, 51, which of the following values of `target` would make this method fail?

(A)   3
(B)   4
(C)   35
(D)   42
(E)   51

Questions 39-40 refer to the following class `SortX`.

```
public class SortX
{
  public static void sort(String[] items)
  {
    int n = items.length;
    while (n > 1)
    {
      sortHelper(items, n - 1);
      n--;
    }
  }

  private static void sortHelper(String[] items, int last)
  {
    int m = last;
    for (int k = 0; k < last; k++)
    {
      if (items[k].compareTo(items[m]) > 0)
        m = k;
    }
    String temp = items[m];
    items[m] = items[last];
    items[last] = temp;
  }
}
```

39. Suppose `names` is an array of `String` objects:

```
String[] names =
          {"Dan", "Alice", "Claire", "Evan", "Boris"};
```

If `SortX.sort(names)` is running, what is the order of the values in `names` after two complete iterations through the `while` loop in the `sort` method?

(A) "Boris", "Alice", "Claire", "Dan", "Evan"
(B) "Alice", "Claire", "Boris", "Dan", "Evan"
(C) "Alice", "Boris", "Claire", "Evan", "Dan"
(D) "Alice", "Claire", "Dan", "Evan", "Boris"
(E) None of the above

40. If `items` contains five values and `SortX.sort(items)` is called, how many times, total, will `items[k].compareTo(items[m])` be called in the `sortHelper` method?

   (A) 5
   (B) 10
   (C) 15
   (D) 25
   (E) Depends on the values in `items`

Practice Exam #3

Time — 1 hour and 45 minutes
Number of questions — 4
Percent of total grade — 50

1. In computerized monitoring of electrocardiograms (ECG), one of the tasks is detecting the most prominent spikes in the signal, called R-peaks.

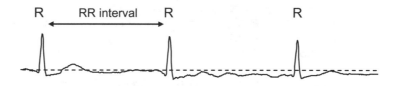

Measuring the time intervals between R-peaks allows the device to compute the patient's heart rate. In this question you will write two methods of the class `ECGAnalysis`, which help detect all R-peaks, and a method that calculates the patient's heart rate.

In a computer program, the ECG voltage signal is digitized at a certain sampling rate and the resulting values are stored in an array; an integer constant `SAMPLING_RATE` in the `ECGAnalysis` class indicates how many consecutive elements in the array represent one second of ECG recording. In the `ECGAnalysis` class, when we say "R-peak" we mean the point in time when the peak occurred, not its magnitude; more precisely, R-peak is the <u>index in the voltage array</u> that corresponds to the point in time when the peak occurred.

A partial definition of the `ECGAnalysis` class is shown below.

```
public class ECGAnalysis
{
  /** Defines how many consecutive elements in the voltage
   *  array correspond to 1 second of ECG recording */
  public static final int SAMPLING_RATE = 300;

  /** The length of a time interval used in the R-peak
   *  detection algorithm (about 100 ms) */
  public static final int DELTA = SAMPLING_RATE / 10;

  /** Returns true if r, the index in the array v,
   *  is an R-peak; otherwise returns false.  r is an
   *  R-peak if three conditions are satisfied:
   *  (1) v[r] > 1.0;
   *  (2) v[r] is equal to the maximum value among v[k]
   *      for all k in the interval r - DELTA ≤ k ≤ r + DELTA;
   *  (3) v[k] is negative somewhere on the interval
   *      r - DELTA ≤ k ≤ r and also somewhere on the interval
   *      r ≤ k ≤ r + DELTA.
   *  Precondition: DELTA <= r < v.length - DELTA
   */
  public static boolean isRpeak(double[] v, int r)
  { /* to be implemented in part (a) */ }

  /** Returns a list of positions of all R-peaks in v
   *  between v[DELTA] and v[v.length-1 - DELTA],
   *  preserving their sequence in time.  R-peaks are
   *  represented as Integer objects.  An R-peak
   *  is determined by a call to the method isRpeak.
   *  R-peaks must be at least DELTA apart.
   */
  public static ArrayList<Integer> allRpeaks(double[] v)
  { /* to be implemented in part (b) */ }

  /** Determines the heart rate from a list of R-peaks
   *  @return heart rate in beats per minute
   *  Precondition: rPeaks.size() >= 2
   */
  public static int heartRate(List<Integer> rPeaks)
  { /* to be implemented in part (c) */ }

  /** Returns the largest value among v[i], v[i+1], ..., v[j]
   *  Precondition: 0 <= i <= j < v.length;
   */
  private static double max(double[] v, int i, int j)
  { /* implementation not shown */ }

  /** Returns the smallest value among v[i], v[i+1], ..., v[j]
   *  Precondition: 0 <= i <= j < v.length;
   */
  private static double min(double[] v, int i, int j)
  { /* implementation not shown */ }
}
```

The code for the private methods `max` and `min` in `ECGAnalysis` is not shown. Write them yourself for additional practice.

(a) Write the `boolean` method `isRpeak(v, r)`. This method returns `true` if the index `r` in the given voltage array `v` is an R-peak; otherwise it returns `false`. In this project we use a simple algorithm for detecting R-peaks: `r` is an R-peak in `v` if the following three conditions are satisfied:

1. `v[r] > 1.0`

2. `v[r]` is equal to the maximum value among `v[k]` for all `k` in the interval `r - DELTA ≤ k ≤ r + DELTA`, where `DELTA` is a constant defined in `ECGAnalysis`.

3. `v[k]` is negative somewhere on the interval `r - DELTA ≤ k ≤ r` and also somewhere on the interval `r ≤ k ≤ r + DELTA`.

Complete the method `isRpeak` below.

```
/** Returns true if r, the index in the array v,
 *  is an R-peak; otherwise returns false.  r is an
 *  R-peak if three conditions are satisfied:
 *  (1) v[r] > 1.0;
 *  (2) v[r] is equal to the maximum value among v[k]
 *      for all k in the interval r - DELTA ≤ k ≤ r + DELTA;
 *  (3) v[k] is negative somewhere on the interval
 *      r - DELTA ≤ k ≤ r and also somewhere on the interval
 *      r ≤ k ≤ r + DELTA.
 *  Precondition: DELTA <= r < v.length - DELTA
 */
public static boolean isRpeak(double[] v, int r)
```

(b) Write the method `allRpeaks(v)`. The method returns an `ArrayList` of all R-peaks found in `v` between `v[DELTA]` and `v[v.length-1 - DELTA]`, preserving their sequence in time. R-peaks are represented as `Integer` objects. Note that we do not want to detect the same R-peak multiple times. To avoid that, when an R-peak `r` is found, we do not look for the next one in the interval from `r` to `r+DELTA-1`. Complete the method `allRpeaks` below.

```
/** Returns a list of positions of all R-peaks in v
 *  between v[DELTA] and v[v.length-1 - DELTA],
 *  preserving their sequence in time.  R-peaks are
 *  represented as Integer objects.  An R-peak
 *  is determined by a call to the method isRpeak.
 *  R-peaks must be at least DELTA apart.
 */
public static ArrayList<Integer> allRpeaks(double[] v)
```

(c)   Write the method `heartRate` that takes a list of R-peaks (indices in the voltage array where R-peaks occur) and returns patient's heart rate in beats per <u>minute</u>, rounded to the nearest integer. The heart rate is derived from the average length between consecutive R-peaks in the list. To obtain the average length, take the interval between the first and the last R-peak in the list and divide its length by the number of RR-intervals between these two R-peaks. Use `SAMPLING_RATE` to convert indices into real time. For example, if the average RR-interval is 250 (indices) and `SAMPLING_RATE` is 300, then the average length of the RR-interval is 250/300 = 5/6 seconds. This corresponds to 72 beats per minute. Complete the method `heartRate` below.

```
/** Determines the heart rate from a list of R-peaks
 *   @return heart rate in beats per minute
 *   Precondition: rPeaks.size() >= 2
 */
public static int heartRate(List<Integer> rPeaks)
```

2. Web pages on the Internet are formatted in HTML (HyperText Markup Language). HTML text contains embedded *tags* — formatting commands enclosed in angle brackets < and >. Simple formatting tags often come in pairs where the opening tag indicates the beginning of some formatting (for example, italics, bold, underline) and the closing tag indicates the end of the formatting. The closing tag contains the same command as the opening tag, but preceded by a slash (the "/" character). The following example shows a line of HTML text and illustrates the way it might be displayed on the screen.

```
The <i>quick</i> <b>brown</b> fox <b>jumps
<u>over</b> the lazy</u> dog
```

> The *quick* **brown** fox **jumps** <u>**over** the lazy</u> dog

In this question, text is represented as a `String` object. We assume that text contains only complete tags: all "<" and ">" characters properly delimit tags and do not otherwise occur inside tags or anywhere else in the text. Segments of text formatted with different tags may overlap. In the above example, the word "**<u>over</u>**" falls into the overlapping bold and underlined segments.

You will write a small class `Tag` and a method of the `HTMLProcessor` class that uses `Tag`.

(a) Write a class `Tag` that implements the following interface that represents a tag embedded into a string.

```java
public interface Embedded
{
    /** Returns the index of the opening bracket */
    int getStartIndex();

    /** Returns the index of the closing bracket */
    int getEndIndex();

    /** Returns the substring inside brackets */
    String getCommand();
}
```

Provide a constructor

```java
public Tag(int startIndex, int endIndex, String cmd)
{
    ...
}
```

(b) Write the `findFirstTag` method of the `HTMLProcessor` class. The method finds and returns the first tag in a given text string. The method returns `null` if no tags were found. Complete the method `findFirstTag` below.

```
/** Returns the first tag in text, or null if none
 *  were found.
 *  Precondition: text is properly formatted HTML text
 */
public static Tag findFirstTag(String text)
```

For additional practice, write a method `removeAllTags` for the `HTMLProcessor` class. The method deals only with a subset of HTML tags: it assumes that a given text contains only complete simple tags, such as `<u>` and `</u>` or `<cite>` and `</cite>`, where a closing tag differs from the corresponding opening tag only by the `"/"` character after `"<"`. The closing tag must come after the opening tag. For properly formatted HTML, the method returns the text with all tags removed (or the original text if no tags were found). The method returns `null` if the tags in `text` do not match (no matching closing tag found after an opening tag or a closing tag found before a matching opening tag). Do not duplicate code from `findFirstTag`.

3.   This question involves reasoning about the GridWorld case study. Reference materials
     are provided in the appendices.

     A `Bee` is a `Critter` that interacts with `Clover` objects in the grid. A `Clover` is a kind
     of `Flower` that can be pollinated. Partial code of the `Clover` class is shown below.

```
public class Clover extends Flower
{
  /** Pollinates this clover (typically called by a Bee)
   */
  public void pollinate()
  { /* implementation not shown */ }

  /** Returns true if this clover has been pollinated;
   *   otherwise returns false
   */
  public boolean hasBeenPollinated()
  { /* implementation not shown */ }

  < variables, constructors, and other methods not shown >
}
```

     A `Bee` first pollinates all `Clover` flowers it finds in the adjacent locations, then moves
     toward the nearest clover that has not been pollinated yet. A partial definition of the `Bee`
     class is shown below.

```
public class Bee extends Critter
{
  /** Creates a yellow Bee
   */
  public Bee()
  {
    setColor(Color.YELLOW);
  }

  /** Processes the elements of actors; pollinates all
   *  Clover objects among them
   */
  public void processActors(ArrayList<Actor> actors)
  {   /* to be implemented in part (a) */   }

  /** Returns the location chosen among locs and this Bee's
   *  current location that is nearest to an unpollinated
   *  clover; if several locations are at the same distance
   *  from an unpollinated clover, returns any one of them;
   *  if the grid does not have any unpollinated clovers,
   *  returns this Bee's current location
   */
  public Location selectMoveLocation(ArrayList<Location> locs)
  {   /* to be implemented in part (b) */   }

  /** Turns toward loc, then moves into loc like a
   *  regular Critter
   */
  public void makeMove(Location loc)
  {   /* to be implemented in part (c) */   }

  /** Returns the location of a Clover that has not
   *  yet been pollinated and that is nearest to loc;
   *  if the grid does not contain any unpollinated clovers,
   *  returns null
   *  Precondition: loc != null
   */
  private Location findNearestClover(Location loc)
  { /* implementation not shown */ }

  /** Returns the distance between loc1 and loc2
   *  Precondition: loc1 != null and loc2 != null
   */
  private int distance(Location loc1, Location loc2)
  { /* implementation not shown */ }
}
```

For additional practice, write the methods of the Bee class whose implementation is not shown.

(a) Write the `processActors` method. This method pollinates each `Clover` in the `actors` list passed to it. Complete the method `processActors` below.

```
/** Processes the elements of actors; pollinates all
 *  Clover objects among them
 */
public void processActors(ArrayList<Actor> actors)
```

(b) Write the `selectMoveLocation` method. This method takes the `Bee`'s current location plus all the locations in the given list and finds among them the one that is nearest to any unpollinated clover. If several locations are at the same minimal distance to an unpollinated clover, any one of them can be selected. If the grid contains no unpollinated `Clover`s, `selectMoveLocation` should return this `Bee`'s current location. Do not duplicate code from the `findNearestClover` method. Complete the method `selectMoveLocation` below.

```
/** Returns the location chosen among locs and this Bee's
 *  current location that is nearest to an unpollinated
 *  clover; if several locations are at the same distance
 *  from an unpollinated clover, returns any one of them;
 *  if the grid does not have any unpollinated clovers,
 *  returns this Bee's current location
 */
public Location selectMoveLocation(ArrayList<Location> locs)
```

(c) Write the `makeMove` method. A `Bee` turns toward `loc`, then moves like a regular `Critter`. Complete the method `makeMove` below.

```
/** Turns toward loc, then moves into loc like a
 *  regular Critter
 */
public void makeMove(Location loc)
```

4. An app that helps arrange furniture in a room represents the floor plan as a rectangular grid of square cells. A cell may be not available for placing furniture; for example, it may be near the door or window or too close to another furniture piece placed earlier. In the app, the grid is represented as a two-dimensional array of integers; a value of 0 means the cell is empty and available for placing furniture; a value of 1 means the cell is not available. For example:

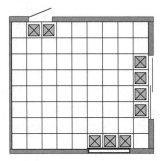

```
0 1 1 0 0 0 0 0
0 0 0 0 0 0 0 0
0 0 0 0 0 0 0 1
0 0 0 0 0 0 0 1
0 0 0 0 0 0 0 1
0 0 0 0 0 0 0 1
0 0 0 0 0 0 0 0
0 0 0 0 0 1 1 1 0
```

A rectangular region on a floor plan is described by its top and bottom rows and its left and right columns. For example, the pictures below show two regions:

```
0 1 1 0 0 0 0 0          0 1 1 0 0 0 0 0
0 0 0 0 0 0 0 0          0 0 0 0 0 0 0 0
0 0 0 0 0 0 0 1          0 0 0 0 0 0 0 1
0 0 0 0 0 0 0 1          0 0 0 0 0 0 0 1
0 0 0 0 0 0 0 1          0 0 0 0 0 0 0 1
0 0 0 0 0 0 0 1          1 0 0 0 0 0 0 1
0 0 0 0 0 0 0 0          1 0 0 0 0 0 0 0
0 0 0 0 0 1 1 1 0        0 0 0 0 1 1 1 1 0
```

The first region has `top = 1`, `bottom = 3`, `left = 2`, and `right = 6`. This region is empty because all the cells in it are empty and available for placing furniture on them (the corresponding elements of the `room` array have values 0). The second region has `top = 5`, `bottom = 7`, `left = 4`, and `right = 6`. This region is not empty.

A piece of furniture is represented on a floor plan by a rectangular region that covers several entire cells. We call the rectangle's horizontal dimension on the plan *width* and its vertical dimension *height*. The location of the piece on the plan is always identified by the row and column of its upper left corner.

The row and column can be combined in one object of the class `Location`. The `Location` class has a constructor that takes two integer parameters, row and column of the location, and public methods `getRow()` and `getCol()`, which return `Location`'s row and column, respectively. The location of the upper left corner of the room is `(0, 0)`, and the location of the lower right corner of the room is `(ROWS-1, COLS-1)`.

The floor plan is represented in the app by the Java class `FloorPlan`. A partial definition of the `FloorPlan` class is shown below. Your task is to write three methods of this class.

```
public class FloorPlan
{
  /** The number of rows in this floor plan */
  private final int ROWS;

  /** The number of columns in this floor plan */
  private final int COLS;

  /** room[r][c] == 0 means the cell at location (r, c)
   *   is empty and available for placing furniture;
   *   room[r][c] == 1 means the location is not available
   */
  private int[][] room;

  /** Constructs a two-dimensional array with given
   *   dimensions, filled with zeroes
   */
  public FloorPlan(int rows, int cols)
  { /* implementation not shown */

  /** Returns true if the rectangular region between top and
   *   bottom and between left and right, including the borders,
   *   contains only zeroes; otherwise returns false.
   *   Precondition: top <= bottom, left <= right;
   *                 the entire region is within room limits
   */
  private boolean isEmptyRegion(int top, int bottom,
                                      int left, int right)
  { /* to be implemented in part (a) */

  /** Returns true if a piece of furniture with given dimensions
   *   fits into this floor plan at a specified location.
   *   To fit, all the cells under the piece  must be within the
   *   room and all the cells within a slightly larger region
   *   must be empty. The larger region consists of all the cells
   *   under the piece plus all the adjacent cells that are
   *   within the room limits.
   *   @param width the horizontal dimension of the piece
   *   @param height the vertical dimension of the piece
   *   @param ulCorner location of the upper left corner of
   *          the piece
   */
  public boolean fits(int width, int height, Location ulCorner)
  { /* to be implemented in part (b) */ }

  /** Returns a list of all locations where a piece of furniture
   *   with given dimensions can fit.
   *   @param width the horizontal dimension of the piece
   *   @param height the vertical dimension of the piece
   */
  public ArrayList<Location> whereFits(int width, int height)
  { /* to be implemented in part (c) */ }
}
```

(a) Write the `boolean` method `isEmptyRegion` of the `FloorPlan` class. The method takes four parameters: the top row, the bottom row, the left column, and the right column of the region. `isEmptyRegion` returns `true` if all the cells in the region, including the borders, are empty (the corresponding values in the `room` array are zeroes). The precondition for the method stipulates that the entire region fits into the room, so there is no need to check for that. Complete the method `isEmptyRegion` below.

```
/** Returns true if the rectangular region between top and
 *  bottom and between left and right, including the borders,
 *  contains only zeroes; otherwise returns false.
 *  Precondition: top <= bottom, left <= right;
 *                the entire region is within room limits
 */
private boolean isEmptyRegion(int top, int bottom,
                              int left, int right)
```

(b) The `boolean` method `fits` of the `FloorPlan` class returns `true` if a piece of furniture with given horizontal and vertical dimensions fits at a specified location in the room. For a piece of furniture to fit, two conditions must be satisfied:

(1) All the cells in the rectangular region under the piece must be within the room limits;

(2) All the cells in a slightly larger rectangular region must be empty. The larger region includes all the cells under the piece and all the adjacent cells that are within the room limits.

For example, the following pictures show that a 4 by 2 piece of furniture fits into the floor plan at locations (2, 2), (2, 0), and (6, 0):

```
0 1 1 0 0 0 0 0        0 1 1 0 0 0 0 0        0 1 1 0 0 0 0 0
0 0 0 0 0 0 0 0        0 0 0 0 0 0 0 0        0 0 0 0 0 0 0 0
0 0 0 0 0 0 0 1        0 0 0 0 0 0 0 1        0 0 0 0 0 0 0 1
0 0 0 0 0 0 0 1        0 0 0 0 0 0 0 1        0 0 0 0 0 0 0 1
0 0 0 0 0 0 0 1        0 0 0 0 0 0 0 1        0 0 0 0 0 0 0 1
0 0 0 0 0 0 0 1        0 0 0 0 0 0 0 1        0 0 0 0 0 0 0 1
0 0 0 0 0 0 0 0        0 0 0 0 0 0 0 0        0 0 0 0 0 0 0 0
0 0 0 0 0 1 1 1 0      0 0 0 0 0 1 1 1 0      0 0 0 0 0 1 1 1 0
```

The same piece does not fit, for example, at locations (1, 2), (2, 4), and (6, 1):

```
0 1 1 0 0 0 0 0        0 1 1 0 0 0 0 0        0 1 1 0 0 0 0 0
0 0 0 0 0 0 0 0        0 0 0 0 0 0 0 0        0 0 0 0 0 0 0 0
0 0 0 0 0 0 0 1        0 0 0 0 0 0 0 1        0 0 0 0 0 0 0 1
0 0 0 0 0 0 0 1        0 0 0 0 0 0 0 1        0 0 0 0 0 0 0 1
0 0 0 0 0 0 0 1        0 0 0 0 0 0 0 1        0 0 0 0 0 0 0 1
0 0 0 0 0 0 0 1        0 0 0 0 0 0 0 1        0 0 0 0 0 0 0 1
0 0 0 0 0 0 0 0        0 0 0 0 0 0 0 0        0 0 0 0 0 0 0 0
0 0 0 0 0 1 1 1 0      0 0 0 0 0 1 1 1 0      0 0 0 0 0 1 1 1 0
```

Write the method `fits` of the `FloorPlan` class. Assume that `isEmptyRegion` works and specified, regardless of what you wrote in Part (a), and do not duplicate `isEmptyRegion`'s code in your `fits` method. Complete the method `fits` below.

```
/** Returns true if a piece of furniture with given dimensions
 *  fits into this floor plan at a specified location.
 *  To fit, all the cells under the piece  must be within the
 *  room and all the cells within a slightly larger region
 *  must be empty. The larger region consists of all the cells
 *  under the piece plus all the adjacent cells that are
 *  within the room limits.
 *  @param width the horizontal dimension of the piece
 *  @param height the vertical dimension of the piece
 *  @param ulCorner location of the upper left corner of
 *         the piece
 */
public boolean fits(int width, int height, Location ulCorner)
```

(c)   Write the method `whereFits` of the `FloorPlan` class that returns an `ArrayList` of all locations where a piece of furniture with given horizontal and vertical dimensions fits in the room. Complete the method `whereFits` below.

```
/** Returns a list of all locations where a piece of furniture
 *  with given dimensions can fit.
 *  @param width the horizontal dimension of the piece
 *  @param height the vertical dimension of the piece
 */
public ArrayList<Location> whereFits(int width, int height)
```

For additional practice, write the entire `Location` class and the constructor of the `FloorPlan` class. To extend the project further, introduce the vertical and horizontal orientation of a piece of furniture. Add an instance variable to the `Location` class to describe the direction of a piece, and modify the `whereFits` method to try all horizontal and vertical orientations of the same piece. A more difficult project is to write a method that lists all possible configurations of several pieces of furniture.

Practice Exam #4

Time — 1 hour and 15 minutes
Number of questions — 40
Percent of total grade — 50

1. Assuming that x and y are `int` variables, the expression

    ```
    !(x > y && y <= 0)
    ```

    is equivalent to which of the following?

    (A) `!(x <= y) || (y > 0)`
    (B) `x > y && y <= 0`
    (C) `x <= y || y > 0`
    (D) `x > y || y < 0`
    (E) `x <= y && y <= 0`

2. Which of the following describes the return value of the following method?

    ```
    /** Precondition: amt represents a positive value in dollars
     *               and cents (for example, 1.15 represents
     *               one dollar and fifteen cents)
     */
    private int process(double amt)
    {
      return (int)(amt * 100 + 0.5) % 100;
    }
    ```

    (A) the cent portion in `amt`
    (B) the number of whole dollars in `amt`
    (C) `amt` converted into cents
    (D) `amt` rounded to the nearest dollar
    (E) the smallest number of whole dollars that is greater than or equal to `amt`

3.   What is the output of the following code segment?

```
int sum = 0, d = -1;

for (int count = 10; count > 0; count--)
{
  sum += d;
  if (d > 0)
  {
    d++;
  }
  else
  {
    d--;
  }
  d = -d;
}

System.out.println(sum);
```

(A)   0
(B)   5
(C)   -5
(D)   10
(E)   -10

4.   The following code segment is supposed to calculate and display the sum $1 + 2 + ... + 20$.

```
int count = 0, sum = 0;
while (count < 20)
{
  sum += count;
}
System.out.println(sum);
```

Which of the following statements best describes the result?

(A)   The total displayed will be correct.
(B)   The total displayed will be 20 too small.
(C)   The output will be the number 0.
(D)   The output will be the number 20.
(E)   There will be no output because the program goes into an infinite loop.

5. What is the result when the following code segment is compiled/executed?

```
Integer n = new Integer(Integer.MIN_VALUE); // Line 1
Double x = new Double(n.intValue());        // Line 2
System.out.print(x);
```

    (A) 0 is displayed
    (B) 0.0 is displayed
    (C) -2147483648.0 is displayed
    (D) Syntax error on Line 1
    (E) Syntax error on Line 2

6. Which of the following Boolean expressions implement a comparison for equality of two String objects str1 and str2 and evaluate to true if and only if str1 and str2 hold the same values?

    I.   `str1 == str2`

    II. `str1.equals(str2)`

    III. `str1.compareTo(str2) == 0`

    (A) I only
    (B) II only
    (C) I and II only
    (D) II and III only
    (E) I, II, and III

7. Consider the following class.

```
public class Sphere
{
  public static final double PI = 3.14159;

  public static double volume(int r)
  {
    return 4 / 3 * PI * Math.pow(r, 3);
  }
}
```

    Which of the following statements about this code is true?

    (A) The class will not compile because no constructors are defined.
    (B) The class will not compile because pi cannot be declared public.
    (C) The class will not compile because the volume method is declared static.
    (D) Math.pow(r, 3) cannot be used because r is an int.
    (E) The class compiles with no errors but the volume method returns a smaller value than the expected $\frac{4}{3}\pi r^3$.

8.   Consider the following code segment.

```
int n = IO.readInt();    // read an int value
n = Math.abs(n);

while (n >= 2)
{
   n = n/2 - 1;
}
System.out.println(n);
```

Which of the following is the list of all the possible outputs?

(A)   0
(B)   -1, 0
(C)   0, 1
(D)   -1, 1
(E)   -1, 0, 1

9.   Consider the following method.

```
private int swap(int a,  int b)
{
   if (a < b)
   {
      b = a;
      a = b;
   }
   return b - a;
}
```

What are the values of the variables a, b, and c after the following statements are executed?

```
int a = 2,  b = 5;
int c = swap(a, b);
```

(A)   2, 5, 0
(B)   2, 5, 3
(C)   2, 5, -3
(D)   2, 2, 0
(E)   5, 2, 3

10. Consider the following class.

```
public class Rectangle
{
  private int width, height;

  public Rectangle(int w, int h) { width = w; height = h; }
  public int getArea() { return width * height; }

  < other methods not shown >
}
```

Suppose this class also overrides `Object`'s `equals` method in such a way that `Rectangle` objects with the same area are deemed equal. Which of the following `equals` methods will accomplish this?

(A)
```
public int equals(int area)
{
  return getArea() - area;
}
```

(B)
```
public boolean equals(int area)
{
  return getArea() == area;
}
```

(C)
```
public boolean equals(Rectangle other)
{
  return getArea() == other.getArea();
}
```

(D)
```
public boolean equals(Object other)
{
  return this.getArea() == other.getArea();
}
```

(E)
```
public boolean equals(Object other)
{
  return getArea() == ((Rectangle)other).getArea();
}
```

11. Consider the following method.

```
// Precondition: a != null; a.length > 0
private static void doIt(double[] a)
{
  for (int k = 0; k < a.length / 2; k++)
  {
    double temp = a[k];
    a[k] = a[a.length - 1 - k];
    a[a.length - 1 - k] = temp;
  }
}
```

Which of the following best describes the task performed by this method?

(A)   Sorts an array in ascending order
(B)   Sorts an array in descending order
(C)   Swaps the first and last elements of an array
(D)   Reverses the order of elements in an array
(E)   None of the above tasks is implemented correctly

12. Consider the following method.

```
public String filter(String str, String pattern)
{
  int pos = str.indexOf(pattern);
  if (pos == -1)
    return str;
  else
    return filter(str.substring(0, pos) +
                  str.substring(pos + pattern.length()), pattern);
}
```

What is the output of

```
System.out.println(filter("papaya", "pa"));
```

(A)   p
(B)   pa
(C)   ya
(D)   aya
(E)   paya

13. Consider the following method, intended to use Binary Search to find the location of `target` within the `ArrayList a`.

```
public int findLocation(ArrayList<String> a, String target)
{
  int first = 0, last = a.size() - 1;
  while (first <= last)
  {
    int middle = (first + last) / 2;
    int compResult = target.compareTo(a.get(middle));
    if (compResult == 0)
      return middle;
    if (compResult < 0)
      last = middle - 1;
    else
      first = middle + 1;
  }
  return -1;
}
```

This method may fail if it is applied to a list that is not sorted. For which of the following lists will `findLocation(a, "C")` return -1?

(A) "A", "B", "C", "D", "E", "F", "G"
(B) "G", "F", "E", "D", "C", "B", "A"
(C) "A", "C", "D", "G", "E", "B", "F"
(D) "B", "A", "D", "C", "F", "E", "G"
(E) "D", "F", "B", "A", "G", "C", "E"

14. Consider the following code segment.

```
String abc = "AAABBBCCC";
String abc1 = abc.substring(0, abc.length() - 1);
abc1 = abc1.substring(1, abc1.length());
System.out.println(abc.indexOf(abc1));
```

What is printed as a result of executing the code?

(A) -1
(B) 0
(C) 1
(D) 7
(E) IndexOutOfBoundsException

Questions 15-16 refer to the following `sort` method.

```
public void sort(int[] a)
{
  for (int i = 1; i < a.length; i++) // Line 1
  {
    int current = a[i];                 // Line 2
    int j = 0;                          // Line 3

    while (a[j] < current)              // Line 4
    {
      j++;                              // Line 5
    }

    for (int k = i; k > j; k--)         // Line 6
    {
      a[k] = a[k-1];                    // Line 7
    }

    a[j] = current;                     // Line 8
  }
}
```

15. The sorting algorithm implemented in the `sort` method can be best described as:

    (A) Selection Sort
    (B) Insertion Sort
    (C) Quicksort
    (D) Mergesort
    (E) Incorrect implementation of a sorting algorithm

16. Given

    ```
    int[] a = {24, 16, 68, 56, 32};
    ```

    what will be the result after the statement on Line 8 in `sort` completes for the second time?

    (A) The values in a are 16, 24, 68, 56, 32
    (B) The values in a are 16, 24, 32, 56, 68
    (C) The values in a are 24, 16, 32, 56, 68
    (D) The code has failed with an `ArrayIndexOutOfBoundsException` on Line 4
    (E) The code has failed with an `ArrayIndexOutOfBoundsException` on Line 8

17. The class `PlayList` provides methods that allow you to represent and manipulate a list of songs, but you are not concerned with how these operations work or how the list is stored in memory. You only know how to initialize and use `PlayList` objects and have no direct access to the implementation of the `PlayList` class or its private data fields. This is an example of:

    (A) encapsulation
    (B) overriding
    (C) inheritance
    (D) polymorphism
    (E) method overloading

18. Consider the following class.

```
public class FrequentFlyer
{
  private int miles = 0;

  public FrequentFlyer(int m) { miles = m; }
  public void addMiles(int m) { miles += m; }
  public int getMiles() { return miles; }
}
```

    What is the output from the following code segment in a client class?

```
FrequentFlyer alex = new FrequentFlyer(20000);
FrequentFlyer beth = new FrequentFlyer(10000);
FrequentFlyer cindy = new FrequentFlyer(0);
FrequentFlyer[] friends = {alex, beth, cindy};
int total = 0;
for (FrequentFlyer p : friends)
{
  p.addMiles(1000);
  total += p.getMiles();
}
System.out.println(total);
```

    (A) 0
    (B) 3000
    (C) 30000
    (D) 33000
    (E) None of the above

Questions 19 and 20 refer to the following class.

```
public class Sample
{
  private double[][] amps;

  public Sample(int n)
  {
    < missing statements >
  }

  public double get(int j, int k)
  {
    return amps[j][k];
  }
}
```

19. Which of the following code segments can replace < *missing statements* > in `Sample`'s constructor so that it initializes `amps` to hold a table of values with n rows and n columns and fills them with random values $0.0 \le$ `amps[j][k]` < 1.0?

    I.

```
amps = new double[n][n];
```

    II.

```
amps = new double[n][n];
for (int j = 0; j < n; j++)
{
  for (int k = 0; k < n; k++)
  {
    amps[j][k] = Math.random();
  }
}
```

    III.

```
amps = new double[n][n];
for (int j = 0; j < n; j++)
{
  for (int k = j; k < n; k++)
  {
    amps[j][k] = Math.random();
    amps[k][j] = Math.random();
  }
}
```

(A)   I only
(B)   II only
(C)   I and II only
(D)   II and III only
(E)   I, II, and III

20. Given

```
int size = 100;
Sample s = new Sample(size);
```

which of the following statements assigns to x the value in the last row and the first column of amps in s?

(A)   `double x = s.amps[amps.length - 1][0];`
(B)   `double x = s.get(amps.length - 1, 0);`
(C)   `double x = s.get[s.length - 1, 0];`
(D)   `double x = s.get(size - 1, 0);`
(E)   `double x = s[99][0];`

21. Consider the following method.

```
public void splat(String s)
{
  if (s.length() < 8)
    splat(s + s);
  System.out.println(s);
}
```

What is displayed when `splat("**")` is called?

(A)   `**`

(B)   `****`

(C)   `********`

(D)   `********`
        `**`

(E)   `********`
        `****`
        `**`

22. Suppose `ArrayList<Integer>` numbers and `ArrayList<String>` names **are** created as follows:

```
ArrayList<Integer> numbers = new ArrayList<Integer>();
Integer x = new Integer(1);
numbers.add(x);
numbers.add(x);

ArrayList<String> names = new ArrayList<String>();
names.add(0, "Anya");
names.add(0, "Ben");
names.add(0, "Cathy");
```

What is the result of the following code segment?

```
for (Integer i : numbers)
{
   names.remove(i.intValue());
}
for (String name : names)
{
   System.out.print(name + " ");
}
```

(A) `Cathy`
(B) `Cathy Anya`
(C) `Anya Cathy`
(D) `IndexOutOfBoundsException`
(E) `NoSuchElementException`

23. Which outputs from the following statements are possible?

```
int x = (int)(2*Math.random()) + (int)(2*Math.random());
System.out.println(x);
```

(A) 0 only
(B) 2 only
(C) 0 and 2 only
(D) 1 and 2 only
(E) 0, 1 and 2

24. Consider the following class definitions.

```
public class Airplane
{
  private int fuel;

  public Airplane() { fuel = 0; }
  public Airplane(int g) { fuel = g; }

  public void addFuel() { fuel++; }
  public String toString() { return fuel + " "; }
}

public class Jet extends Airplane
{
  public Jet(int g) { super(2*g); }
}
```

What is the result when the following code is compiled and run?

```
Airplane plane = new Airplane(4);
Airplane jet = new Jet(4);

System.out.print(plane);
plane.addFuel();
System.out.print(plane);

System.out.print(jet);
jet.addFuel();
System.out.print(jet);
```

(A)   A syntax error, "undefined addFuel," is reported for the `jet.addFuel();` statement.

(B)   A run-time error, `ClassCastException`, occurs when `jet.addFuel()` is attempted.

(C)   The code compiles and runs with no errors; the output is 4 5 5 6

(D)   The code compiles and runs with no errors; the output is 4 5 8 9

(E)   The code compiles and runs with no errors; the output is 8 9 9 10

Questions 25-29 refer to the code from the GridWorld case study. Reference materials are provided in the appendices.

25. Which of the following code segments will compile with no errors?

I.
```
BoxBug bb = new BoxBug();
if (!bb.canMove())
{
   bb.turn();
}
```

II.
```
BoxBug bb = new BoxBug(5);
bb.setColor(Color.BLUE);
```

III.
```
BoxBug bb = new BoxBug(Color.BLUE);
bb.move();
```

    (A)   I only
    (B)   II only
    (C)   I and II only
    (D)   II and III only
    (E)   I, II, and III

26. Suppose we want to create a variation of `Bug` that acts like a regular `Bug` but turns 45 degrees randomly left or right after each move. Which of the following is the most economical approach, in terms of the amount of code to be written?

    (A)   Extend `Actor` and override the `act` method
    (B)   Extend `Bug` and override the `move` method
    (C)   Extend `Bug` and override the `turn` method
    (D)   Extend `Bug` and override both `move` and `turn` methods
    (E)   Extend `Bug` and override both `move` and `canMove` methods

27. Given

```
Rock rock = new Rock();
```

and assuming that all the necessary `import` statements are present, which of the following statements will cause a syntax error?

    (A)   `rock.moveTo(null);`
    (B)   `rock.setDirection(0);`
    (C)   `rock.setColor(Color.GRAY);`
    (D)   `rock.setGrid(null);`
    (E)   `Grid<Actor> gr = rock.getGrid();`

28. Consider the following class.

```
public class IntGrid extends BoundedGrid<Integer>
{
  < constructors not shown >

  /** Increments by 1 Integer objects in all occupied
   *  locations
   */
  public void increment()
  {
    < missing code >
  }
}
```

Which of the following code segments could replace < *missing code* > so that the method increment works as specified?

(A)
```
for (Location loc : getOccupiedLocations())
{
  Integer i = get(loc);
  i = new Integer(i.intValue() + 1);
}
```

(B)
```
for (Location loc : getOccupiedLocations())
{
  put(loc, new Integer(get(loc).intValue() + 1));
}
```

(C)
```
for (Location loc : grid.getOccupiedLocations())
{
  Integer i = grid.get(loc);
  i.setValue(i.intValue() + 1);
}
```

(D)
```
for (Location loc : getOccupiedLocations())
{
  Integer i = get(loc);
  i.setValue(i.intValue() + 1);
  put(loc, i);
}
```

(E)
```
for (Location loc : grid.getOccupiedLocations())
{
  grid.put(loc, new Integer(grid.get(loc).intValue() + 1));
}
```

29. Which of `Critter`'s methods calls `selectMoveLocation`?

   (A)   `act`
   (B)   `processActors`
   (C)   `makeMove`
   (D)   `moveTo`
   (E)   None of the above

Questions 30-31 refer to a project that includes the following classes.

```
public class Cake
{
  private String name;
  private int price;

  public Cake(String _name, int _price)
  { name = _name; price = _price; }

  public int getPrice() { return price; }

  < other constructors and methods not shown >
}

public class BakeSale
{
  private ArrayList<Cake> cakes;

  public BakeSale() { items = new ArrayList<Cake>(); }
  public void add(Cake cake) { items.add(cake); }

  public int getTotal()
  {
    int total = 0;

    for (Cake cake : items)
      total += cake.getPrice();

    return total;
  }
}
```

The project designer has instructed the programmer to modify the code as follows: to introduce

```
public interface Priced
{
  int getPrice();
}
```

into the project, add `implements Priced` to the `Cake` class header, and replace `Cake` with `Priced` everywhere in the `BakeSale` class.

30. Which design principle is applied here, and which Java feature makes it possible for the modified code to work?

    (A)   Encapsulation and polymorphism
    (B)   Abstraction and encapsulation
    (C)   Abstraction and polymorphism
    (D)   Information hiding and encapsulation
    (E)   Information hiding and Java Virtual Machine

31.   Which of the following are good reasons for this change?

    I.   In a future version of the project, the `items` list in a `BakeSale` object may hold items of the type of a subclass of `Cake`.

    II.   In a future version of the project, different types of `Priced` objects can be intermixed in the `items` list in a `BakeSale` object.

    III.   The `Cake` class can be reused in other projects dealing with a different type of `Priced` items.

    (A)   I only
    (B)   II only
    (C)   I and II only
    (D)   II and III only
    (E)   I, II, and III

Questions 32-35 use the classes `Track` and `CD`:

```
public class Track
{
  private String name;
  private int duration;

  public Track(String nm, int dur)
  { name = nm; duration = dur; }

  public String getName() { return name; }
  public int getDuration() { return duration; }
}

public class CD
{
  private String title;
  private String band;
  private int numTracks;
  private ArrayList<Track> tracks;

  public CD(String t, int n)
  { title = t; numTracks = n; }

  /** Initializes all the instance variables and copies
   *   all the data from songs into tracks
   */
  public CD(String t, String b, int n, ArrayList<Track> songs)
  {
    title = t; band = b; numTracks = n;

    < missing code >
  }

  public int totalPlayTime()
  { /* implementation not shown */ }

  /** Returns duration of the k-th track
   *  Precondition: 1 <= k <= numTracks
   */
  public int getDuration(int k)
  { /* implementation not shown */

  < other methods not shown >
}
```

32. Which one of the following declarations is INVALID?

(A)   `Track tune = new Track();`
(B)   `Track tune = new Track("Help", 305);`
(C)   `Track[] playList = new Track[20];`
(D)   `CD top = new CD("throwing copper", 13);`
(E)   `CD[][] rack = new CD[3][40];`

33. Which of the following expressions correctly refers to the duration of the *k*-th track inside CD's `totalPlayTime` method?

    (A) `getDuration(k);`
    (B) `tracks[k-1].duration;`
    (C) `tracks.getDuration(k);`
    (D) `tracks.get(k-1).duration;`
    (E) `getDuration(tracks[k-1]);`

34. What is the result of the following code?

```
Track t = new Track("lightning crashes", 200);
ArrayList<Track> tracks = new ArrayList<Track>();   // Line **
for (int count = 1; count <= 13; count++)
{
   tracks.add(t);
}
CD live = new CD("throwing copper", "live", 13, tracks);
System.out.println(live.totalPlayTime());
```

    (A) Syntax error on Line **
    (B) Run-time `IndexOutOfBoundsException`
    (C) 0 is displayed
    (D) 200 is displayed
    (E) 2600 is displayed

35. Which of the following can replace < *missing code* > in the CD class's constructor?

    I.
```
for (Track t : songs)
   tracks.add(t);
```

    II.
```
tracks = new ArrayList<Track>();
for (Track t : songs)
   tracks.add(t);
```

    III.
```
tracks = new ArrayList<Track>();
for (int i = 0; i < songs.size(); i++)
   tracks.set(i, songs.get(i));
```

    (A) I only
    (B) II only
    (C) I and II only
    (D) II and III only
    (E) I, II, and III

36. A programmer wants to write a method `swap` that swaps two integer values. Which of the following three ways of representing the values and corresponding methods successfully swap the values?

I.
```
// a and b are Integer objects that represent
// the values to be swapped
public static void swap(Integer a, Integer b)
{
    Integer temp = a; a = b; b = temp;
}
```

II.
```
// a[0] and a[1] contain the values to be swapped
public static void swap(int[] a)
{
    int temp = a[0]; a[0] = a[1]; a[1] = temp;
}
```

III.
```
// a[0] and b[0] contain the values to be swapped
public static void swap(int[] a, int[] b)
{
    int temp = a[0]; a[0] = b[0]; b[0] = temp;
}
```

(A)   I only
(B)   II only
(C)   I and II only
(D)   II and III only
(E)   I, II, and III

37. Suppose an interface `Solid` specifies the `getVolume()` method. Two classes, `Cube` and `Pyramid`, implement `Solid`. Which Java feature makes it possible for the following code segment to print the correct values for the volume of a pyramid and a cube?

```
Solid[] solids = new Solid[2];
solids[0] = new Cube(100);
solids[1] = new Pyramid(150, 100);
System.out.println("Cube: " + solids[0].getVolume());
System.out.println("Pyramid: " + solids[1].getVolume());
```

(A)   abstraction
(B)   encapsulation
(C)   polymorphism
(D)   platform-independence
(E)   method overloading

38. Consider the following code segment.

```
if (!somethingIsFalse())
  return false;
else
  return true;
```

Which of the following replacements for this code will produce the same result?

(A) `return true;`
(B) `return false;`
(C) `return somethingIsFalse();`
(D) `return !somethingIsFalse();`
(E) None of the above

39. Consider the following code segment.

```
List<String> list = new ArrayList<String>();
list.add("One");
list.add("Two");
String[] msg = new String[2];
list.add(msg[0]);
< another statement >
```

Which of the following choices for < *another statement* > will cause a `NullPointerException` when the code is compiled and executed?

(A) `msg[0] = "Three";`
(B) `msg[0] = list.get(list.size());`
(C) `if (!"Three".equals(list.get(2))) msg[0] = "Three";`
(D) `list.add(2, msg[0]);`
(E) `msg[1] = msg[0].substring(0, 2);`

40. A programmer is trying to choose between an `ArrayList` and a standard one-dimensional array for representing data. Which of the following is NOT a correct statement?

(A) Both an `ArrayList` and a standard array allow direct access to the *k*-th element.
(B) A standard array may hold elements of a primitive data type, such as `int` or `double`; an `ArrayList` may only hold objects.
(C) An `ArrayList<Object>` may hold objects of different types, such as `Integer` and `Double`, simultaneously.
(D) An `ArrayList` has a convenient method for inserting a value at a specified location in the middle.
(E) Both an `ArrayList` and a standard array are expanded automatically when the number of values stored exceeds their capacity.

Practice Exam #4

SECTION II

Time — 1 hour and 45 minutes
Number of questions — 4
Percent of total grade — 50

1. The College Board grants an AP Scholar award to students who earn grades of 3 or higher on three or more AP Exams. The College Board also grants an AP Scholar with Honor award to students with an average AP Exam grade of at least 3.25 on all exams taken and with grades of 3 or higher on four or more of these exams. The College Board also grants a similar AP Scholar with Distinction award. These three awards are summarized in the table below.

	AP Scholar	AP Scholar with Honor	AP Scholar with Distinction
Average grade on all AP exams taken, at least	No effect	3.25	3.25
Minimum grade that counts toward an award	3	3	3
Number of exams not below the minimum grade	3	4	5

Note that a student may have low grades on some AP exams and still meet the requirements for any of the above awards.

(a) A class `APStudent` has an instance variable `exams`, which represents a list of all AP exams taken by a student. `exams` is defined as

```
private List<Exam> exams;
```

where `Exam` is the following interface:

```
public interface Exam
{
  String getSubject();
  int getGrade();
}
```

Write a method `getAwardLevel()` of the `APStudent` class that examines the list of all exams taken by the student and returns the AP Scholar award level for that student: 0 for none, 1 for AP Scholar, 2 for AP Scholar with Honor, and 3 for AP Scholar with Distinction. Complete the method `getAwardLevel` below.

```
/** Returns the award level obtained by this student:
 *   0 for no award, 1 for AP Scholar, 2 for AP Scholar
 *   with Honor, and 3 for AP Scholar with Distinction.
 *   Precondition: exams.size() > 0
 */
public int getAwardLevel()
```

(b) Write a static method `getStats` of a client class of `APStudent` that takes a non-empty list of `APStudent` objects, calculates the percentages of students with no award, AP Scholars, AP Scholars with Honor, and AP Scholars with Distinction, and returns the result in an array of respective values. For example, if a list holds 10 AP students of whom 6 received no award, 3 are AP Scholars, and 1 is an AP Scholar with Distinction, then `getStats` returns an array with the values 60.0, 30.0, 0.0, and 10.0. Assume that the method `getAwardLevel` from Part (a) works as specified. Complete the method `getStats` below.

```
/** Returns an array p of length 4 in which p[0], p[1],
 *   p[2], and p[3] are the percentages of all students
 *   from a given list with no award, AP Scholars,
 *   AP Scholars with Honor, and AP Scholars with
 *   Distinction, respectively.
 *   @param students list of students
 *   @return the array of percentages for four awards
 *   Precondition: students.size() > 0
 */
public static double[] getStats(List<APStudent> list)
```

2. The Appelsino restaurant uses a computer to manage its dinner reservations. Reservations are accepted at half-hour increments from 5 to 9:30 pm, and each group of diners is given three half-hour slots at the table. The restaurant closes at 11, so there are 12 half-hour slots for dinner each evening.

The schedule for a given table is represented as a string of 12 characters, "." or "x": a dot means the time slot is available, an x means it is taken. For example, "............" indicates that there are no reservations for the table yet; "..xxx..xxx.." means the table has two reservations: for 6:00 and 8:30. The computer program works with tables of a fixed size, and it is assumed that each group of diners fits at one table (Appelsino's manager handles larger groups separately).

Each table is identified by its number (an integer), which ranges from 1 to the total number of tables. The schedules for all the tables for one evening are kept in a list of Strings. The string at index k represents the schedule for the table with that number (the list element at index 0 is null, not used). Each string is of length 12 and contains only "." and "x" characters.

The following class TablesSchedule represents the schedules for all the tables for one evening and provides methods for handling them.

```
public class TablesSchedule
{
  /** Holds reservation schedules for all tables; the
      first element is not used (null) */
  List<String> schedules;

  /** Creates schedules for the evening for a given number of
   *  tables, 12 empty time slots for each table.
   *  @param numTables the number of tables in the restaurant
   */
  public TablesSchedule(int numTables)
  { /* implementation not shown */ }

  /** For a given table, marks as occupied three consecutive
   *  time slots in its schedule, starting from timeSlot.
   *  @param k table number
   *  @param timeSlot the starting time of reservation
   *  Precondition: 1 <= k < schedules.size();
   *                0 <= timeSlot <= 9
   *  Postcondition: the substring of length 3 starting
   *           at timeSlot in the schedule for the table is
   *           replaced with "xxx"; all other reservations
   *           remain unchanged
   */
  public void reserve(int k, int timeSlot)
  { /* to be implemented in part (a) */ }

  /** Returns the total number of occupied time slots for
   *  a given table
   *  @param k table number
   *  Precondition: 1 <= k < schedules.size();
   */
  public int occupiedSlots(int k)
  { /* to be implemented in part (b) */ }

  /** Finds the best table available for three consecutive
   *  time slots, starting from timeSlot, and returns that
   *  table's number. The best table is the one with
   *  the maximum total reserved time (or the first one of
   *  them if several have the same maximum reserved time).
   *  If none of the tables is available for the three time
   *  slots, returns 0.
   *  @param timeSlot the starting time slot for this
   *           reservation
   *  Precondition: 0 <= timeSlot <= 9
   */
  public int findTable(int timeSlot)
  { /* to be implemented in part (c) */ }
}
```

For additional practice, write `TablesSchedule`'s constructor.

(a) Write the `reserve` method of the `TablesSchedule` class. This method takes two
     `int` parameters: k, a table number (an index in the `schedules` list), and
     `timeSlot`, which represents the time of a dinner reservation. The method marks
     three consecutive slots, starting at `timeSlot`, as occupied for the *k*-th table,
     leaving all other reservations unchanged. Complete the method `reserve` below.

```
/** For a given table, marks as occupied three consecutive
 *  time slots in its schedule, starting from timeSlot.
 *  @param k table number
 *  @param timeSlot the starting time of reservation
 *  Precondition: 1 <= k < schedules.size();
 *                0 <= timeSlot <= 9
 *  Postcondition: the substring of length 3 starting
 *          at timeSlot in the schedule for the table is
 *          replaced with "xxx"; all other reservations
 *          remain unchanged
 */
public void reserve(int k, int timeSlot)
```

(b) Write the `occupiedSlots` method of the `TablesSchedule` class. This method
     returns the total number of occupied half-hour slots for the *k*-th table. Complete the
     method `occupiedSlots` below.

```
/** Returns the total number of occupied time slots for
 *  a given table
 *  @param k table number
 *  Precondition: 1 <= k < schedules.size();
 */
public int occupiedSlots(int k)
```

(c) `TablesSchedule`'s `findTable` method finds the best table available for three consecutive time slots, starting at a given time slot, and returns that table's number. The best table is the one with most total time slots occupied (or the first one, if there are several of them). If none of the tables is available for a dinner reservation starting at the specified time slot, the method returns 0. For example, if the restaurant has five tables with the following reservations —

```
                                11
         time slot:     012345678901
         Table 1:       xxx......xxx
         Table 2:       .xxx.xxx....
         Table 3:       .....xxx....
         Table 4:       ....xxxxxx..
         Table 5:       .xxx.xxx....
```

— then `findTable(1)` returns 4, because both Table 3 and Table 4 have the slots 1, 2, and 3 available, but Table 4 has more total slots occupied. `findTable(9)` returns 2, because Tables 2, 3, and 5 have slots 9, 10, and 11 available, the maximum total slots occupied for them is 6, and Table 2 is the first one among them that has 6 slots occupied. `findTable(7)` returns 0 because none of the tables has all three slots 7, 8, and 9 available.

Complete the method `findTable` below.

```
/** Finds the best table available for three consecutive
 *  time slots, starting from timeSlot, and returns that
 *  table's number. The best table is the one with
 *  the maximum total reserved time (or the first one of
 *  them if several have the same maximum reserved time).
 *  If none of the tables is available for dinner starting
 *  at timeSlot, returns 0.
 *  @param timeSlot the starting time slot for this
 *         dinner reservation
 *  Precondition: 0 <= timeSlot <= 9
 */
public int findTable(int timeSlot)
```

For additional practice, write an alternative version of the `findTable` method, which defines the "best table" as the first one that already has a reservation that is immediately before or after the requested three time slots. If such a table does not exists, the best table is the one with most reserved slots, as before.

3.   This question involves reasoning about the GridWorld case study.* Reference materials are provided in the appendices.

`BusyAnt` is a subclass of `Critter`. A `BusyAnt` moves only within a 5 by 5 area of the grid (rows and columns ranging from 0 to 4), each time choosing a random neighboring location within the 5 by 5 area, with equal probability. In this project we consider only four locations to be the neighbors of a given location: to the north, south, east, and west (diagonally adjacent locations do not count as neighbors).

There are a few "seeds" scattered in the area. `BusyAnt`'s task is to collect the seeds, one by one, and arrange them along the top row (row 0). For example:

<table>
<tr><td>Start</td><td>Finish</td></tr>
</table>

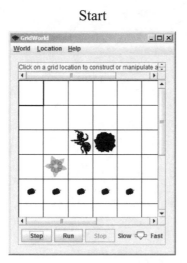 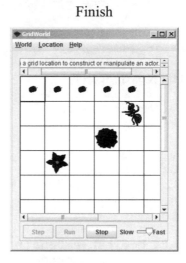

A seed is represented by an object of the class `Seed` (a subclass of `Actor`). It has one constructor that takes no parameters.

 For additional practice, write the `Seed` class.

The ant can carry only one seed at a time. If the ant is not carrying a seed and "steps" on one anywhere in the area, except row 0, it "picks up" the seed. When the ant is carrying a seed and steps on any empty location in row 0, the ant "drops" the seed there. The ant can "crawl over" other `Actors`, including `Seeds`, in the grid: when the ant steps on an `Actor`, the ant temporarily removes it from the grid, then restores it back on the ant's next move (unless the ant picked up the seed and intends to carry it). The ant also counts the number of moves it has made, and displays it when the program is paused and the user hovers over the ant.

A partial definition of the `BusyAnt` class is shown below.

_____

* This question is inspired by Project Euler Problem #280, `http://projecteuler.net/problem=280`.

```
public class BusyAnt extends Critter
{
    /** The number of moves made by this ant so far */
    private int movesCount;

    /** Indicates whether this ant is carrying a seed */
    private boolean haveSeed;

    /** If there is an actor temporarily "under" the ant,
     *    a reference to that actor; otherwise null */
    private Actor actorUnder;

    /** Sets this ant's color to Color.BLACK and initializes
     *  all instance variables
     */
    public BusyAnt()
    {   /* implementation not shown */ }

    public void act()
    {
        if (!amDone())
            super.act();
    }

    /** Returns true if the ant is not carrying a seed,
     *  has no seed under itself, and there are no seeds
     *  anywhere in the grid except in row 0; otherwise
     *  returns false
     */
    private boolean amDone()
    { /* to be implemented in part(a) */ }

    /** Overrides Critter's processActors */
    public void processActors(ArrayList<Actor> actors)
    { /* do nothing */ }

    /** Returns a list of locations where this ant can move:
     *  adjacent to this ant's location and within the 5 by 5
     *  area 0 <= row <= 4 and 0 <= col <= 4
     */
    public ArrayList<Location> getMoveLocations()
    {   /* implementation not shown */ }

    /** If the ant is not carrying a seed and Location next
     *  holds a seed and is not in row 0, the ant "picks up" the
     *  seed and changes its own color to red.  If the ant is
     *  carrying a seed and Location next is empty and in row 0,
     *  the ant drops the seed there and changes its own color
     *  back to black.  In any case, the ant moves to Location
     *  next and increments movesCount.
     */
    public void makeMove(Location next)
    { /* to be implemented in part(b) */ }
}
```

In this question you will write `BusyAnt`'s private method `amDone` and the method `makeMove` that overrides `Critter`'s `makeMove`.

For additional practice, write `BusyAnt`'s constructor and the `getMoveLocations` method, too.

(a) Write the private method `amDone` of the `BusyAnt` class. The method returns `true` if the ant is not carrying a seed (`haveSeed` is `false`), the actor under the ant, if any, is not a seed, and there are no seeds left anywhere in the grid except in row 0. Otherwise `amDone` returns `false`. Complete the method `amDone` below.

```
/** Returns true if the ant is not carrying a seed,
 *  has no seed under itself, and there are no seeds
 *  anywhere in the grid except in row 0; otherwise
 *  returns false
 */
private boolean amDone()
```

(b) Write the method `makeMove(Location next)` of the `BusyAnt` class. Follow these steps:

1. If `next` is `null`, remove this ant from the grid.

2. If this ant is not carrying a seed but is standing on one (`actorUnder` is a `Seed`) and `next` is not in row 0, "pick up" the seed, that is, change the ant's color to `Color.RED` and update the `haveSeed` and `actorUnder` variables appropriately.

3. If this ant is carrying a seed and is standing on an empty location (`actorUnder` is `null`) and `next` is in row 0, "drop" the seed, that is, change the ant's color back to `Color.BLACK` and update the `haveSeed` and `actorUnder` variables appropriately.

4. Move this ant to `next`, but first save the actor from the `next` location in a temporary variable. Restore `actorUnder` (if any) in the ant's old location, and set `actorUnder` to the saved actor from `next`.

5. Increment `movesCount`.

Complete the method `makeMove` below.

```
/** If the ant is not carrying a seed and Location next
 *  holds a seed and is not in row 0, the ant "picks up" the
 *  seed and changes its own color to red.  If the ant is
 *  carrying a seed and Location next is empty and in row 0,
 *  the ant drops the seed there and changes its own color
 *  back to black.  In any case, the ant moves to Location
 *  next and increments movesCount.
 */
public void makeMove(Location next)
```

4. This question is concerned with the design and implementation of classes for a school bus transportation system. In this system, a `Student` object represents a student in a given school. A student has a name and an address, represented as a street name (a `String`) and a house number on the street (an `int`). The class `Student` implements the following interface:

```
public interface Person
{
    String getName();
    String getStreet();
    int getNumber();
}
```

(a) Write the `distance(Student other)` method of the `Student` class. If `this` student lives on the same street as `other`, then `distance` returns the absolute value of the difference in the numbers of their houses; otherwise it returns 99999.

For additional practice, write the entire class `Student`. Provide a `toString` method that returns all the information about the `Student` object combined in one string.

Complete the method `distance` below.

```
/** If this student and other live on the same street,
 *  returns the absolute value of the difference in the
 *  numbers of their houses; otherwise returns 99999
 *  Precondition: other is not null
 */
public int distance(Student other)
```

(b) A `SchoolBus` object corresponds to one bus route and holds a list of students assigned to that bus. `SchoolBus` <u>extends</u> `ArrayList<Student>`. `SchoolBus` has a constructor that creates a bus with a given number of seats. `SchoolBus`'s `boolean` method `isFull` returns `true` if there are no vacant seats left on this bus; otherwise it returns `false`. Write the entire `SchoolBus` class. Do not duplicate any methods inherited from `ArrayList<Student>`.

(c) A `SchoolTransport` object handles bus assignments for a given school. It has an
     `ArrayList` of `SchoolBus` objects:

```
/** List of all bus routes for this school */
private List<SchoolBus> buses;
```

Your task is to write `SchoolTransport`'s `enroll` method.

The `enroll` method tries to find a bus on which it makes sense to place a new
student. On all the buses that are not already full, it looks for a student already
enrolled who lives on the same street and is closest to the new student (such that the
distance between that student and the new student, as defined by `Student`'s
`distance` method, is the smallest). If such a student is found, then the method
places the new student on the same bus and returns `true`. Otherwise the method
returns `false`, indicating that the bus placement decision is left to the school's
transportation manager. Complete the method `enroll` below.

```
/** Looks in all buses for someone whose bus is not
 *  yet full and who lives on the same street, the
 *  closest to student (in terms of distance defined
 *  for Student objects); if found, adds student to the
 *  same bus and returns true; otherwise returns false
 */
public boolean enroll(Student student)
```

For additional practice, write the whole `SchoolTransport` class, including a
constructor, a method that adds a `SchoolBus` to the list, and a `toString` method.

Practice Exam #5

Time — 1 hour and 15 minutes
Number of questions — 40
Percent of total grade — 50

1. Which of the following statements displays `1234`?

    I.   `System.out.print(12 * 100 + 34);`
    II. `System.out.print("12" + 34);`
    III. `System.out.print(12 + "34");`

    (A) None of the above
    (B) I only
    (C) I and II only
    (D) II and III only
    (E) I, II, and III

2. What is the output of the following code segment?

    ```
    String url = "http://www.usa.gov";
    int pos = url.indexOf("http://");
    if (pos >= 0)
    {
      System.out.println("<" + url.substring(0, pos) + ">");
    }
    else
    {
      System.out.println("not found");
    }
    ```

    (A) `<>`
    (B) `<www.usa.gov>`
    (C) `<http://www.usa.gov>`
    (D) `not found`
    (E) `IndexOutOfBoundsException`

3.   Consider the following method.

```
public void reduce(int[] arr, int len)
{
  for (int k = 0; k < len; k++)
  {
    arr[k]--;
  }

  len--;
}
```

What is the output of the following code segment?

```
int[] counts = {3, 2, 1, 0};
int len = 3;
reduce(counts, len);

for (int c : counts)
{
  System.out.print(c + " ");
}
System.out.println(len);
```

(A)   2 1 0 -1 2
(B)   2 1 0 -1 3
(C)   2 1 0 0 2
(D)   2 1 0 0 3
(E)   2 1 1 0 3

4.   What values are stored in `arr` after the following code segment has been executed?

```
int[] arr = {1, 2, 3, 4, 5, 6, 7, 8};

for (int k = 1; k <= 6; k += 2)
{
  arr[7] = arr[k];
  arr[k] = arr[k+1];
  arr[k+1] = arr[7];
}
```

(A)   1 3 2 5 4 7 6 6
(B)   1 3 2 5 4 7 6 8
(C)   2 1 4 3 6 5 8 7
(D)   2 1 4 3 6 5 7 8
(E)   2 1 4 3 6 5 7 5

5. What is printed as a result of executing the following code segment?

```
int k = 0;
while (k < Integer.MAX_VALUE)
{
   k += 4;
}
System.out.println(k);
```

(A) `Integer.MAX_VALUE`
(B) `Integer.MAX_VALUE - 4`
(C) `Integer.MAX_VALUE + 4`
(D) 3
(E) Nothing — the program goes into an infinite loop

6. A two-dimensional array `image` holds brightness values for pixels (picture elements) in an image. The brightness values range from 0 to 255. Consider the following method.

```
public int findMax(int[][] image)
{
   int[] count = new int[256];
   int i, iMax = 0;

   for (int r = 0; r < image.length; r++)
   {
      for (int c = 0; c < image[0].length; c++)
      {
         i = image[r][c];
         count[i]++;
      }
   }

   for (i = 1; i < 256; i++)
   {
      if (count[i] > count[iMax])
         iMax = i;
   }

   return iMax;
}
```

What does this method compute?

(A) The column with the highest sum of brightness values in `image`
(B) The maximum brightness value for all pixels in `image`
(C) The most frequent brightness value in `image`
(D) The maximum sum of brightness values in any 256 by 256 square in `image`
(E) The maximum sum of brightness values in any 256 consecutive rows in `image`

7. Consider the following method.

```
public String encrypt(String word)
{
  int pos = word.length() / 2;
  if (pos >= 1)
  {
    word = encrypt(word.substring(pos)) +
           encrypt(word.substring(0, pos));
  }
  return word;
}
```

Which of the following strings is returned by encrypt("SECRET")?

(A) TERCES
(B) TSECRE
(C) RETSEC
(D) CESTER
(E) ETRECS

8. What is printed as a result of executing the following code segment?

```
int i = 2;
for (int k = 0; k <= 12; k += i)
{
  System.out.print(k + " ");
  i++;
}
```

(A) 0 3 7
(B) 0 3 7 12
(C) 2 5 8 11
(D) 0 3 6 9 12
(E) 0 2 4 6 8 10

9. Consider the following method.

    ```
    /** Returns the index of searchVal, if found in list;
     *  otherwise returns -1
     */
    public int binarySearch(ArrayList<String> list,
                                        String searchVal)
    {
      int first = 0, last = list.size() - 1;
      while (first <= last)
      {
        int mid = (first + last) / 2;

        if (searchVal.compareTo(list.get(mid)) < 0)
          last = mid - 1;
        else if (searchVal.compareTo(list.get(mid)) > 0)
          first = mid + 1;
        else
          return mid;    // Statement 1
      }
      return -1;         // Statement 2
    }
    ```

    We want to modify this method: if searchVal is not already in the list, we want
    binarySearch to return the position where it can be inserted, keeping the list sorted.
    Which of the following could be used for *Statement 1* and *Statement 2*?

	Statement 1	*Statement 2*
(A)	return mid;	return mid;
(B)	return mid;	return first;
(C)	return mid;	return last;
(D)	return mid - 1;	return first;
(E)	return mid - 1;	return last;

10. Given that x is true, y is true, and z is false, which of the following expressions will
    evaluate to false?

    (A) (x && y) || z
    (B) (x || y) && z
    (C) y || (x && z)
    (D) x || (y && z)
    (E) x && (y || z)

11. Consider the following three implementations of a method `rotate90degrees` and the code segment (in the same class) used to test it.

I.
```
public int[] rotate90degrees(int[] v)
{
  int[] w = new int[2];
  w[0] = -v[1];
  w[1] = v[0];
  return w;
}


  int[] v = {1, 2};
  v = rotate90degrees(v);
  System.out.println(v[0] + ", " + v[1]);
```

II.
```
public void rotate90degrees(int[] v)
{
  int  temp  = v[0];
  v[0] = -v[1];
  v[1] = temp;
}

  int[] v = {1, 2};
  rotate90degrees(v);
  System.out.println(v[0] + ", " + v[1]);
```

III.
```
public int[] rotate90degrees(int[] v)
{
  int  temp  = v[0];
  v[0] = -v[1];
  v[1] = temp;
  return v;
}

  int[] v = {1, 2};
  rotate90degrees(v);
  System.out.println(v[0] + ", " + v[1]);
```

Which of these implementations will compile with no errors and print -2, 1?

(A)   I only
(B)   II only
(C)   I and II only
(D)   II and III only
(E)   I, II, and III

12. Consider the following method.

```
/** Returns the number of times the digit d occurs in the
 *  decimal representation of n
 *  Precondition: n and d are non-negative integers
 */
private int findDigit(int n, int d)
{
  int count = 0;
  < statement 1 >

  while (n > 0)
  {
    if (n % 10 == d)
    {
      count++;
    }
    < statement 2 >
  }

  return count;
}
```

Which of the following could replace < *statement 1* > and < *statement 2* > to make findDigit work as specified?

	< *statement 1* >	< *statement 2* >
(A)	`if (n == 0) return 1;`	`n /= 10;`
(B)	`if (n == 0) return 1;`	`d *= 10;`
(C)	`if (d == 0) count++;`	`n -= n % 10;`
(D)	`if (n == 0 && d == 0) count++;`	`n /= 10;`
(E)	`if (n == 0 && d != 0) return 0;`	`n *= 10;`

13. What is printed when the following code segment is executed?

```
List<Integer> list = new ArrayList<Integer>();
list.add(new Integer(1));
list.add(new Integer(2));
for (int i = 1; i <= 3; i++)
{
   list.add(i, new Integer(i));
}
System.out.println(list);
```

(A) `[1, 1, 2, 2, 3]`
(B) `[1, 1, 2, 3, 2]`
(C) `[1, 2, 1, 2, 3]`
(D) `[1, 2, 3, 1, 2]`
(E) `IndexOutOfBoundsException`

14. Consider the following code segment.

```
int[][] t = new int[2][3];
for (int i = 0; i < t.length; i++)
{
  for (int j = 0; j < t[0].length; j++)
  {
    t[i][j] = i + j + 1;
  }
}
```

What is the result when the code segment is executed?

(A)   t holds the values

```
1 2 3
4 5 6
```

(B)   t holds the values

```
1 2 0
2 3 0
```

(C)   t holds the values

```
1 2 3
2 3 4
```

(D)   t holds the values

```
3 4 5
4 5 6
```

(E)   `ArrayIndexOutOfBoundsException`

15. Which of the following tasks are made easier when information hiding is practiced?

    I.   Implementing IS-A relationships for classes
   II.   Making changes to the implementation of one of the classes in a project
  III.   Producing specifications for individual programmers working on the same project

(A)   I only
(B)   II only
(C)   I and II only
(D)   II and III only
(E)   I, II, and III

16. Consider the following method.

```
public boolean examine(String[] letters)
{
  int count = 0;
  for (String letter1 : letters)
  {
    for (String letter2 : letters)
    {
      if (letter1.equals(letter2))
        count++;
    }
  }
  return count > 0;
}
```

What will examine return for the following arrays?

```
String[] letters1 = {"A", "B", "C"};
String[] letters2 = {"A", "B", "B"};
String[] letters3 = {"A", "A", "B"};
```

	letters1	letters2	letters3
(A)	true	true	true
(B)	true	true	false
(C)	false	true	true
(D)	false	false	true
(E)	false	false	false

17. What is printed as a result of executing the following code segment?

```
int[] factors = {2, 3, 5};
List<Integer> products = new ArrayList<Integer>();
products.add(new Integer(1));
for (int f : factors)
{
  int n = products.size();
  for (int k = 0; k < n; k++)
  {
    products.add(new Integer(f * products.get(k)));
  }
}
int n = products.size();
System.out.println(n + " " + products.get(n-2) +
                            " " + products.get(n-1));
```

(A)   4 3 5
(B)   4 6 15
(C)   8 10 15
(D)   8 10 30
(E)   8 15 30

18. Consider the following classes.

```
public class APTestResult
{
  private String subject;
  private int score;

  public int getScore() { return score; }

  < constructors and other methods not shown >
}

public class APScholar
{
  private String name;
  private int id;
  private ArrayList<APTestResult> exams;

  public ArrayList<APTestResult> getExams() { return exams; }

  < constructors and other methods not shown >
}
```

Given

```
APScholar[] list = new APScholar[100];
```

which of the following expressions correctly represents the third AP score of the sixth APScholar in list?

(A)   `list[5].exams[2].score`
(B)   `list[5].exams.getScore(2)`
(C)   `list[5].exams[2].getScore()`
(D)   `list[5].getExams(2).getScore()`
(E)   `list[5].getExams().get(2).getScore()`

19. In a regular pentagon, the ratio of the length of a diagonal to the length of a side is equal to the Golden Ratio (defined as $\frac{1+\sqrt{5}}{2} \approx 1.618$). Consider the following class `Pentagon`, which represents a regular pentagon.

```
public class Pentagon
{
  public static final double goldenRatio =
                            (1 + Math.sqrt(5.0)) / 2;
  private double side;

  public Pentagon (double x)
  {
    side = x;
  }

  public double getDiagonalLength()
  {
    return side * goldenRatio;
  }
}
```

Which of the following code segments will compile with no errors and display the correct length of a diagonal in a regular pentagon with side 3.0?

I.   `System.out.println(3/2 * (1 + Math.sqrt(5.0)));`

II.   `System.out.println(3.0 * Pentagon.goldenRatio);`

III.   `Pentagon p = new Pentagon(3);`
        `System.out.println(p.getDiagonalLength());`

(A) I only
(B) II only
(C) III only
(D) I and II only
(E) II and III only

Questions 20-21 refer to the following implementation of Mergesort.

```
public class Mergesort
{
  /** Returns a new array which holds the values
   *  arr[m], arr[m+1], ... arr[n] arranged in ascending order
   *  Precondition: 0 <= m <= n < arr.length
   */
  public static int[] sort(int[] arr, int m, int n)
  {
    int[] result = new int[n - m + 1];

    if (m == n)
    {
      result[0] = arr[m];
    }
    else
    {
      int mid = (n + m) / 2;
      int[] result1 = sort(arr, m, mid);
      int[] result2 = sort(arr, mid + 1, n);
      result = merge(result1, result2);
    }

    return result;
  }

  /** Merges arr1 and arr2 in ascending order and returns the
   *  resulting array.
   *  Precondition: arr1 and arr2 are sorted in ascending order
   */
  private static int[] merge(int[] arr1, int[] arr2)
  { /* implementation not shown */ }
}
```

20. If `int[] arr` holds eight values and `Mergesort(arr, 0, 7)` is called, how many times in total will `Mergesort`'s `merge` method be called?

    (A) 1
    (B) 3
    (C) 7
    (D) 8
    (E) 15

21. If `Mergesort.sort(arr, 0, 999)` takes on average 40 ms and
`Mergesort.merge(arr1, arr2)` takes on average
`0.01*(arr1.length + arr2.length)`, what is the average run time for
`Mergesort.sort(arr, 0, 1999)`?

(A) 50 ms
(B) 100 ms
(C) 160 ms
(D) 170 ms
(E) 180 ms

22. Consider the following method.

```
private double compute(int x, int y)
{
  double r = 0;
  if (!(y == 0 || x / y <= 2))
    r = 1 / ((x - 2*y) * (2*x - y));
  return r;
}
```

For which of the following values of x and y will `compute(x, y)` throw an exception?

(A) x = 0, y = 0
(B) x = 1, y = 2
(C) x = 2, y = 1
(D) x = 3, y = 5
(E) None of the above

23. The Binary Search algorithm is designed to work with an array sorted in ascending order. Under which of the following circumstances will the algorithm find a given target value even if the array is not sorted?

I.   The array has an odd number of elements and the target value is located exactly in the middle of the array.

II. The array is partially sorted: the left third of the array has values all in ascending order and the target value is among them.

III. The array is partially sorted: all the values to the left of the target are smaller than the target and all the values to the right of the target are larger than the target.

(A) I only
(B) I and II only
(C) I and III only
(D) II and III only
(E) I, II, and III

Questions 24-27 refer to the following class `House` and its subclass `HouseForSale`.

```
public class House
{
  private int mySize;

  public House(int size) { mySize = size; }
  public int getSize() { return mySize; }
  public void setSize(int size) { mySize = size; }

  public int compareToOther(House other)
  {
    return getSize() - other.getSize();
  }
}

public class HouseForSale extends House
{
  private int myPrice;

  public HouseForSale(int size, int price)
  {
    < missing statement >

    myPrice = price;
  }

  public int getPrice() { return myPrice; }

  public int compareToOther(House other)
  {
    return getPrice() - ((HouseForSale)other).getPrice();
  }

  < other constructors, methods, and fields not shown >
}
```

24. Which of the following is the most appropriate replacement for < *missing statement* > in
    `HouseForSale`'s constructor?

    (A) `mySize = size;`
    (B) `setSize(size);`
    (C) `super.setSize(size);`
    (D) `super(size);`
    (E) `super = new House(size);`

25. Suppose that while writing the `HouseForSale` class the programmer accidentally misspelled "compareToOther" in his code. What will happen when he tries to compile and run his class and the following statements in a client class?

```
HouseForSale house1 = new HouseForSale(2000, 129000);
HouseForSale house2 = new HouseForSale(1800, 149000);
System.out.println(house1.compareToOther(house2));
```

(A) A syntax error "undefined compareToOther method"
(B) A syntax error "HouseForSale should be declared abstract"
(C) The code compiles with no errors and displays 200.
(D) The code compiles with no errors but throws a `ClassCastException`.
(E) The code compiles with no errors but throws a `NoSuchMethodException`.

26. If the classes `House` and `HouseForSale` compile with no errors, which of the following declarations will result in a syntax error?

(A) `House[] houses = new House[2];`

(B) `HouseForSale[] houses = {new House(2000), new House(1800)};`

(C) `House[] houses = {new HouseForSale(2000, 129000),`
`                     new HouseForSale(1800, 149000)};`

(D) `HouseForSale[] houses = {new HouseForSale(2000, 129000),`
`                           new HouseForSale(1800, 149000)};`

(E) All of the above compile with no errors.

27. Which of the following is the most appropriate way to define the `getSize` method in `HouseForSale`?

(A) `public int getSize() { return mySize; }`
(B) `public int getSize() { return super.mySize; }`
(C) `public int getSize() { return super(mySize); }`
(D) `public int getSize() { return super.getSize(); }`
(E) No definition is necessary, because the same code is already written in `House`.

Questions 28-32 refer to the code from the GridWorld case study. Reference materials are provided in the appendices.

28. How does a `Bug` act if there is a `Rock` directly in front of it in the grid?

  (A)   The `Bug` is removed from the grid.
  (B)   The `Bug` remains in its current state — no action is taken.
  (C)   The `Rock` is removed, and the `Bug` moves forward, leaving a new `Flower` in its old location.
  (D)   The `Bug` turns 45 degrees to the right.
  (E)   The `Bug` turns 180 degrees.

29. Consider the following subclass of `Bug`.

```
public class SpinningBug extends Bug
{
  public void act()
  {
    super.act();
    turn();
  }

  public void turn()
  {
    setDirection(getDirection() + Location.LEFT);
  }
}
```

If a `SpinningBug` is put into a grid, among other actors, how does it act?

  (A)   The `SpinningBug` throws a `NoSuchMethodException`, because the `canMove` and `move` methods are undefined.
  (B)   The `SpinningBug` acts like a regular `Bug` but turns 90 degrees to the left after each move.
  (C)   If the `SpinningBug` can move, it moves forward, then turns 90 degrees to the left; otherwise the bug turns 180 degrees.
  (D)   If the `SpinningBug` can move, it moves forward, then turns 90 degrees to the left; otherwise the bug turns 45 degrees to the left.
  (E)   If the `SpinningBug` can move, it moves forward, then turns 90 degrees to the left; otherwise the bug turns 45 degrees to the right.

30. When a `ChameleonCritter` object is first created, what are its initial color and direction?

    (A) blue color and north
    (B) red color and north
    (C) blue color and random direction
    (D) random color and random direction
    (E) the color passed to `ChameleonCritter`'s constructor as a parameter and random direction

31. A `RockChameleonCritter` "acts" exactly like a `ChameleonCritter`, except it changes color to the color of a randomly chosen adjacent `Rock`. If there are no rocks among its neighbors, `RockChameleonCritter`'s color remains unchanged. Which of the following approaches to implementing the `RockChameleonCritter` class can work?

    I.   Derive `RockChameleonCritter` from `Critter` and override the `processActors` and `makeMove` methods

    II. Derive `RockChameleonCritter` from `ChameleonCritter` and override only the `processActors` method

    III. Derive `RockChameleonCritter` from `ChameleonCritter` and override only the `getActors` method

    (A) I only
    (B) II only
    (C) I and II only
    (D) II and III only
    (E) I, II, and III

32. Which of the following is NOT an example of polymorphism?

    (A) The appropriate `act` method is called for `Rocks`, `Bugs`, `Flowers`, and `Critters`
    (B) `BoxBug`'s `act` method calls `move` and `turn` inherited from `Bug`
    (C) `ChameleonCritter`'s `act` method, inherited from `Critter`, calls `ChameleonCritter`'s `processActors` and `makeMove`
    (D) `Bug`'s `canMove` method calls the appropriate `Grid`'s `isValid` for different implementations of `Grid`
    (E) All of the above are examples of polymorphism.

33. Consider the following code segment with a missing "for" loop.

```
List<String> letters = new ArrayList<String>();

letters.add("A");
letters.add("B");
letters.add("C");

< missing "for" loop >

System.out.println(letters);
```

Suppose, when executed, the above code segment displays

```
[A*, B*, C*]
```

Which of the following could replace *< missing "for" loop >*?

I.
```
for (int i = 0; i < letters.size(); i++)
{
    letters.set(i, letters.get(i) + "*");
}
```

II.
```
for (int i = 0; i < letters.size(); i++)
{
    String s = letters.get(i);
    s = s + "*";
}
```

III.
```
for (String s : letters)
{
    s = s + "*";
}
```

(A) I only
(B) II only
(C) I and II only
(D) II and III only
(E) I, II, and III

34. Consider the following class.

```
public class Game
{
  private static int bestScore;
  private int score;
  private String player;

  < constructors and methods not shown >
}
```

Which of the following constructors or methods in Game will cause a syntax error?

I.   `public static void resetScore()`
     `{ score = 0; bestScore = 0; }`

II. `public Game()`
     `{ score = 0; bestScore = 0; }`

III. `public void setPlayer(String name)`
     `{ player = name; }`

(A) I only
(B) II only
(C) I and II only
(D) II and III only
(E) I, II, and III

35. Consider the following method.

```
public int guess(int num1, int num2)
{
  if (num1 % num2 == 0)
    return num2;
  else
    return guess(num2, num1 % num2);
}
```

What is the value of num after the following statement is executed?

```
int num = (6 * 14) / guess(6, 14);
```

(A) 6
(B) 12
(C) 28
(D) 42
(E) 84

36. Consider two different designs for a data structure to hold the total number of home runs hit in a season by baseball players. There are *n* players (*n* > 1000), and each total is in the range from 0 to 80.

Design A

Use an array of length 81. Each index into the array corresponds to a number of home runs, and each element of the array is a reference to a list containing the names of the players who hit that many home runs, in no particular order.

Design B

Use an array of length *n* so that each element of the array corresponds to one player. Each element of the array is an object that represents a player, holding his name and the number of home runs he has hit. The elements of the array are sorted alphabetically by player name.

This data structure will be used to support three operations:

Operation 1: Print the names of all players who hit over 50 home runs.

Operation 2: Given a player's name, look up that player's home run total.

Operation 3: Given the names of two players, determine whether they hit the same number of home runs.

Which of the three operations could be performed more efficiently using Design A rather than Design B?

(A)   Operation 1 only
(B)   Operation 2 only
(C)   Operation 3 only
(D)   Operations 1 and 2
(E)   Operations 2 and 3

37. Consider the following incomplete method that shuffles a list of `Card` objects, so that any card can end up at any index in the list with equal probability.

```
public void shuffle(List<Card> cards)
{
  int n = cards.size();
  while (n > 1)
  {
    < missing statement >

    Card temp = cards.set(k, cards.get(n-1));
    cards.set(n-1, temp);
    n--;
  }
}
```

Which of the following can replace < *missing statement* >?

(A)   `int k = Math.random(n);`
(B)   `int k = Math.random(cards.size());`
(C)   `int k = Math.random(cards.size() - 1);`
(D)   `int k = (int)(n * Math.random());`
(E)   `int k = (int)((n-1) * Math.random());`

38. Consider the following classes.

```
public class MyList1 extends ArrayList<Double>
{
  public MyList1() { }

  < other constructors, methods and data fields not shown >
}

public class MyList2 implements List<Double>
{
  public MyList2() { }

  < other constructors, methods and data fields not shown >
}
```

Which of the following statements will cause a compile-time error?

(A)   `MyList1 list = new MyList1();`
(B)   `ArrayList<Double> list = new MyList1();`
(C)   `List<Double> list = new MyList1();`
(D)   `List<Double> list = new MyList2();`
(E)   All of the above will compile with no errors

39. Suppose a programmer has written a method that implements Insertion Sort for an array of integers. The method has no preconditions. Which of the following is NOT a useful test for this method?

(A) An array of length 5 with random values
(B) An array of length 5 with values sorted in ascending order
(C) An empty array (length 0)
(D) An array of length 1
(E) All of the above are useful tests.

40. Consider the following class.

```java
public class ArrayProcessor
{
  public static void run(int[] arr)
  {
    for (int i = 0; i < arr.length; i++)
    {
      for (int j = arr.length - 1; j > i; j--)
      {
        if (arr[j] < arr[i])
        {
          swap(arr, i, j);
        }
      }
    }
  }

  private static void swap(int[] arr, int i, int j)
  {
    int temp = arr[i];
    arr[i] = arr[j];
    arr[j] = temp;
  }
}
```

How many times will ArrayProcessor's swap method be called when the following code segment is executed?

```java
int[] counts = {1, 2, 3, 4, 5, 0};
ArrayProcessor.run(counts);
```

(A) 1
(B) 5
(C) 15
(D) 30
(E) 35

Practice Exam #5

Time — 1 hour and 45 minutes
Number of questions — 4
Percent of total grade — 50

1. All emails received by the Office of Complaints in Appaloosa County are assigned a
    priority rank from 0 to 9 and answered in the order of priority; emails with a higher
    priority are answered first; emails with the same priority are answered in the order in
    which they were received. In the Java application that handles email in Appaloosa, each
    message is represented by an object of a class that implements the following interface.

```
public interface Message
{
   /** Returns the priority of this message, an int value
    *   in the range from 0 to 9
    */
   int getPriority();
}
```

In this question you will write three methods for the MessagePriorityQueue class,
which is used to store all incoming messages and retrieve them in order of priority.

A MessagePriorityQueue object holds ten lists, one list for messages of a particular
priority from 0 to 9. Each of these ten lists is implemented as an
ArrayList<Message>. The ten lists are collected in one
ArrayList<ArrayList<Message>>. The MessagePriorityQueue class also has
an instance variable that holds the total number of messages stored in all ten lists
combined. This variable is updated appropriately when a message is added or removed
from the queue.

An incomplete definition of the MessagePriorityQueue class is shown below.

```
public class MessagePriorityQueue
{
  /** The list of lists; each list holds messages of
   *   a particular priority */
  private ArrayList<ArrayList<Message>> messageLists;

  /**  The total number of messages in this priority queue */
  private int numMessages;

  /** Constructs an empty priority queue with 10 empty
   *   lists of messages, one for each priority
   */
  public MessagePriorityQueue()
  { /* implementation not shown */ }

  /** Returns the total number of messages in this
   *   priority queue
   */
  public int size()
  { /* implementation not shown */ }

  /** Returns true if this priority queue is empty;
   *   otherwise returns false
   */
  public boolean isEmpty()
  { /* to be implemented in part(a) */ }

  /** Adds a message at the end of the list that holds
   *   messages of the same priority as this message;
   *   increments the total number of messages in the queue
   */
  public void add(Message msg)
  { /* to be implemented in part(b) */ }

  /** If this priority queue is not empty, removes and returns
   *   the first message of the highest priority from this
   *   priority queue and decrements the total number of messages
   *   in the queue; otherwise returns null
   */
  public Message remove()
  { /* to be implemented in part(c) */ }
}
```

(a)   Write the method `isEmpty` of the `MessagePriorityQueue` class. This method returns `true` if the priority queue is empty (contains no messages); otherwise it returns `false`. Complete the method `isEmpty` below.

```
public boolean isEmpty()
```

(b)   Write the method `add(Message msg)` of the `MessagePriorityQueue` class. This method retrieves the priority of `msg` and adds `msg` at the end of the list that holds all the messages of that priority. `add` also increments the total number of messages in this priority queue. Complete the method `add` below.

```
/** Adds a message at the end of the list that holds
 *  messages of the same priority as this message;
 *  increments the total number of messages in the queue
 */
public void add(Message msg)
```

(c)   Write the method `remove` of the `MessagePriorityQueue` class. This method removes from this priority queue the first message of the highest priority and returns it. It also decrements the count of messages in the queue. If the queue is empty, `remove` returns `null`. Complete the method `remove` below.

```
/** If this priority queue is not empty, removes and returns
 *  the first message of the highest priority from this
 *  priority queue and decrements the total number of messages
 *  in the queue; otherwise returns null
 */
public Message remove()
```

2.   This question involves reasoning about the GridWorld case study. Reference materials
are provided in the appendices.

A `MazeBug` is a bug that can find its way out of a maze. The walls of a maze are made of
rocks (`Rock` objects). <u>A `MazeBug` can move only in four directions: north, east, south,
and west</u>.

`MazeBug`'s strategy is to cling to the wall on its left: when the wall turns left, the bug
turns left, too. The picture below shows a bug's path in a small maze.

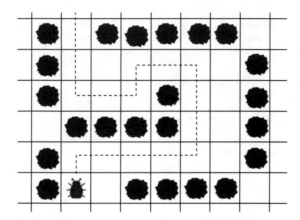

In this project assume that the grid contains only `MazeBug`, `Rock`, and `Flower` objects.

`MazeBug` extends `Bug`. It overrides two methods, `act` and `turn`, and adds two new
methods: `moveLeft` and `canMoveLeft`. Your task is to write the `MazeBug` class.

`MazeBug`'s `moveLeft` method turns the bug 90 degrees to the left, then moves it forward
to the adjacent location, putting a `Flower` into the location it previously occupied. In
other words, after turning 90 degrees to the left, a `MazeBug` moves like a regular `Bug`.
Do not duplicate `Bug`'s `move` code in `moveLeft`. (You may not receive full credit if you
do that.)

If a `MazeBug` can move left, it does so; otherwise it acts like a regular bug (with the
exception of the four directions restriction).

A `MazeBug` can move left whenever the adjacent location to the left of the bug is valid and does not hold a rock while the adjacent location diagonally to the left and back is either invalid or holds a rock. If, for example, the bug is facing east, the adjacent location to the north should be empty (or hold a `Flower`) and the adjacent location to the northwest should hold a rock (or be invalid). The picture below illustrates such a situation.

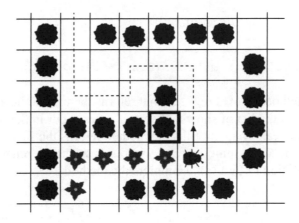

Write the entire `MazeBug` class.

For additional practice, allow a `MazeBug` to turn and move in all eight directions and "cut corners," but don't allow the bug to move diagonally between two adjacent rocks:

3.   In a survey, a small group of TV viewers were asked to name a few of their favorite TV shows. The results were compiled in one list of shows, in no particular order. In this question you will write three static methods of the class `Survey` that will help process the resulting list.

(a)   Write a method `matches` that returns the number of times a given title occurs in a list of strings. Complete the method `matches` below.

```
/** Returns the number strings in the list shows that are
 *  equal to title.
 */
public static int matches(List<String> shows, String title)
```

(b)   Write a method `leastPopular` that returns the title of the show that occurs least frequently in the list of shows. If several titles occur in the list the same number of times as the least frequent title, the method returns the first one of them. In writing `leastPopular`, assume `matches` works as specified, regardless of what you wrote in your solution to Part (a). Complete the method `leastPopular` below.

```
/** Returns the title that occurs in shows least frequently;
 *  if several titles occur in shows with the same minimum
 *  frequency, returns the first one of them
 *  Precondition: shows is not empty
 */
public static String leastPopular(List<String> shows)
```

(c)   Write a method `removeLeastPopular` that removes all occurrences of the least popular show from the list of shows, as determined by the `leastPopular` method from Part (b). Assume `leastPopular` works as specified, regardless of what you wrote in your solution to Part (b). Complete the method `removeLeastPopular` below.

```
/** Removes all occurrences of the least popular title
 *  from the list shows.
 *  Precondition: shows is not empty
 */
public static void removeLeastPopular(List<String> shows)
```

For additional practice, write the following method.

```
/** Returns the list of unique strings from shows,
 *  arranged in order of popularity, without duplicates,
 *  starting with the most popular (or one of the most
 *  popular if there are several shows of equal popularity).
 *  Postcondition: The list shows is empty
 */
public static ArrayList<String> popularShows
                              (List<String> shows)
```

4. An exam development committee is in charge of writing multiple-choice questions for a national exam. In order to judge the difficulty of proposed questions, the committee recruited a group of student volunteers and offered the questions to them. The results of this trial test are summarized in a two-dimensional `boolean` array `answered`: `answered[s][k]` is `true` if student number `s` answered correctly the *k*-th question. The difficulty of a question is measured on the scale from 0 to 100 and computed as percent of students who chose the <u>wrong</u> answer to that question, rounded to the nearest integer. For example, if 30 students out of 200 answered a certain question incorrectly, the difficulty level of that question is 15. For convenience, questions are identified by their nicknames.

A question is represented as an object of the class `ExamQuestion`. This class has a constructor

```
public ExamQuestion(String nickname, int difficulty) {...}
```

`ExamQuestion` also has a method

```
public int compareTo(ExamQuestion other) {...}
```

that compares questions based on their difficulty. The method returns a positive integer if this question is "more difficult" than `other`, a negative integer if this question is less difficult than `other`, and 0 if they are of the same difficulty.

For additional practice, write the `ExamQuestion` class. Make sure it implements `Comparable<ExamQuestion>` interface and has a `toString` method.

The results of the trial test are processed with the help of the class `ExamAnalysis`. A partial definition of this class is shown below. You will write three methods of this class.

```
public class ExamAnalysis
{
  /** Nicknames of the questions */
  private String[] nicknames;

  /** Holds the results of the trial test:
   *  answered[s][k] is true if student number s answered the
   *  k-th question correctly.  (Student and question numbers
   *  start from 0.)
   */
  private boolean[][] answered;

  /** Returns the percent of students who DID NOT answer the
   *  k-th question correctly, rounded to the nearest integer
   *  @param k question number
   *  Precondition: 0 <= k < the number of columns in answered
   */
  public int getDifficulty(int k)
  { /* to be implemented in part (a) */ }

  /** Generates and returns an array of ExamQuestion objects from
   *  nicknames and corresponding difficulty values.
   *  Precondition: array answered has been initialized;
   *                nicknames.length is equal to the number of
   *                of columns in answered
   */
  public ExamQuestion[] makeQuestionsList()
  { /* to be implemented in part (b) */ }

  /** Sorts the array questions in ascending order of
   *  difficulty using Selection Sort
   */
  public static void sort(ExamQuestion[] questions)
  { /* to be implemented in part (c) */ }
}
```

(a) Write the method `getDifficulty` of the `ExamAnalysis` class. This method
assumes that the `boolean` array `answered` holds the trial test results. It computes
the difficulty of the *k*-th question as the percentage of students who made a mistake
in that question. The percent is rounded to the nearest integer. Complete the
method `getDifficulty` below.

```
/** Returns the percent of students who DID NOT answer the
 *  k-th question correctly, rounded to the nearest integer
 *  @param k question number
 *  Precondition: 0 <= k < the number of columns in answered
 */
public int getDifficulty(int k)
```

(b) Write the method `makeQuestionsList` of the `ExamAnalysis` class. This method
assumes that the array `nicknames` and the `boolean` array `answered` hold valid
data. The method creates and returns an array of `ExamQuestion` objects. The
returned array has the same length as `nicknames`. The *k*-th element in the returned
array has the nickname `nicknames[k]` and difficulty computed by the
`getDifficulty(k)` method. Complete the method `makeQuestionsList` below.

```
/** Generates and returns an array of ExamQuestion objects from
 *  nicknames and corresponding difficulty values.
 *  Precondition: array answered has been initialized;
 *                nicknames.length is equal to the number of
 *                of columns in answered
 */
public ExamQuestion[] makeQuestionsList()
```

(c) Write the static method `sort` of the `ExamAnalysis` class. This method sorts a
given array of `ExamQuestion` objects in order of increasing difficulty, using the
Selection Sort algorithm. Note that Java library sorting methods use more
sophisticated algorithms; do not use these methods. Your `sort` method must sort
the array "in place" — do not use any temporary arrays or lists. Complete the
method `sort` below.

```
/** Sorts the array questions in ascending order of
 *  difficulty using Selection Sort
 */
public static void sort(ExamQuestion[] questions)
```

Answers and Solutions

Exam #1 ~ Multiple Choice

1.	A	11.	E	21.	A	31.	A
2.	A	12.	A	22.	E	32.	D
3.	C	13.	A	23.	B	33.	B
4.	B	14.	D	24.	E	34.	B
5.	E	15.	A	25.	A	35.	C
6.	B	16.	D	26.	C	36.	E
7.	C	17.	E	27.	D	37.	B
8.	C	18.	C	28.	B	38.	B
9.	D	19.	D	29.	E	39.	B
10.	A	20.	D	30.	C	40.	E

Notes:

1. `17/5` gives 3; `3 % 3 = 0`; `85 % 3 = 1`.
2. Strings are immutable; a method cannot change a `String` object.
3. The elements in the 2 by 2 square in the middle are set to 1.
4. Can't convert a `String` into an `Integer` — not allowed in Java.
5. `1 < x/y < 2` and `4 < x*y < 5`; truncated to integers gives 1 + 4 = 5.
6. It is easier to negate each of the expressions (using De Morgan's Laws when necessary) and check whether the result is equivalent to "all three values are the same." In Choice B, `!(a != b || b != c)` is the same as `(a == b && b == c)`, which is `true` if and only if `a == b` and `b == c` and `a == c`.
7. `(m + n)/2` evaluates to 4.
8. Either way, `a > 10`. Try `a = 15` with `b = 10` or `b = 20`.
9. When the *k*-th element is removed from the list in the second `for` loop, the subsequent elements are shifted to the left, and their indices are decremented by one. As a result, this loop removes every other element, 1, 3, and 5 (with the original indices 0, 2, and 4). These values are added at the end of the list.
10. In I and II, `fun` returns `true` when `a >= b >= c`.
11. The code in Option I first sets all the elements to 1, then sets the elements on the diagonal to 0; the code in Option II first sets all the elements on the diagonal to 0, then all the elements not on the diagonal to 1; the code in Option III checks whether the element is on the diagonal or not and sets it accordingly. All three work.
12. Choice A is false: the main purpose of testing a program is to make sure it works as specified, not just that it doesn't crash.
13. Pat's design is inferior in every way. The statements in Options I and II are true for both designs. The statement in Option III is simply false.
14. Implementation 1 has two multiplications and one addition in each of the 6 iterations, 18 operations total. Implementation 2 has one addition and one multiplication in each of the 5 iterations, 10 operations total.

15. Every third element from 3 to 48 is set to 0 — 16 elements. Every fifth element from 5 to 50 is set to 0 — 10 elements. Total 10 + 16 = 26. But we counted the 15-th, the 30-th, and the 45-th elements twice. 26 − 3 = 23.

16. For each element `p[i]`, `countSomething` adds to the total the length of the cycle `p[p[p...[i]...]] = i`. This is 1 for 0 and 3 for each of the other three elements.

17. Options II and III are valid because `Salsa` IS-A `Dance` IS-A(n) `Object`, and `Swing` IS-A `Dance` IS-A(n) `Object`.

18. On each iteration through the `while` loop, the code takes the elements from 0 to `n-1` and repeats that segment of the array, adding 1 to each element. Thus {0, ...} becomes {0, 1, ...}, then {0, 1, ...} becomes {0, 1, 1, 2, ...}, then {0, 1, 1, 2, ...} becomes {0, 1, 1, 2, 1, 2, 2, 3}. Note that `nums[k]` is the number of binary digits equal to 1 in the binary representation of `k`. The sequence can grow in the same manner up to any power of 2. An interesting property of this sequence is that it is a "fractal" sequence: If you take every second element, starting from 0, you will get the same sequence!

19. Choices A and C won't work, because `x` is private in `Point`.

20. The code in Options II and III does the same thing. Option I doesn't work because `x` is private in `Point`.

21. The concept of "privacy" applies to the whole class, not a particular object, so Choice A works.

22. In Options I and III, we copy `words` into `temp`, then reconstitute `words` according to the values in `indices`. In Option II, we build `temp` according to the values in `indices`, then copy it back into `words`. All three options work.

23. The code first adds `"0"`, `"1"`, `"2"`, ..., `"9"` to `digits`, then replaces each of the 5 pairs of elements `"a"`, `"b"`, with `"a+b"`.

24. This is basically a Binary Search algorithm. We need 1 iteration for one element, 2 iterations for three elements, 3 iterations for seven elements, 4 iterations for 15 elements, 5 iterations for 31 elements. There is no "best" or "worst" case.

25. In the best case, all the values in the shorter array are smaller than the first value in the longer array. We need 10 comparisons to establish that. In the worst case, neither array "runs out of values", so we need one comparison for each element of the resulting array, except the last one.

26. `s1 = "BCD"`, so `printSomething(s1)` cannot print any A's. The only "A" is printed in the `println` statement for the original string. `printSomething(s)` prints 1 letter if `n` is 1, 1 + 2 + 1 = 4 letters if `n` is 2, 4 + 3 + 4 = 11 letters if `n` is 3, and 11 + 4 + 11 = 26 letters if `n` is 4.

27. The most significant (the leftmost) bit in the binary representation of an integer in Java is the sign. When we add 2 to `Integer.MAX_VALUE`, this bit gets set, so the result is interpreted as a negative number. In fact, $(2^{31} - 1) + 2 + (2^{31} - 1) = 2^{32}$, which is interpreted as 0, so `Integer.MAX_VALUE + 2 = - Integer.MAX_VALUE`.

28. In Choice B, the compiler would report an error.

29. `countSomething` returns the number of times the maximum value occurs in the array. If a new maximum is found, the count is reset to 1.

30. Choices A and E use non-existing methods. Choice D applies `equals` to `int`s, which is a syntax error. Choice B works only for an adjacent `loc2`. Choice C is correct — see the documentation for the `Location` class.

31. See `Bug`'s code.

32. Option I won't work because the `ZipBug` might turn several times in one call to `act`. Option II is a little fancy, but it works. So does Option III: `ZipBug`'s `move` won't be called if it can't move at least once.

33. In `Caterpillar` as a subclass of `Bug`, each of the two constructors takes a couple of lines, and the following `move` method will make it work:

```
public void move()
{
  ArrayList<Actor> actors = getGrid().getNeighbors(getLocation());
  for (Actor a : actors)
  {
    if (a instanceof Flower && !a.getLocation().
        getAdjacentLocation(getDirection()).equals(getLocation()))
      a.removeSelfFromGrid();
  }
  super.move();
}
```

34. `getMoveLocations` should return a list of locations that includes valid jump locations.

35. Choice A: `Animal` is not necessarily a `Mammal`; Choice B: `Mammal` must have a constructor that takes a `String` parameter; Choice D: No relation to the situation; Choice C works.

36. `yx` and `xy` refer <u>to the same array</u>, so after the assignment `yx[0] = xy[1]`, `yx[0]` and `xy[0]` are both set to `"Y"`.

37 When a class implements a method specified in an interface, the method's number, types, and order of parameters in the class and in the interface must match. Choice C: overloaded methods are allowed.

38. Note that `Game`'s `getPlayer(k)` returns `players.get(k-1)`. Choices C and D don't work because `players` is private in `Game`; Choice E doesn't work because `Game` has no method `getPlayers`.

39. Option I doesn't work because `Game` has no constructor that takes three parameters. Option II is fine. Option III doesn't work because `super(...)`, a call to a superclass's constructor, must be the first statement in the subclass's constructor.

40. In Version 1, `choose(4, 2)` calls `choose(4, 1)`, which in turn calls `choose(4, 0)` — three calls total. In Version 2, there is a branching progression of calls —

```
                                (4, 2)
                     /                        \
                    /                          \
              (3, 1)                            (3, 2)
             /      \                          /      \
        (2, 0)      (2, 1)                 (2, 1)      (2, 2)
        / \          / \                   / \          / \
  (1, -1) (1, 0)  (1, 0) (1, 1)      (1, 0) (1, 1)  (1, 1) (1, 2)
           / \      / \    / \         / \    / \      / \
     (0, -1) (0, 0) ..  .. ..  ..     ..  .. ..  ..    ..  ..
```

— 27 calls total.

Answers and Solutions

Exam #1 ~ Free Response

1. (a)
```
public static String replaceOne(String text, int i,
                                    int n, String sub)
{
  return text.substring(0, i) + sub +
                    text.substring(i + n);
}
```

(b)
```
public static String replaceAll(String text,
                            String what, String sub)
{
  savedText.add(text);

  int i = 0, n = what.length();
  while (i >= 0)
  {
    i = text.indexOf(what);
    if (i >= 0)
      text = replaceOne(text, i, n, sub);
  }
  return text;
}

public static String undoReplaceAll()
{
  if (savedText.size() == 0)
    return null;
  return savedText.remove(savedText.size() - 1); [1]
}
```

Notes:

1. `savedText` is used in the "LIFO" (Last-In-First-Out) manner. Such data structure is called a *stack*.

2.   (a)

```
public class BagelsOrderItem implements OrderItem
{
  private double price;
  private int quantity;

  public BagelsOrderItem(double pr, int qty)
  {
    price = pr;
    quantity = qty;
  }

  public int getQuantity()
  {
    return quantity;
  }

  public double getPrice()
  {
    return price;
  }

  public double getCost()
  {
    return getPrice() * getQuantity();
  }
}
```

(b)

```
public class BakersDozen extends BagelsOrderItem
{
  public BakersDozen(double price)
  {
    super(price, 13);
  }

  public double getCost()
  {
    return super.getCost() - getPrice();
  }
}
```

3. (a)
```
public void destroy()
{
  Grid<Actor> gr = getGrid();
  ArrayList<Location> locs = gr.getOccupiedLocations();

  for (Location loc : locs)
  {
    Actor a = gr.get(loc);
    if (a.getLocation().getCol() == getLocation().getCol() &&
        a.getLocation().getRow() > getLocation().getRow())
      a.removeSelfFromGrid();
  }
}
```

(b)
```
public void move()
{
  int dir;
  if (Math.random() < 0.5)
    dir = Location.EAST;
  else
    dir = Location.WEST;
  Location next = getLocation().getAdjacentLocation(dir);
  if (getGrid().isValid(next))
    moveTo(next);
  else
    removeSelfFromGrid();
}
```

4. (a)

```
public boolean canSwitchLane(int lane, int dir, int x)
{
  int lanes = hwy.length;

  int newLane = lane + dir;
  if (newLane < 0 || newLane >= lanes)
    return false;

  while (newLane >= 0 && newLane < lanes)
  {
    if (hwy[newLane][x] != 0)
      return false;
    newLane += dir;
  }
  return true;
}
```

(b)

```
public void moveAllForward()
{
  int lanes = hwy.length;
  int xMax = hwy[0].length - 1;
  for (int lane = 0; lane < lanes; lane++)
  {
    int saved = hwy[lane][xMax];

    for (int x = xMax; x > 0; x--)
      hwy[lane][x] = hwy[lane][x-1];

    hwy[lane][0] = saved;
  }
}
```

Answers and Solutions

Exam #2 ~ Multiple Choice

1.	B	11.	D	21.	C	31.	D
2.	D	12.	D	22.	B	32.	A
3.	E	13.	A	23.	D	33.	E
4.	D	14.	D	24.	B	34.	D
5.	E	15.	C	25.	C	35.	C
6.	A	16.	C	26.	C	36.	D
7.	E	17.	B	27.	C	37.	B
8.	E	18.	D	28.	E	38.	E
9.	B	19.	A	29.	E	39.	E
10.	A	20.	D	30.	A	40.	B

Notes:

1. The last iteration starts with `num = 1`.
2. `12%7` gives 5; `(double)(12/5)` results in 2.0; `n` remains unchanged because it is passed to `goFigure` by value.
3. Applying one of De Morgan's Laws, we can see that the expressions in Options I and II are identical. The expression in Option III is `true` when x ≠ y, the same as I and II.
4. `Integer.MIN_VALUE` is -2^{31}; $2^{30} < \left| -2^{31} + 1 \right| < 2 \cdot 2^{30} \Rightarrow 1 < \dfrac{\left| -2^{31} + 1 \right|}{2^{30}} < 2$

   $\Rightarrow -2^{31} + 1$, a negative number, when divided by 2^{30} is truncated to -1.
5. Use De Morgan's Laws: `!(x > y && x % y != 0)` is the same as `(x <= y || x % y == 0)`.
6. `printVals(names, 0)` and `printVals(names, 1)` do nothing.
   `printVals(names, 2)` prints `"Ann"`.
   `printVals(names, 3)` prints `"Ann"`, then `"Cal"`.
   `printVals(names, 4)` prints `"Ann"`, then `"Cal"`, then `"Amy"`, then `"Ann"`.
7. `printVals(names, 2)` results in 1 + 1 + 1 = 3 calls.
   `printVals(names, 3)` results in 1 + 3 + 1 = 5 calls.
   `printVals(names, 4)` results in 1 + 5 + 3 = 9 calls.
8. Inheritance hierarchies are at the heart of OOP for the reasons listed in the question.
9. Selection Sort finds the largest element among 2000, then among the remaining 1999, and so on.
10. It is usually impossible to test the program with all possible values of input data.
11. Option I doesn't work, because `doNothing` returns a `List`, not an `ArrayList`, and you can't assign a `List` object to an `ArrayList` variable.
12. `product` returns 6·4·2.
13. When an `int` gets out of range, it might be interpreted as negative because the sign bit gets set to 1.

14. The last element remains unchanged.

15. The first version quits as soon as the target value is found; the second version always scans the whole array.

16. Options I and II do not work, because `buddies` is private in `BuddyList`.

17. A call to `Counter`'s `setCount` method has no effect, because `setCount` introduces and sets a local variable `count`, as opposed to modifying the field `count`. The code prints 1. The correct method would be

```
public void setCount(int c) { count = c; }  // Line 3
```

18. The "for each" loops in Choices A and B are wrong because `m` is not a one-dimensional array. Choice C is wrong because the outer loop has to iterate over the first index (the Java convention is that the first index is row, the second is column). Choice E is wrong because the number of rows is `m.length` and the number of columns is `m[0].length`.

19. `n` remains unchanged, because it is passed to `change` by value.

20. `list.remove(i)` shifts the subsequent elements to the left by one, so only every other element is removed.

21. `mat[0][0]` remains equal to 2, `mat[1][1]` becomes $2*2 + 1 = 5$; `mat[2][2]` becomes $2*5+2 = 12$.

22. The statement `s = t;` has no effect in this code. The last element of `list` is set in turn to the first element, then the second element, and then to its own value, so it remains equal to the second element.

23. Option I does not work, because in the second "for each" loop, `x` acts like a local variable; you cannot replace the value of an array element using a "for each" loop.

24. With 160,000 numbers, it will take 18 ms to sort each half. Then merging together the two sorted halves with 80,000 numbers in each of them takes $40-2*18 = 4$ ms. For 320,000 elements, it will take 2*40 ms to sort each half and 2*4 (twice as long) to merge the sorted halves with 160,000 numbers in each, for the total of $2*40+8 = 88$ ms.

25. For example, a subclass of `Athlete` may be a wrapper class for `Athlete`, which has an embedded `Athlete` object and channels all method calls to it, while `numMedals` remains 0 (this design pattern is called "Decorator").

26. If a bug cannot move, it turns to the right by 45 degrees.

27. In Option III, the bug leaves a `Flower` behind, while it is supposed to leave behind an empty cell.

28. See the documentation for the `Grid` interface.

29. You cannot instantiate (create) an object of an abstract class.

30. The change does not affect other methods.

31. Using De Morgan's Laws, negate the condition in the `while` loop.

32. Binary Search will look at `arr[63]`, `arr[31]`, `arr[47]`, and `arr[39]`.

33. In Choice C, a method cannot change `START_POS`, because it is declared `final`.

34. `product = (3%2) * (7%4) * (5%2) = 1 * 3 * 1`.

35. Can't make a `Party` object an element of `BirthdayParty[]` array: not every party is a birthday party.

36. `theGuests` is private in `Party`.

37. The method `getOccasion` must be defined, and it should return
```
"Birthday " + getName();
```

38. Actually, a "for each" loop is more efficient when the list happens to be a `LinkedList`.

39. `Math.random` returns a random `double` in the range $0 \le x < 1$.

40. Must provide the methods specified in the interface `Student` — the rest are optional.

Answers and Solutions

Exam #2 ~ Free Response

1. (a)

```
public Mancala(int n)
{
  board = new int[BOARD_SIZE];
  for (int k = 0; k < BOARD_SIZE; k++)
    board[k] = n;
  board[store1] = 0;
  board[store2] = 0;
}  1
```

(b)

```
public boolean move(int k)
{
  int myStore, opponentsStore;
  if (k < store1)
  {
    myStore = store1;
    opponentsStore = store2;
  }
  else
  {
    myStore = store2;
    opponentsStore = store1;
  }

  int seeds = board[k];
  board[k] = 0;
  while (seeds > 0)
  {
    k++;
    if (k >= BOARD_SIZE)
      k = 0;

    if (k != opponentsStore)
    {
      board[k]++;
      seeds--;
    }
  }

  return k == myStore;
}
```

Notes:

1. Or:

```
for (int k = 0; k < BOARD_SIZE; k++)
{
  if (k == store1 || k == store2)
    board[k] = 0;
  else
    board[k] = n;
}
```

Or, using the fact that array elements are initialized to zeroes by default:

```
for (int k = 0; k < BOARD_SIZE; k++)
{
  if (k != store1 && k != store2)
    board[k] = n;
}
```

2.

```
public class Dahlia extends Flower
{
  private Color nativeColor;
  private int age;

  public Dahlia()
  {
    nativeColor = getColor();  ¹
    age = 0;
  }

  public Dahlia(Color color)
  {
    super(color);
    nativeColor = color;
    age = 0;
  }

  public void act()
  {
    age++;
    if (age <= 5)
      super.act();
    else
    {
      Grid<Actor> gr = getGrid();
      ArrayList<Location> locs =
              gr.getValidAdjacentLocations(getLocation());

      for (int k = 1; k <= 3; k++)
      {
        int r = (int)(Math.random() * locs.size());
        Location loc = locs.get(r);
        if (gr.get(loc) == null)
        {
          DahliaSeed seed = new DahliaSeed(nativeColor);
          seed.putSelfInGrid(gr, loc);
        }
      }

      removeSelfFromGrid();
    }
  }
}
```

Notes:

1. Must save the initial color, because a Dahlia darkens with age, like a regular Flower.

3.   (a)

```
public double likenessScore(Movie other)
{
  int count = 0;

  for (int k = 0; k < features.length(); k += 3)
    if (features.substring(k, k+3).equals
                      (other.features.substring(k, k+3)))
      count++;

  return (double)count / (features.length() / 3);
}
```

(b)

```
public static void removeOutliers(List<Movie> movies)
{
  double[] coefficients = getFitCoefficients(movies);

  double sum = 0.0;
  for (double c : coefficients)
    sum += c;

  double threshold = (sum / coefficients.length) / 2;

  for (int k = coefficients.length - 1; k >= 0; k--) [1]
    if (coefficients[k] < threshold)
      movies.remove(k);
}
```

Notes:

1.   Traverse in reverse to avoid problems with shifting indices when an element is removed. Or:

```
int k = 0;
for (int c = 0; c < coefficients.length; c++)
  if (coefficients[c] < threshold)
    movies.remove(k);
  else
    k++;
```

4. (a)
```
public int findRemotestCity()
{
  int iMax = -1;
  int maxSum = 0;
  for (int i = 0; i < distances.length; i++)
  {
    int sum = 0;
    for (int j = 0; j < distances.length; j++)
      sum += distances[i][j];
    if (sum > maxSum)
    {
      iMax = i;
      maxSum = sum;
    }
  }
  return iMax;
}
```

(b)
```
public List<String> makeItinerary()
{
  List<String> itinerary = new ArrayList<String>();
  boolean[] visited = new boolean[cityNames.size()];

  for (int i = 0; i < cityNames.size(); i++)
    visited[i] = false;  [1]

  int i = findRemotestCity();
  itinerary.add(cityNames.get(i));
  visited[i] = true;

  for (int count = 2; count <= cityNames.size(); count++)
  {
    i = findNearestCity(i, visited);
    itinerary.add(cityNames.get(i));
    visited[i] = true;
  }

  return itinerary;
}
```

Notes:

1. This `for` loop is optional: all elements of a `boolean` array are initialized to `false` by default.

Answers and Solutions

Exam #3 ~ Multiple Choice

1.	A	11.	D	21.	D	31.	E
2.	D	12.	B	22.	C	32.	C
3.	A	13.	E	23.	E	33.	E
4.	A	14.	A	24.	C	34.	D
5.	A	15.	E	25.	B	35.	D
6.	D	16.	D	26.	D	36.	E
7.	C	17.	D	27.	C	37.	B
8.	C	18.	B	28.	E	38.	E
9.	B	19.	B	29.	B	39.	A
10.	A	20.	B	30.	E	40.	B

Notes:

1. In Option II, `(double)(q / 2)` evaluates to 1.0; in Option III, `(double)(p * q / 2)` evaluates to 7.0.
2. `mystery(0, 16)` prints 0, then calls `mystery(5, 15)`; that call prints 5, then calls `mystery(10, 14)`; that call prints 10, then calls `mystery(15, 13)`; that call prints 15 and quits.
3. `b = fun2(a, b)` sets `b` to 4, `a` remains 3 (because `a` and `b` are passed to `fun2` by value); then `a = fun2(b, a)` sets `a` to –1, `b` remains 4.
4. This is equivalent to `(a && !b) || (!a && b)`.
5. Two subclasses of *A* normally cannot be cast one into another — they represent different "animals."
6. In Option I, the loops go "too far," flipping `m[r][c]` and `m[c][r]` twice.
7. The code adds 2, 4, 8, 16, and 32 to the elements of `v`, respectively. `v[4]`, the last element, becomes 33.
8. Private methods are identified by the keyword `private`.
9. In this code segment, we add to `lst` the next number that is not evenly divisible by any of the numbers already in the list. This results in the list of the first five primes.
10. Options II and III are not convincing, because `Fun` can have a `playWith` method but not state that it `implements Game`.
11. Each of the 3 elements equals only to itself.
12. The smallest possible value of `x` is 0 when `Math.random()` returns a number close to 0 (any number < 1/16). The largest possible value of `x` is 2 when `Math.random()` returns a number close enough to 1 (any number ≥ 9/16).
13. `Integer.MAX_VALUE` is determined by the size of `int`, which is four bytes.
14. Before the loop, `words` contains `["ban", "an", "a"]`; the `for` loop concatenates all the elements together to make `"banana"`. The first occurrence of `"an"` in `"banana"` is at index 1.

15. `smile(4)` prints `"smile!"` 4 times, then calls `smile(3)`, and so on. The total number of times `"smile!"` will be printed is $4 + 3 + 2 + 1 = 10$.

16. `smile` is called in succession with parameters 4, 3, 2, 1, and 0.

17. If `targetValue` is not in `a`, the `while` loop eventually causes `ArrayIndexOutOfBoundsException`.

18. To compare two strings you must use `compareTo`, which returns an `int`.

19. `r` does not have to be a `double` (`x/y` results in an `int` anyway); `r` can be either a static variable or an instance variable in `ClassX`.

20. A cast to `int` truncates the `double` value 31415.9 toward zero.

21. All three print 13579. In Option III, the loop is entered with i = 0, 2, 4, 6, and 8.

22. Take, for instance, $a = 2$, $b = 1$, $c = 2$. The code in Option III gives 0 instead of 1.

23. The concept of privacy applies to the class as a whole. Any method of a class has access to private fields of all objects of that class.

24. In Option III, you cannot instantiate an interface.

25. Array indices start from 0; need `arr[i]` to be both positive and odd.

26. `isGood(s)` returns `true` if `s` has no duplicate (not necessarily consecutive) characters.

27.
```
public boolean canMove()
{
    ...
    Actor neighbor = gr.get(next);
    return (neighbor == null) || (neighbor instanceof Flower);
    // ok to move into empty location or onto flower
    // not ok to move onto any other actor
}
```

28. See `Bug`'s code for an example.

29. `Rock` will inherit the empty `act` method from `Actor`.

30. Options II and III work, because `Bug` extends `Actor`. In addition, in Option II, `Bug` has a constructor that takes a parameter of the type `Color`.

31. If, for example, both `getActors` and `processActors` must be empty methods, in the new design you need to override only `processActors`.

32. The `boolean` variable `flag` "accumulates" the `v[i] == v[i+1]` conditions.

33. The sequence of calls: `B`'s constructor ==> `A`'s constructor ==> `B`'s `methodOne` (not `A`'s `methodOne`, due to polymorphism) ==> print `"B"` in `B`'s `methodOne` ==> print `"*"`, finishing `B`'s constructor.

34. `LibraryBook` does not override `Object`'s `toString` method, so Option I is out. Options II and III do the same thing.

35. Choice A doesn't work, because `numCopies` and `info` are private in `LibraryBook`.

36. It is your choice to use `getNumCopies` / `setNumCopies` methods or to manipulate the `numCopies` variable directly within the `LibraryBook` class.

37. `list.remove(i)` shifts to the left all the subsequent elements. Therefore, it is a mistake to increment `i` when an element is removed: the subsequent element won't be examined.

38. The code goes into an infinite loop when `first` is 3 and `last` is 4.

39. `SortX` implements Selection Sort. First `"Boris"` is swapped with `"Evan"`, then `"Boris"` is swapped with `"Dan"`.

40. $4 + 3 + 2 + 1 = 10$

Answers and Solutions

Exam #3 ~ Free Response

1. (a)
```java
public static boolean isRpeak(double[] v, int r)
{
  return v[r] > 1.0 &&
          v[r] == max(v, r - DELTA, r + DELTA) &&
          min(v, r - DELTA, r) < 0 &&
          min(v, r, r + DELTA) < 0;
}
```

(b)
```java
public static ArrayList<Integer> allRpeaks(double[] v)
{
  ArrayList<Integer> rPeaks = new ArrayList<Integer>();

  int r = DELTA;
  while (r < v.length - DELTA)
  {
    if (isRpeak(v, r))
    {
      rPeaks.add(new Integer(r));
      r += DELTA;
    }
    else
      r++;
  }
  return rPeaks;
}
```

(c)
```java
public static int heartRate(List<Integer> rPeaks)
{
  int r0 = rPeaks.get(0).intValue();
  int r1 = rPeaks.get(rPeaks.size() - 1).intValue();
  double rr = (double)(r1 - r0) / (rPeaks.size() - 1);
  return (int)(60 * SAMPLING_RATE / rr + 0.5);
}
```

2.   (a)

```
public class Tag implements Embedded
{
  private int startIndex;
  private int endIndex;
  private String command;

  public Tag(int i, int j, String cmd)
  {
    startIndex = i;
    endIndex = j;
    command = cmd;
  }

  public int getStartIndex()
  {
    return startIndex;
  }

  public int getEndIndex()
  {
    return endIndex;
  }

  public String getCommand()
  {
    return command;
  }
}
```

(b)

```
public static Tag findFirstTag(String text)
{
  int i1 = text.indexOf("<");
  if (i1 == - 1)
    return null;

  int i2 = text.indexOf(">");
  return new Tag(i1, i2, text.substring(i1+1, i2));
}
```

3. (a)
```java
public void processActors(ArrayList<Actor> actors)
{
  for (Actor a : actors)
  {
    if (a instanceof Clover)
    {
      Clover clover = (Clover)a;
      if (!clover.hasBeenPollinated())
        clover.pollinate();
    }
  }
}
```

(b)
```java
public Location selectMoveLocation(ArrayList<Location> locs)
{
  Location next = getLocation();
  Location cloverLoc = findNearestClover(next);
  if (cloverLoc == null)
    return next;
  int minDistance = distance(next, cloverLoc);
  for (Location loc : locs)
  {
    int d = distance(loc, findNearestClover(loc));
    if (d < minDistance)
    {
      minDistance = d;
      next = loc;
    }
  }
  return next;
}
```

(c)
```java
public void makeMove(Location loc)
{
  setDirection(getLocation().getDirectionToward(loc));
  super.makeMove(loc);
}
```

4. (a)

```
private boolean isEmptyRegion(int top, int bottom,
                                          int left, int right)
{
   for (int r = top; r <= bottom; r++)
     for (int c = left; c <= right; c++)
       if (room[r][c] != 0)
         return false;

   return true;
}
```

(b)

```
public boolean fits(int width, int height, Location ulCorner)
{
   int top = ulCorner.getRow();
   int bottom = top + height - 1;
   int left = ulCorner.getCol();
   int right = left + width - 1;

   if (top < 0)
     return false;
   else if (top > 0)
     top--;

   if (bottom >= ROWS)
     return false;
   else if (bottom < ROWS - 1)
     bottom++;

   if (left < 0)
     return false;
   else if (left > 0)
     left--;

   if (right >= COLS)
     return false;
   else if (right < COLS - 1)
     right++;

   return isEmptyRegion(top, bottom, left, right);
}
```

(c)

```
public ArrayList<Location> whereFits(int width, int height)
{
  ArrayList<Location> locs = new ArrayList<Location>();

  for (int r = 0; r < ROWS; r++) ¹
  {
    for (int c = 0; c < COLS; c++)
    {
      Location loc = new Location(r, c);
      if (fits(width, height, loc))
        locs.add(loc);
    }
  }
  return locs;
}
```

Notes:

1.   It is easier here to scan all rows and columns — the `fits` method will filter out locations where the width-height rectangle does not fit within the room.

Answers and Solutions

Exam #4 ~ Multiple Choice

1. C	11. D	21. E	31. D
2. A	12. C	22. A	32. A
3. B	13. B	23. E	33. A
4. E	14. C	24. D	34. E
5. C	15. B	25. B	35. B
6. D	16. A	26. B	36. D
7. E	17. A	27. D	37. C
8. C	18. D	28. B	38. C
9. A	19. D	29. A	39. E
10. E	20. D	30. C	40. E

Notes:

1. Use De Morgan's Laws.
2. `% 100` leaves the last 2 digits.
3. $0 - 1 + 2 - 3 + 4 - \ldots + 10 = 0 + (-1 + 2) + (-3 + 4) + \ldots (-9 + 10) = 5$
4. `count` is not incremented.
5. `Integer.MIN_VALUE` is a negative number with a large absolute value.
6. In Option 1, the expression compares the addresses of `str1` and `str2`.
7. `4/3` yields 1.
8. n remains positive and eventually is reduced either to 0 or to 1.
9. First of all, a and b are passed to `swap` by value, so `swap` cannot change their values. This rules out Choices D and E. Inside `swap`, a and b act as local variables. The assignment `b = a` makes them equal, so `swap` returns 0.
10. The correct signature for `equals` is in Choices D and E, but in D a cast of `other` into a `Rectangle` is missing.
11. This is pretty standard way to reverse an array.
12. `filter` makes a new string from `str` with all the occurrences of `pattern` in `str` removed.
13. In Choice B, after the first comparison with `"D"` in the middle, `findLocation` will continue searching in the left half of the array.
14. `abc1` is first set to `"AAABBBCC"`, then to `"AABBBCC"`; it is a substring of `abc`, starting at index 1.
15. The `while` loop finds the right spot to insert `current`; the `for` loop shifts the elements in a to the right to make room.
16. `a[1]` and `a[2]` have been inserted into the right places, so the first three elements in a must be now in ascending order.

17. ... and information hiding.

18. The three friends are created with the sum of their miles equal to 30000. The "for each" loop gives 1000 additional miles to each friend.

19. By default, an array is initialized with 0.0 values, so Option I doesn't work.

20. Choices A and B do not work, because `amps` is private in `Sample`.

21. `splat("**")` calls `splat("****")`, then prints `**`.
     `splat("****")` calls `splat("********")`, then prints `****`.
     `splat("********")` prints `********`.

22. `numbers` holds two elements: two copies of an `Integer` with value 1. `names` holds `["Cathy", "Ben", "Anya"]`. Then the element at index 1 is deleted twice from `names`.

23. Each of the two addends can have a value 0 or 1, independently. Their sum can have values 0, 1, or 2 (actually, 1 will be twice as likely as 0 or 2).

24. `Jet` inherits `addFuel` from `Airplane`. `plane` is created with fuel 4, `jet` is created with fuel 8.

25. `BoxBug` has only one constructor and it takes an `int` parameter.

26. You cannot override the `turn` method in `Bug` (without also changing `act`), because `turn` is called when a bug cannot move.

27. `Actor` doesn't have a method `setGrid`.

28. The `for` loop is set up correctly in Choices A, B, and D. The code in Choice A fails to place the new object `i` into the grid; the code in Choice C calls a non-existent `Integer`'s method `setValue` (`Integer`s are immutable objects).

29. See `Critter`'s code.

30. Replacing `Cake` with `Priced` is neither encapsulation nor information hiding.

31. Option I is already guaranteed — no change is necessary for that.

32. `Track` does not have a no-args constructor.

33. `duration` is private in `Track`, so Choices B and D are wrong.

34. `tracks` holds 13 copies of the same track of duration 200.

35. Option I fails to create `ArrayList tracks`. Option III attempts to set a non-existing element, which would cause `IndexOutOfBoundsException`.

36. Option I won't work: in it `swap` receives and swaps <u>copies</u> of references to the objects. An array is passed to a method as a reference to the original array, so both Option II and Option III will work.

37. This is a typical example of polymorphism.

38. Suppose `somethingIsFalse` returns `true`. Then the `else` clause is executed in the code segment and it returns `true`, and so does the statement in Choice C.

39. `msg[0]` has not been initialized (`null`), so you can't call its methods.

40. A standard array has a fixed size.

Answers and Solutions

Exam #4 ~ Free Response

1. (a)
```java
public int getAwardLevel()
{
  int count = 0, sum = 0;

  for (Exam e : exams)
  {
    int grade = e.getGrade();
    if (grade >= 3)
      count++;
    sum += grade;
  }
  double avg = (double)sum / exams.size();

  int award;
  if (count >= 5 && avg >= 3.25)
    award = 3;
  else if (count >= 4 && avg >= 3.25)
    award = 2;
  else if (count >= 3)
    award = 1;
  else
    award = 0;

  return award;
}
```

(b)

```
public static double[] getStats(List<APStudent> list)
{
  int[] counts = new int[4];

  for (APStudent s : list)
  {
    int award = s.getAwardLevel();
    counts[award]++;
  }

  double[] percent = new double[4];

  for (int award = 0; award <= 3; award++)
    percent[award] = 100.0 *
            (double)counts[award] / list.size();  [1]

  return percent;
}
```

Notes:

1. The cast to `double` is optional here, because 100.0 is a `double`.

2. (a)

```
public void reserve(int k, int timeSlot)
{
  String s = schedules.get(k);
  schedules.set(k, s.substring(0, timeSlot) + "xxx" +
                s.substring(timeSlot + 3));  1
}
```

(b)

```
public int occupiedSlots(int k)
{
  String s = schedules.get(k);
  int count = 0;

  for (int t = 0; t < s.length(); t++)
    if (s.substring(t, t+1).equals("x"))
      count++;

  return count;
}
```

(c)

```
public int findTable(int timeSlot)
{
  int bestTable = 0;
  int mostOccupiedSlots = -1;

  for (int k = 1; k < schedules.size(); k++)  2
  {
    String s = schedules.get(k);
    if (s.substring(timeSlot, timeSlot + 3).equals("..."))
    {
      int x = occupiedSlots(k);
      if (x > mostOccupiedSlots)
      {
        bestTable = k;
        mostOccupiedSlots = x;
      }
    }
  }
  return bestTable;
}
```

Notes:

1. Not

```
s = s.substring(0, timeSlot) + "xxx" +
            s.substring(timeSlot + 3);
```

2. `schedules` at index 0 is `null`, not used.

3.   (a)

```
private boolean amDone()
{
  if (actorUnder instanceof Seed || haveSeed)
    return false;

  Grid<Actor> gr = getGrid();
  ArrayList<Location> locs = gr.getOccupiedLocations();
  for (Location loc : locs)
  {
    if (loc.getRow() > 0 && gr.get(loc) instanceof Seed)
      return false;
  }
  return true;
}
```

(b)

```
public void makeMove(Location next)
{
  if (next == null)
    removeSelfFromGrid();

  Grid<Actor> gr = getGrid();
  Location loc = getLocation();

  if (!haveSeed && loc.getRow() > 0 &&
                   actorUnder instanceof Seed)
  {
    haveSeed = true;
    setColor(Color.RED);
    actorUnder = null;
  }

  if (haveSeed && loc.getRow() == 0 && actorUnder == null)
  {
    haveSeed = false;
    setColor(Color.BLACK);
    actorUnder = new Seed();
  }

  Actor temp = gr.get(next);
  moveTo(next);
  if (actorUnder != null)
    actorUnder.putSelfInGrid(gr, loc);
  actorUnder = temp;

  movesCount++;
}
```

4. (a)
```
public int distance(Student other)
{
  if (getStreet().equals(other.getStreet()))
    return Math.abs(getNumber() - other.getNumber());
  else
    return 99999;
}
```

(b)
```
public class SchoolBus extends ArrayList<Student>
{
  private int numSeats;

  public SchoolBus(int seats)
  {
    numSeats = seats;
  }

  public boolean isFull()
  {
    return size() == numSeats;
  }
}
```

(c)
```
    public boolean enroll(Student student)
    {
      int minDistance = 99999;
      SchoolBus bestBus = null;

      for (SchoolBus bus : buses)
      {
        if (!bus.isFull())
        {
          for (int k = 0; k < bus.size(); k++)
          {
            int d = student.distance(bus.get(k));
            if (d < minDistance)
            {
              minDistance = d;
              bestBus = bus;
            }
          }
        }
      }

      if (bestBus != null)
      {
        bestBus.add(student);  [1]
        return true;
      }
      else
        return false;
    }
```

Notes:

1. The add method is inherited from ArrayList<Student>.

Answers and Solutions

Exam #5 ~ Multiple Choice

1. E	11. E	21. B	31. E
2. A	12. D	22. E	32. B
3. D	13. B	23. C	33. A
4. A	14. C	24. D	34. A
5. E	15. D	25. C	35. D
6. C	16. A	26. B	36. A
7. A	17. E	27. E	37. D
8. B	18. E	28. D	38. E
9. B	19. E	29. C	39. E
10. B	20. C	30. A	40. B

Notes:

1. When one of the operands in the + operator is a string, the other is converted into a string, and the two strings are concatenated.
2. `url.indexOf(...)` sets `pos` to 0; `url.substring(0,0)` returns an empty string.
3. `arr` is passed as a reference to the original array, `len` is passed by value.
4. `arr[0]` is never changed, and, on the last iteration, `arr[7]` is assigned the value of `arr[5]`, which is 6.
5. `Integer.MAX_VALUE` is $2^{31} - 1$, an odd number. `k` is incremented by 4, never "hits" `Integer.MAX_VALUE`. When `k` "goes above" `Integer.MAX_VALUE`, its sign bit gets set to 1, so `k` becomes negative. The process continues indefinitely.
6. `findMax` first counts the number of times each brightness value occurs in `image`, then finds the largest count.
7. `encrypt("SEC")` returns `"CES"`; `encrypt("RET")` returns `"TER"`.
8. At the end of an iteration, `i` is 3, then 4, then 5; `k` changes from 0 to 3 to 7 to 12.
9. "`return mid;`" must remain unchanged for the method to work when the `searchVal` is in `list`. Try a list of size 1 to see where to insert `searchVal`: at the beginning, both `first` and `last` are 0; after the loop `mid` is undefined and `last` becomes -1 when `searchVal < list.get(0)`, so `last` cannot be used as the insert position.
10. "`&& z`" in Choice B gives it away.
11. There are no tricks in this question: Options I, II, and III are all fine.
12. `n /= 10` is the correct choice for < *statement 2* > (to eliminate the rightmost digit). This leaves only Choices A and D. If *n* = 0, the return should be 1 only when *d* = 0, so Choice A is wrong.
13. `[] => [1] => [1, 2] => [1, 1, 2] => [1, 1, 2, 2] => [1, 1, 2, 3, 2]`.
14. The nested `for` loops correctly traverse the whole array and fill all its elements in a diagonal pattern, starting with 1 in the upper left corner.
15. Option I has nothing to do with information hiding (it is inheritance).

16. `examine` returns `true` even when all the letters in the array are different, because in the inner `for` loop, each letter is also compared to itself.

17. After the first iteration through the outer "for each" loop, with `f = 2`, the `products` list will hold `[1, 2]`. After the second iteration, with `f = 3`, the `products` list will hold `[1, 2, 3, 6]`. After the third iteration, with `f = 5`, the `products` list will hold `[1, 2, 3, 6, 5, 10, 15, 30]`.

18. `list` is an array; `getExams` returns an `ArrayList<APTestResult>`, `getExams().get(2)` returns an `APTestResult`.

19. Option I doesn't work, because `3/2` evaluates to 1.

20. 4 times for each pair plus 2 times for each quadruplet plus 1 time at the top level.

21. 40 ms + 40 ms to sort both halves + 0.01 * 2000 = 20 ms to merge them.

22. Simplify using De Morgan's Laws and notice short-circuit evaluation.

23. Option II does not necessarily work: consider {2, 3, 4, 0, 1, 5, 6, 7, 8} and `target = 3`.

24. Since `House` doesn't have a no-args constructor, `super(someInt)` must be the first statement in its subclass's constructor.

25. Superclass's `compareToOther` method will be called, which returns the difference in sizes, `2000 - 1800 = 200`.

26. Can't assign a `House` to a `HouseForSale` (because not every house is for sale).

27. `getSize` is inherited from `House`.

28. `if (canMove()) move(); else turn();`

29. When a `SpinningBug` cannot move, `super.act()` calls `turn`, then `act()` calls `turn` for the second time. Both times `SpinningBug`'s `turn` is called, due to polymorphism. The two 90-degree turns produce a 180-degree turn.

30. `ChameleonCritter`'s implicit default no-args constructor calls `Critter`'s default no-args constructor, which in turn calls `Actor`'s no-args constructor.

31. Recall that a `ChameleonCritter` turns in the direction of the move, so if you derive `RockChameleonCritter` from `Critter` (Option I), you need to override the `makeMove` method. In Option II, you can consider only rocks in `processActors`. In Option III, you can select only rocks in `getActors`.

32. Inheritance and polymorphism are not the same thing.

33. The code segments in Options II and III essentially fail the same way: in both of them `"*"` is appended to a local variable, not an element of `letters`.

34. In Option I, you cannot access an instance variable `score` from a static method. You are allowed, of course, to access static variables in constructors and instance methods.

35. You might notice that `guess` implements Euclid's Algorithm for finding the greatest common factor.

36. For Operations 2 and 3, finding a player in a sorted list (Design B) using a binary search takes less time than finding a player in Design 1.

37. The shuffling algorithm is similar to Selection Sort. In each iteration in the `while` loop, a random card among the first `n` is selected and swapped places with the n-th card.

38. `ArrayList<Double>` implements the `List<Double>` interface, so `MyList1`, a subclass of `ArrayList<Double>`, also implements `List<Double>`.

39. It is important to test the basic operation but also any special and boundary conditions.

40. After the first pass through the outer loop: `counts` holds 0, 2, 3, 4, 5, 1; 1 swap.
After the second pass through the outer loop: `counts` holds 0, 1, 3, 4, 5, 2; 1 swap.
After the third pass through the outer loop: `counts` holds 0, 1, 2, 4, 5, 3; 1 swap.
And so on.

Answers and Solutions

Exam #5 ~ Free Response

1. (a)
```
public boolean isEmpty()
{
  return numMessages == 0;
}
```

    (b)
```
public void add(Message msg)
{
  int pr = msg.getPriority();
  ArrayList<Message> lst = messageLists.get(pr);
  lst.add(msg);
  numMessages++;
}
```

    (c)
```
public Message remove()
{
  for (int pr = 9; pr >= 0; pr--)
  {
    ArrayList<Message> lst = messageLists.get(pr);

    if (!lst.isEmpty())
    {
      numMessages--;
      return lst.remove(0);
    }
  }

  return null;
}
```

2.

```
public class MazeBug extends Bug
{
  public void act()
  {
    if (canMoveLeft())
      moveLeft();
    else
      super.act();
  }

  public void turn()
  {
    super.turn();
    super.turn();
  }

  public void moveLeft()
  {
    setDirection(getDirection() + Location.LEFT);
    super.move();
  }

  public boolean canMoveLeft()
  {
    Grid<Actor> gr = getGrid();
    if (gr == null)
      return false;
    Location loc = getLocation();
    Location next = loc.getAdjacentLocation(
                getDirection() + Location.LEFT);
    Location leftnext = loc.getAdjacentLocation(
                getDirection() + 3 * Location.HALF_LEFT);
    return gr.isValid(next) &&
           !(gr.get(next) instanceof Rock) &&
           (!gr.isValid(leftnext) || gr.get(leftnext)
                                   instanceof Rock);
  }
}
```

3. (a)
```
public static int matches(List<String> shows, String title)
{
  int count = 0;

  for (String s : shows)
  {
    if (s.equals(title))
      count++;
  }
  return count;
}
```

(b)
```
public static String leastPopular(List<String> shows)
{
  int minCount = shows.size() + 1;
  String infreqTitle = null;

  for (String title : shows)
  {
    int count = matches(shows, title);
    if (count < minCount)
    {
      minCount = count;
      infreqTitle = title;
    }
  }
  return infreqTitle;
}
```

(c)
```
public static void removeLeastPopular(List<String> shows)
{
  String title = leastPopular(shows);
  int k = 0;
  while (k < shows.size())
  {
    if (title.equals(shows.get(k)))
      shows.remove(k);
    else
      k++;
  } 1
}
```

Notes:

1.   Or:

```
for (k = shows.size() - 1; k >= 0; k--)
  if (title.equals(shows.get(k)))
    shows.remove(k);
```

4. (a)
```
public int getDifficulty(int k)
{
  int count = 0;

  for (int s = 0; s < answered.length; s++)
    if (!answered[s][k])
      count++;

  return (int)(count * 100.0 / answered.length  + 0.5 );
}
```

(b)
```
public ExamQuestion[] makeQuestionsList()
{
  ExamQuestion[] questions =
            new ExamQuestion[nicknames.length];

  for (int k = 0; k < nicknames.length; k++)
    questions[k] = new ExamQuestion(nicknames[k],
                               getDifficulty(k));

  return questions;
}
```

(c)
```
public static void sort(ExamQuestion[] questions)
{
  int n = questions.length;
  while (n > 1)
  {
    int kMax = 0;

    for (int k = 1; k < n; k++)
      if (questions[k].compareTo(questions[kMax]) > 0)
        kMax = k;

    ExamQuestion temp = questions[n-1];
    questions[n-1] = questions[kMax];
    questions[kMax] = temp;
    n--;
  }
}
```

Index

Index to Free-Response Questions
in Practice Exams

Other Computer Science and Mathematics Titles from Skylight Publishing

Java Methods: Object-Oriented Programming and Data Structures, Second AP Edition ISBN 978-0-9824775-7-1

250 Multiple-Choice Computer Science Questions in Java, E-Edition Part 978-0-9727055-J-E

100 Multiple-Choice Questions in C++
ISBN 978-0-9654853-0-2

Mathematics for the Digital Age and Programming in Python, Second Edition ISBN 978-0-9824775-4-0

Be Prepared for the AP Calculus Exam, Second Edition
ISBN 978-0-9824775-5-7

800 Questions in Calculus with Solutions, E-Edition
Part 978-0-9727055-E-E

Calculus Calculator Labs Student Pack
Part 978-0-9727055-S-L

Calculus Calculator Labs Teacher Pack
Part 978-0-9727055-T-L

---

www.skylit.com
sales@skylit.com
Toll free: 888-476-1940
Fax: 978-475-1431

Skylight Publishing, 9 Bartlet Street, Suite 70, Andover, MA 01810